Programming
for the Absolute Beginner,
Second Edition

Jerry Lee Ford, Jr.

Cengage Learning PTR

CENGAGE
Learning·

Professional • Technical • Reference

D0911867

Australia, Brazil, Japan, Korea, Mexico, Singapore, Spain, United Kingdom, United States

Programming for the Absolute Beginner, Second Edition
Jerry Lee Ford, Jr.

Publisher and General Manager, Cengage Learning PTR:
Stacy L. Hiquet

Associate Director of Marketing:
Sarah Panella

Manager of Editorial Services:
Heather Talbot

Senior Product Manager:
Mitzi Koontz

Project Editor/Copy Editor:
Karen A. Gill

Technical Reviewer:
Keith Davenport

Interior Layout:
Shawn Morningstar

Cover Designer:
Mike Tanamachi

Indexer:
Valerie Haynes Perry

Proofreader:
Jenny Davidson

Cover Image:
© antishock/Shutterstock.com

© 2016 Cengage Learning PTR.

WCN: 01-100

CENGAGE and CENGAGE LEARNING are registered trademarks of Cengage Learning, Inc., within the United States and certain other jurisdictions.

For product information and technology assistance, contact us at
Cengage Learning Customer & Sales Support, 1-800-354-9706.

For permission to use material from this text or product, submit all requests online at **cengage.com/permissions.**

Further permissions questions can be emailed to **permissionrequest@cengage.com.**

Microsoft and Windows are registered trademarks of Microsoft Corporation in the United States and other countries. Just BASIC is © Shoptalk Systems 2004.

All other trademarks are the property of their respective owners.

All images © Cengage Learning unless otherwise noted.

Library of Congress Control Number: 2014953142
ISBN-13: 978-1-305-50443-1
ISBN-10: 1-305-50443-7

Cengage Learning PTR
20 Channel Center Street
Boston, MA 02210
USA

Cengage Learning is a leading provider of customized learning solutions with office locations around the globe, including Singapore, the United Kingdom, Australia, Mexico, Brazil, and Japan. Locate your local office at: **international.cengage.com/region.**

Cengage Learning products are represented in Canada by Nelson Education, Ltd.

For your lifelong learning solutions, visit **cengageptr.com.**

Visit our corporate website at **cengage.com.**

Printed in the United States of America
Print Number: 01   Print Year: 2015

To my father and my children, Alexander, William, and Molly,
and to my beautiful wife, Mary.

Acknowledgments

There are numerous individuals to whom I owe thanks for their help, guidance, and assistance in the development of the second edition of this book. I should begin thanking Mitzi Koontz who served as the book's acquisitions editor. I wish to thank Karen Gill for bringing her invaluable talents to bear as this book's project editor. I also want to thank the book's technical editor, Keith Davenport, for his technical input and advice. In addition, I would like to thank everyone else at Cengage Learning for all their hard work.

About the Author

Jerry Lee Ford, Jr. is an educator and IT professional with more than 25 years of experience in information technology, including roles as an automation analyst, technical manager, technical support analyst, automation engineer, and security analyst. He is the author of 40 books and the coauthor of two additional books. His published works include *Microsoft WSH and VBScript Programming for the Absolute Beginner*; *Microsoft Visual Basic 2008 Express Programming for the Absolute Beginner*; *HTML, XHTML, and CSS for the Absolute Beginner*; *XNA 3.1 Game Development for Teens*; and *Game Maker Programming for Teens*. Jerry has a master's degree in business administration from Virginia Commonwealth University in Richmond, Virginia, and has more than 5 years of experience as an adjunct instructor teaching networking courses in information technology.

Table of Contents

PART I
INTRODUCTION TO COMPUTER PROGRAMMING

1

2

Creating Programs with Just BASIC 35

3

Creating Graphical User Interfaces 71

PART II
LEARNING HOW TO WRITE BASIC PROGRAMS

4

Working with Variables and Arrays 129

5

Making Decisions with Conditional Logic 159

6

Using Loops to Process Data 189

7

Improving Program Organization with Functions and Subroutines

PART III
ADVANCED PROGRAMMING TOPICS

8

Working with Text Files

9

Working with Sound and Graphics 275

10

Arcade-Style Computer Game Development 305

11

Debugging Your Applications 347

PART IV
APPENDIXES

A
What's on the Companion Website?

B
What's Next?

Introduction

Welcome to the second edition of *Programming for the Absolute Beginner*. This book is designed to provide a gentle and fun introduction to computer programming. For many, the mere thought of attempting to learn how to become a computer programmer is enough to make them turn and head for the hills. However, as you will see, learning how to program really is not that hard, provided you have good instruction and a little patience.

As this book will demonstrate, you do not have to be a computer genius to learn how to program. Think of it this way. Most people have only a limited understanding of the internal mechanics of a car or motorcycle, but they do not let that stop them from getting behind the wheel and learning to drive. Nor do you have to know how to build a computer from scratch or possess detailed understanding of the inner workings of your computer's motherboard, hard drive, or any other hardware component to be able to operate a computer. The same is true of computer programming.

The first edition of this book was specifically written to help first-time programmers get up and running quickly. The second edition expands on this approach through the addition of new examples and simplified explanations. At the same time, the book has been updated to keep things current, and new material has been added that delves into arcade-style computer game programming. You will be provided with enough background information to make sure that you know what is going on without inundating you with an overwhelming amount of technical jargon. Although you will not be a programming guru by the end of this book, you will have learned the fundamentals of computer programming and will have the knowledge required to determine which of the many possible paths you want to pursue with your new programming skills.

What This Book Is All About

There are many programming languages available today, each with its own particular set of strengths and weaknesses. These programming languages run on various operating systems and can be very different from one another. Despite this, all programming languages operate using the same basic set of rules. The purpose of this book is to teach you the rules that govern all programming languages and to explain the steps involved in designing and creating computer applications.

Rather than attempt to provide detailed instruction for a number of different programming languages, I have chosen to focus on one specific language: BASIC. BASIC was originally created as a language for teaching computer programming. As such, I have decided to adopt it as the programming language that this book will use to teach you how to program. Specifically, I have decided to use a version of BASIC called Just BASIC. It does not cost anything and can be downloaded from the Internet. Just BASIC provides a simple streamlined version of BASIC that is easier for first-time programmers to learn than other BASIC programming languages, such as Microsoft Visual Basic, which is a highly complex version of BASIC that is used throughout the world to develop commercial software.

If you are looking for a good introduction to computer programming and are not sure yet which programming language you ultimately want to work with, this book will serve you well. It will give you the skills and knowledge you need to get started programming with Just BASIC. If you are interested in learning an advanced programming language like Visual Basic, Java, or C++, you will be well served by first learning the principles of BASIC programming prior to moving on and tackling these more complex languages.

Who Should Read This Book?

This book is designed to teach you how to become a programmer. By the time you are done with this book, you will not be a programming expert, but you will have a solid understanding of how programming works. You will also have a good understanding of the strengths and weaknesses of different programming languages.

This book teaches you basic programming skills using the free implementation of the BASIC programming language called Just BASIC. BASIC was designed as a programming language to be used to teach beginner programmers. As such, it provides an excellent model through which you can learn the basics of computer programming and will help you build a technical foundation from which you can later make the jump to other programming languages, should that be your goal.

Although previous programming experience is helpful, I wrote this book based on the assumption that you do not have any previous programming experience with BASIC or any other programming language. However, a good understanding of how to work with Microsoft Windows is required.

This book has been specifically designed to help jump-start your programming career. By the time you have finished the book, you will have laid down a strong programming foundation that you can apply to other programming languages. This will help prepare you to learn more advanced BASIC programming languages such as Visual Basic or non-BASIC programming languages such as C#, C++, Java, JavaScript, Python, and Perl.

Regardless of which programming language you eventually decide to learn and master, the purpose of this book is to provide you with a programming foundation that you can build on and use as a starting point to achieve your goals. I believe that you will find this book very helpful as you begin your programming career and that you will be pleased with what the book has in store for you. This book's unique game-based teaching approach will make your learning experience not only easier but a lot more fun.

What You Need to Begin

This book was written using Just BASIC on computers running Windows 7 and Windows 8.1. Therefore, all the figures and examples you will see will show Just BASIC applications running on these two operating systems. If you are running a different Windows operating system, you may notice small differences in the way your applications look. However, these differences will be purely cosmetic, and you should not have trouble following along with the examples presented in this book.

As of the writing of this book, the current version of Just BASIC is 1.01. You can download a free copy of Just BASIC at the Just BASIC website located at www.justbasic.com. The download is only 2.41MB, so it will not take long to download and install. You can install and run Just BASIC on any of the Windows operating systems up through Windows 8.1.

Compared to most programming languages and applications, Just BASIC has modest hardware requirements, as shown in Table I.1. These modest requirements, combined with Just BASIC's broad support for different Windows operating systems, allows you to create Just BASIC applications for any Windows operating system, including older operating systems that many other programming languages no longer support. Of course, the minimum requirements shown in Table I.1 are just that. For best performance, install Just BASIC and create Windows applications on a computer that meets the table's recommended requirements.

TABLE 1.1 MINIMUM REQUIREMENTS FOR RUNNING JUST BASIC		
Requirement	**Minimum**	**Recommended**
Processor	486 or Pentium	Pentium
Memory	24MB	64MB
Hard Disk	6MB	12MB

© 2016 Shoptalk Systems

Hint

Many Windows applications contain graphics. This book supplies you with the graphics you need to create all its sample applications. To create new graphics for your own Just BASIC applications, you need a paint or graphics application. Windows comes with an image editor called Paint, which has basic image-creation and manipulation capabilities. You may, however, prefer a more full-featured image editor, such as Adobe Photoshop or GIMP for Windows, just to name two.

That's it. As long as you are running a supported version of Microsoft Windows and can download a free copy of Just BASIC, you have everything you need to take full advantage of the information and material covered in this book. Everything you need to create Just BASIC applications is provided as part of the programming language.

How This Book Is Organized

Programming for the Absolute Beginner, Second Edition, is organized into four major parts. I have written this book based on the assumption that it will be read sequentially, from cover to cover. If you are a first-time programmer, this is the approach you should take. However, if you already have prior programming experience, you may want to skip around a bit, selecting those topics that are of most interest to you.

Part I of this book consists of three chapters that will provide you with the background information you need to know to get started. You will also learn the steps in creating BASIC applications using Just BASIC and the steps involved in the formulation of graphical user interfaces (GUIs) made up of windows, buttons, and all sorts of other graphical controls.

Part II is made up of four chapters, from which you will learn a number of programming principles and techniques. The topics covered include learning how to store and retrieve data and how to write programs that react differently based on the data input they receive using conditional logic. You will learn how to create and use loops to perform repetitive actions and to process large amounts of data. You will also learn how to improve the overall organization of your BASIC applications using functions and subroutines.

Part III is made up of four chapters that cover a number of advanced topics. These topics include learning how to work with text files, how to integrate sound and graphics into your BASIC applications, and how to create arcade-style computer games. You will also learn the basic steps involved in tracking down and fixing program bugs that inevitably occur as part of the application development process.

Part IV is made up of two appendixes and a glossary. The appendixes outline the additional content that you will find on the book's companion website and provide additional information and guidance that is designed to help you further your programming knowledge and skills.

The basic outline of the book follows:

- **Chapter 1, "Introduction to Programming."** This chapter provides you with a high-level overview of BASIC as well as background information that you will need to know in order to become an effective programmer. This will include a little historical background information as well as a comparison of BASIC to other programming languages. You also learn how to create your first BASIC application: the Knock Knock Joke game.

- **Chapter 2, "Creating Programs with Just BASIC."** In this chapter, you will learn how to work with the Just BASIC editor. You will discover how to navigate the editor's menus and toolbars. You will learn how to work with all of Just BASIC's major features and to customize its settings to suit your personal preferences. You will also learn how to create standalone BASIC applications that can be run without requiring Just BASIC to be installed on the computer.

- **Chapter 3, "Creating Graphical User Interfaces."** This chapter will teach you the basic steps involved in designing and creating graphical user interfaces. You will learn how to create application windows and to populate them with all sorts of controls. You will also learn how to create application menus. In addition, you will learn how to configure the appearance of these controls and how to set them up to execute selected portions of your application code.

- **Chapter 4, "Working with Variables and Arrays."** This chapter will explain how programming languages store and retrieve data. Specifically, you will learn how to define data that never changes as well as how to store individual pieces or groups of related data whose values may change throughout the execution of your applications. You will also learn how to work mathematical and comparison operations and to perform basic text string manipulation.

- **Chapter 5, "Making Decisions with Conditional Logic."** This chapter will teach you how to develop programming logic that can analyze different values and alter its execution based on the results of that analysis. Using this information, you will be able to create applications that can modify their execution based on the data that they are presented with.

- **Chapter 6, "Using Loops to Process Data."** In this chapter, you will learn how to develop applications that are designed to repetitively perform a sequence of actions under the control of loops. You will also learn how to use loops to process large collections of data and to control the overall execution of BASIC applications and games.

- **Chapter 7, "Improving Program Organization with Functions and Subroutines."** This chapter will teach you how to make your applications easier to understand and maintain by helping you organize program code into subroutines and procedures. You will learn how to pass data into procedures and to return it from procedures.

- **Chapter 8, "Working with Text Files."** In this chapter, you will learn how to create applications that interact with the Windows file system. You will also learn how to create, open, and close text files as well as how to write data to and read data from them. Finally, you will learn how to define and access simple database files.

- **Chapter 9, "Working with Sound and Graphics."** In this chapter, you will learn how to integrate sound and graphics into your BASIC applications. This will include displaying animated graphics sequences, making sounds, and playing audio files.

- **Chapter 10, "Arcade-Style Computer Game Development."** In this chapter, you will develop an understanding of fundamental game development techniques, including learning about key features found in most computer games, how to manage game state, and how to control sprite movement and determine when collisions occur. This chapter also reviews the fundamentals of capturing and processing player input.

- **Chapter 11, "Debugging Your Applications."** In this chapter, you will discover how to find and fix program bugs that prevent your applications from running or cause your applications to run inappropriately. You will learn how to locate and fix syntax and logical errors. You will also learn how to use Just BASIC's built-in debugger to locate and fix runtime errors. This will include learning how to trace program execution and set up breakpoints that pause application execution to allow you to check on the status of variable values.

- **Appendix A, "What's on the Companion Website?"** This appendix has an outline of the BASIC source code that you will find on this book's companion website.

- **Appendix B, "What's Next?"** This appendix has some final thoughts that are designed to help you continue your programming education. The information provided in this appendix includes links to websites where you can go to learn more about Just BASIC and other BASIC programming languages. This appendix also has a list of recommended reading that you may find helpful.

- **Glossary.** This unit offers a glossary of key terms that are used throughout the book.

Conventions Used in This Book

To help make the book easier to understand and read, I have incorporated a number of special conventions to help make key points stand out so that they are easy to identify and understand. These conventions are as follows.

HINT

As you read along, I will suggest different or better ways of doing things to help make you a better and more efficient programmer.

TRAP

I will identify places where mistakes are sometimes made and provide advice to help you avoid them.

TRICK

Whenever possible, I will give you shortcuts and other techniques to help you make your work easier.

Challenges

I will end each chapter by offering you a series of suggestions that you can follow up on to enhance and improve the chapter's game project and to advance your programming skills.

Companion Website Downloads

You may download the companion website files from www.cengageptr.com/downloads.

PART I

Introduction to Computer Programming

1

Introduction to Programming

In addition to teaching you the basics of computer programming using Just BASIC, this book seeks to provide you with the background information you need to figure out your place within the grand scope of the programming world. To help get you started, this chapter offers a gentle review of the evolution of computer programming. You will learn about a number of different computer languages and their relative strengths and weaknesses, as well as the types of tasks to which various programming languages are applicable. Along the way, you will pick up some basic terminology. You will discover the origins of the BASIC programming language and create and execute your first BASIC application: the Knock Knock Joke game. By the time you are done with this chapter, you will possess the background knowledge you need to not only begin BASIC programming but start thinking about which programming language or languages you ultimately want to focus on.

Specifically, you will learn the following:

- A brief history of the evolution of computer programming
- Basic programming concepts and terms
- The strengths and weaknesses of various programming languages
- How to create and execute your first BASIC program

Project Preview: The Knock Knock Joke Game

In this chapter and in each chapter that follows, you will learn how to create a new BASIC application. This chapter's project, the Knock Knock Joke game, is a simple computer game that tells the player a series of knock knock jokes. The game begins by displaying the opening prompt for the first joke, as shown in Figure 1.1.

Figure 1.1 The player must respond by entering Who is there? in response to the opening prompt.
© 2016 Cengage Learning®

To minimize the amount of effort required by the player, the game automatically displays the required response in the text field of the pop-up dialog. Therefore, to answer the prompt and proceed to the next part of the joke, all that the player has to do is click on the OK button.

After responding to the opening prompt for the first joke, the game displays the second part of the joke, as shown in Figure 1.2.

Figure 1.2 The player must respond by entering Disease who? to proceed to the end of the joke.
© 2016 Cengage Learning®

Once the game receives the correct response from the player, it displays the first joke's punch line, as shown in Figure 1.3.

Figure 1.3 The punch line for the game's first joke.
© 2016 Cengage Learning®

The player then clicks on OK to dismiss the punch line and proceed to the next joke. All that the player has to do to complete the rest of the game and view its jokes is to continue to click on the OK button. However, if the player instead attempts to retype the correct response and makes a typo in doing so, or if the player clicks on the Cancel button, an error message is displayed similar to that shown in Figure 1.4.

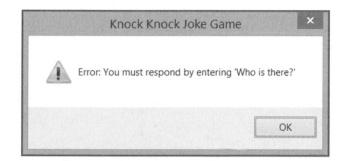

Figure 1.4 Error messages are displayed if the anticipated response is not received.
© 2016 Cengage Learning®

The game automatically ends after the last joke has been told. As you can see, although this is not a particularly challenging game from the player's standpoint, it does possess a number of features upon which you can build and later create more interesting and complex games. For example, the Knock Knock Joke game demonstrates how to interact with the player via dialog windows and how to collect and process input. It also demonstrates how to analyze and process that input.

Getting Started

There are any number of reasons that people decide to learn how to program. For starters, it can be fun, and many people simply enjoy spending time working on challenging tasks and expressing their own unique form of computerized creativity. Some people decide to jump into programming to create an application for which they see a need that has not yet been met. For example, a comic book author might decide to create his own custom word processor with features that make comic book development easier. Of course, many people make the leap into programming to earn more money by switching to or starting a new career.

Programming is a lucrative field, and there is no shortage of jobs for individuals with solid programming skills. Colleges and universities around the world have developed computer sciences degree programs designed to help fill the never-ending need for new programming talent, and sites like Amazon are packed full of books designed to help programmers at all levels learn more about their craft.

For many, taking the first step into programming is the hardest. That is where this book comes into play. One of my objectives of this book was to assist first-time programmers in wading into the sometimes-murky programming waters. This book assumes that, as a beginner programmer, you have not yet made a decision to learn a specific programming language, or you don't have a great deal of understanding as to what the many different programming languages today are capable of or what makes them unique. In addition to teaching you how to program, this book will provide the background you need so that, when you have finished this book, you'll be able to make a well-reasoned and intelligent choice about the next step to take as you continue your programming career.

Programming Overview

All computer programs, regardless of what programming languages they are written in or what operating system they run on, share certain similarities. They all consist of code statements that give the computer instructions. These programs typically accept some type of input, process it in some manner, and then produce output.

The input that is processed might be provided by the program itself, or it might be provided by interacting with a user. Data might also come from files stored on the computer or, in the case of Windows computers, from the Windows registry. Input might also come from data passed to the program at execution time. What the program does with the data that it is given depends on what the programmer designed the application to do. For example, a computer game might accept input from the computer keyboard, mouse, or a joystick and then use this data to guide the movement of an animated spaceship, which would then be displayed as output on the computer screen as part of an arcade-styled game.

Deciding What Programming Language to Learn and Use

In most cases, there are several programming languages available for you to choose from to solve a given problem. For example, you could write a desktop application for Windows using any of several programming languages, including Visual Basic, C++, and Java. Although each of these programming languages has its own particular set of strengths and weaknesses, chances are good that you can create just about any desktop application you would want using any of these languages. In fact, the choice of what language is used is often more a matter of personal preference, based on the programmer's background rather than a technical requirement imposed by the operating system or other external factors. The imagination and experience of the programmer is far more important than the choice of programming language. As a result, in most cases the choice of language is almost immaterial.

Creating Your Own Solutions

For most people, using their computer means running and working with their favorite applications, which may include computer games or Microsoft Office applications like Word and Excel. These applications are examples of software programs written by someone else, typically a commercial software development company like Microsoft. Because commercial software developers want to sell as many copies of their applications as possible, they try to make them appeal to as many people as possible. As a result, compromises are sometimes made, such that a given application may meet most but not all of the needs of every consumer.

Microsoft Word is a general-purpose word processor that is great for creating letters, reports, and all sorts of documents. You can even use it to create resumes and perform desktop publishing. However, it takes a little work to set up Word to perform these kinds of tasks, and the number of features it provides may not meet the needs of every user. Because resume writing and desktop publishing are extremely popular activities, many companies have developed custom applications specifically designed to address these tasks. As you would expect, resume and desktop publishing applications are specifically designed to accomplish their respective tasks and, as such, are more feature rich than Microsoft Word when it comes to polishing your resume or making the company newsletter look good.

Now suppose that you want an application that you can use to create your own electronic diary. You might first look for a commercial application to address your needs. If you find such an application, it might not have the specific set of features that you are looking for, or it might cost more than you think is reasonable to pay. Another option worth pursuing is to visit one of the many shareware websites on the Internet to see if you can find a shareware or freeware application that somebody else has created that may meet your requirements. If this option does not pan out, you may have to settle for using your word processor as your diary. Well, unless, of course, you know how to program. In that case, you can create your own diary application that is perfectly suited to meet your needs. Best of all, once you are done, if you think the application is something that other people might be able to use, you might consider giving it away or even distributing it as shareware. Maybe you can even make a little money from your hard work.

Mastering the Art of Program Logic

Contrary to most people's perception, the programming logic that makes computer applications work is not fundamentally different from the logic that people apply to different aspects of their daily lives. Take, for example, a mother who has been asked by her child to teach him how to play a game. In this scenario, the mother might provide instruction like this:

1. Open the game board and have everybody place their pieces on Go.
2. The first player then rolls the dice and moves his piece the number of spaces indicated by the dice.

3. If a double is rolled, the player rolls again; otherwise, the next player rolls.

4. The player may buy any property he lands on as long as it is not already owned by somebody else and he has the money to do so.

5. If a player lands on someone else's property, he must pay rent.

6. Each time a player successfully makes it around the board, he is rewarded with $200.

7. Players are eliminated from the game as they run out of money.

8. The last player remaining in the game wins.

The logic used to develop a computer program is not fundamentally different from the logic in this list. What makes writing a computer program a little more difficult is that computers do not understand English or any other human language. Instead, to create a new computer program, you must learn how to outline the logic required to perform a given task using a programming language.

Just as there are many different human languages, there are many different computer languages. These languages typically have unusual names like Visual Basic, Java, C#, C ++, and AppleScript. These languages and many other computer languages like them have their own unique set of strengths and weaknesses and are often better suited than other programming languages to perform certain types of tasks. Visual Basic, for example, only runs on Windows computers and is a great language for creating Windows desktop applications. JavaScript, on the other hand, is a web development language that runs inside web browsers and is a great programming language for adding dynamic content and interactivity to websites.

Talking in a Language Computers Understand

Computer languages, like human languages, follow certain sets of rules that define the language and use of specific language keywords. Like human languages, there are thousands of programming languages. In addition, new programming languages are created every year. In the sections that follow, you will learn a little about a great many different programming languages and will come away with an understanding of what each language is used for and where it fits into the grand scheme of computer programming.

Machine Language

Different computers have different types of central processing units (CPUs). Each CPU has its own set of instructions that it understands. These sets of instructions are referred to as *machine language* or *machine code*. Machine code is the only language that a computer can understand. Other languages like BASIC are only intermediary languages that ultimately must be converted into machine language before they can be executed.

Machine code languages consist of patterns of bits, which can take on either of two values—0s or 1s, as demonstrated next. Different bit combinations represent different commands that the CPU recognizes:

```
0011 1101 0001 1010
0010 1001 1000 0011
1111 0001 0101 1011
```

This example is intended to demonstrate that machine languages are enormously difficult programming languages to learn. As such, few programmers know how to write machine code programs. In fact, some of the most talented programmers in the world have never considered learning to work with machine code.

Assembly Language

Programming in machine code is extremely difficult for human beings. As a solution to this problem, assembly language was created in the 1950s. *Assembly languages* use mnemonic codes to represent specific machine code commands. Unlike machine code, which consists of only 0s and 1s, assembly languages are made up of a combination of simple words and numbers.

Assembly language is considered a low-level programming language that is linked to specific CPUs. Therefore, the assembly language used on one type of computer will be slightly different from the assembly language used on another type. When executed, assembly programs are translated line for line into corresponding machine language statements by a program known as an *assembler*.

Assembly language was once widely used in the creation of operating systems such as MS-DOS and applications like the original Lotus 1-2-3 spreadsheet application. Assembly programs were once heavily used on mainframe computers. However, languages such as COBOL and Fortran eventually supplanted it on that platform. Starting in the 1970s, with the advent of the C programming languages, the use of assembly language programs started to fade on personal computers.

Today, assembly languages are used only for specific tasks, such as the development of device drivers where direct hardware access is required or on new computer systems for which high-level languages have not been developed. Regardless, an understanding of assembly language programming is still considered an essential part of a computer science degree in most colleges and universities. Still, assembly language programming has proven to be quite difficult for the average programmer. This, combined with a lack of portability between different types of computers, has relegated assembly language programming to a small number of programmers.

Fortran and COBOL

Despite being a major improvement over machine language coding, assembly language left much to be desired as a general-purpose programming language. Instead, new programming languages were needed to facilitate the development of a new generation of business and scientific applications. In the late 1950s, a pair of new programming languages immerged to address these needs.

Fortran appeared first on the scene in 1957. *Fortran*, which is an acronym for *FORmula TRANslator*, was designed to support complex mathematic calculations. Early versions of Fortran provided for the development of applications whose performance was roughly equivalent to that of assembly programs but which were considerably easier to develop. By the early 1960s, several dozen Fortran compilers had been created for various computing platforms, making it the first truly portable programming language.

Fortran applications are still in use today in various technical areas, including weather and climate modeling and computational chemistry and physics. Once an arcane and difficult language to master, Fortran has been updated and modified over the years and now incorporates many features found in other modern programming languages, including updated syntax and object-oriented features. Although still in use today by the scientific and engineering communities, Fortran is generally regarded as a specialist language.

COBOL, which stands for *Common Business-Oriented Language*, was introduced in the late 1950s. Designed to support the development of business applications, it is still used to support mainframe application development today. In fact, the majority of the world's business applications are still written in COBOL. The current version of COBOL, COBOL 2002, includes many new programming capabilities, such as support for object-oriented programming. Like Fortran, COBOL is a portable programming language that can be written once and ported to other platforms and run, usually with minimal modification.

C

Given that assembly language programming was so difficult to learn, assembly programs were difficult to port from one computer to another, and languages like Fortran and COBOL served specialized purposes, it was clear that an easier-to-learn and far more portable general programming language was needed. This need was answered when C was introduced in the early 1970s.

C was developed at Bell Telephone Laboratories for use on UNIX operating systems. C is far easier to work with than assembly language and provides direct access to computer hardware. It quickly became the most commonly used programming language for writing system and application software.

To run a C program, a special program known as a compiler has to translate its source code into machine code. A *compiler*, like an assembler, is a program that translates a computer program into machine code. C is a relatively small programming language. When compiled, it generates a few machine code statements for each line of C code. C compilers have been developed for just about every computing platform; therefore, C is far easier to port from one computer to another than assembly language programs, often requiring only minimal recoding.

One of C's main features is its ability to directly access computer hardware. This has proven to be a double-edged sword in that only the most experienced and accomplished programmers have the programming skills required to safely use the language in this manner. In the hands of less experienced programmers, C can be a time bomb waiting to go off and crash computers.

C is vastly powerful. As a result, many popular applications have been written using it (and spin-off languages such as C++ and Objective-C), including Microsoft Windows, Linux, and Mac OS X.

To program with a language that was as portable and efficient as C but safer in terms of removing the language's ability to access hardware, a whole new generation of programming languages was created, including C++, Objective-C, Visual Basic, and Java.

C++ and Objective-C

C++ is a general-purpose programming language introduced in the 1980s. C++ is *object oriented*, meaning that it uses an approach where system and key language resources are viewed as objects that come equipped with everything needed to access and manipulate them. C++ was developed out of Bell Telephone Laboratories as an enhancement to C.

Modern implementations of C++ are provided by companies like Microsoft. *Microsoft C++ supports Rapid Application Development*, allowing programmers to create full-featured Windows applications in less time than while using other programming languages.

Hint

Rapid Application Development (RAD) is a programming technique in which programmers begin application development using a drag-and-drop tool that facilitates the creation of graphical user interfaces (GUIs). Once an application's interface has been designed, programmers add the program code required to finish building the application and make it respond when the user interacts with its interface.

C++ incorporates all aspects of C and includes numerous enhancements. As such, it is considered a complicated programming language. Another derivative of C is Objective-C, which was introduced in 1986. Like C++, Objective-C is an object-oriented programming language that is built on top of C. However, unlike C++, Objective-C is relatively small, providing C programming with a faster learning curve than C++. Objective-C applications run on UNIX operating systems, including Mac OS X.

BASIC

Despite the vast improvements introduced by languages like C, C++, and Objective-C, many people, especially first-time programmers, have found that learning how to program using C, C++, and Objective-C is challenging. To reduce the learning curve required to learn how to program, a new language was introduced in the early 1960s called BASIC. *BASIC*, which stands for *Beginner's All-purpose Symbolic Instruction Code*, was created as a programming language that was designed to teach people how to program. However, it soon became obvious that the language was well suited to more than just teaching basic programming concepts.

One of the fundamental design goals of BASIC was to keep things simple. As a result, BASIC soon became the most popular programming language in the world and was ported over to just about every operating system. BASIC programs are much easier to write and typically take less time to create, test, and debug. BASIC programs are also highly portable.

Throughout the 1970s, numerous versions of BASIC were created and made available on various home and desktop computers, including Atari, Apple, and the original IBM PC. As such, BASIC programming was introduced to millions of first-time programmers who used it to create small programs. However, in the 1980s third-party application development companies began to spring up, delivering a host of ready-made applications that soon filled most of the needs of desktop computer owners. As such, individual interest in BASIC programming declined.

BASIC's fortunes began to change in 1991 when Microsoft released Visual Basic 1.0. Visual Basic was a general-purpose RAD programming language. Microsoft has continued to work on and enhance Visual Basic over the years. The current version, Visual Basic 2013, integrates Visual Basic with Microsoft's .NET framework. One particular version of Visual Basic of interest to new programmers is Microsoft Visual Basic Express 2013, which is part of Microsoft Visual Studio Express 2013 for Windows Desktop, shown in Figure 1.5. Microsoft makes this version of Visual Basic available as a free download to attract new Visual Basic programmers.

Hint

The *Microsoft .NET Framework* is a collection of resources designed to support the development and execution of Windows applications that run on desktop computers, local area networks (LANs), and the Internet.

Visual Basic .NET supports desktop, network, and Internet application development as well as the development of database applications. Visual Basic supports the development of software applications that can run on small appliances like handheld computers and cell phones. Visual Basic is also used to develop business and commercial software applications.

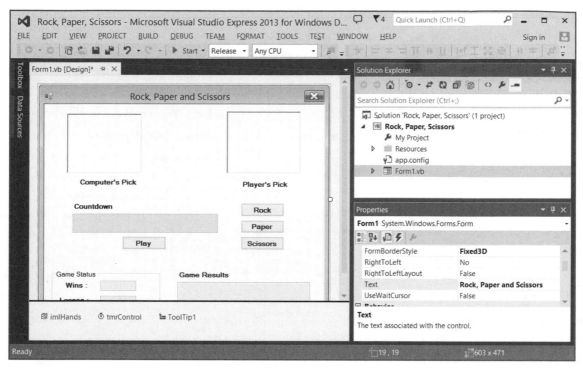

Figure 1.5 Visual Basic Express 2013 is specifically tailored to meet the needs of first-time programmers.
Source: Microsoft Corporation

Hint

To learn more about Visual Basic and other languages based on BASIC, check out Appendix B, "What's Next?"

Java

Another major programming language that has garnered a lot of attention and use in recent years is Java, which Sun Microsystems developed in the early 1990s and first released in 1995. Syntactically, Java is based heavily on C and C++ but lacks these languages' low-level capabilities to access and manipulate system resources. Java programs generally run in one of two forms: either as standalone applications or as applets that can be executed inside web browsers. Standalone applications run like any other software application. Java applets run as programs embedded within web pages that are loaded and executed by a host web browser.

Java is a platform-independent programming language designed to support the development and execution of computer programs that can be run on different operating systems without code modification. To accomplish this goal, Sun designed Java so that the code developed by the program was compiled into an intermediary format known as *bytecode* (also known as *p-code*). This partially compiled code is then loaded into a virtual machine running on the target operating system. It was the job of the virtual machine to finish compiling the Java program into machine language at execution time. For this development model to work, virtual machine programs had to be developed for different operating systems, which Sun developed and made available for free.

Because it runs within a virtual machine, Java programs do not, by default, have a look and feel that mirrors the default appearance of applications native to a particular operating system. Although many programmers were critical of the performance of early versions of Java, improvements have since reduced the amount of memory required while simultaneously increasing processing speed, negating such concerns. Another issue with Java is that Microsoft does not ship it as part of the Windows operating system, forcing individuals to take extra steps to download and install it. However, in the age of the Internet where people are used to constantly downloading and installing browser add-ons and system updates, this hurdle has proven easy to overcome.

Hint

To learn more about Java and to download and install it on your computer, visit www.java.com. You will also find plenty of sample software applications for download.

Other Types of Programming Languages

In addition to the general-purpose, business, and scientific-specific languages already discussed, there are many specialized programming languages in use today that are important to know about. These include the following:

- Scripting languages
- Embedded application languages
- Web development languages
- Database languages

Scripting Languages

A *scripting* language is a computer language that is interpreted into machine code at execution time as opposed to being compiled at development time into machine code. Therefore, whereas an application written in C++ is compiled and converted into machine code just one time at the end of the program processes and can then be executed over and over again, a script is a program that must be reinterpreted and converted to machine code each time it is executed. As a result, scripts take longer to start. In addition, the computers upon which they are executed must have an interpreter installed that is capable of executing them.

Hint

An *interpreter* is a program that converts script statements into machine code at runtime.

There are many scripting languages to choose from, including Perl, Python, JavaScript, VBScript, Ruby, Rexx, and AppleScript, just to name a few. Scripts are saved as plaintext files. As a result, when distributed, the source code for the script is easily accessible by anyone who wants to view and copy or modify it, thus raising concerns regarding a programmer's ability to control the intellectual property rights of his program. However, the trade-off for the lack of speed and visible source code is the speed with which scripts can be developed. To write a script, a programmer typically opens a blank text file, types in its code statements, and then saves and executes the script without ever having to compile anything. As a result, a programmer who runs into an error can quickly open the script's file, fix the error, and run the script again to instantly see if the problem has been fixed.

Scripting is prevalent in most programming environments. For example, Windows computer and network administrators develop scripts using languages like VBScript, Python, Ruby, and Perl to automate a host of time-consuming activities, thus freeing up time to work on other tasks. Web developers also embed scripts within web pages using languages like JavaScript to add dynamic content to websites.

Embedded Application Languages

Many applications provide their own embedded programming language in the form of a scripting language. One such example is Microsoft *VBA* or *Visual Basic for Applications*. VBA is shipped as a standard feature in Microsoft Office. It works with Microsoft Word, Excel, PowerPoint, and Access. Microsoft has also added VBA support to other Windows applications such as Microsoft Visio. In addition, third-party Windows application developers have integrated support for VBA into their applications. For example, Corel has integrated VBA into WordPerfect Office X7.

A programmer who wants to create a new application that includes features found in Microsoft Excel has a couple of options. One option is to create a new application from scratch. Another option is to create a new application that works in conjunction with Microsoft Excel using VBA. VBA allows programs to create custom GUIs and to automate the execution of its host application. In the case of Microsoft Excel, this means that VBA can create a new spreadsheet, populate it with data, perform calculations on that data, and present this data to the user using a customized user interface that handles all the required interaction with Excel, providing the user with a much simpler and more streamlined experience.

Web Development Languages

In its beginning, information on the Internet was delivered as plaintext. Although the Internet certainly represented a great leap in communication, it was not until the introduction of HTML, allowing for the development of the World Wide Web, that things truly became interesting. *HTML* stands for *Hypertext Markup Language*. HTML lets web developers specify how data is displayed. Modern web browsers like Internet Explorer, Opera, and Mozilla Firefox render web pages based on HTML code.

HTML provides the ability to present static information that does not change. As more and more people around the world started surfing the Internet and companies began to look at the Internet as a means of generating revenue, the need for more powerful and robust web page programming languages quickly became evident. In response, a host of new programming languages was created. One of the first was JavaScript. *JavaScript* is a scripting language that lets you embed small scripts inside HTML pages so you can provide interactive content on your web pages. Another similarly named but completely different programming language, Java, came along allowing small programs, referred to as Java applets, to be run within web browsers. Web developers use these advanced programming languages to build web-based applications that enable web commerce.

Web-based programming languages give programmers access to hundreds of millions of Internet users. Unfortunately, even though HTML today is supported by all major web browsers, incompatibilities between web browsers and programming languages create problems for web developers. As a result, there is no guarantee that Internet users surfing the Internet will have the proper combination of software installed to allow them to visit and interact with every website, leading to a unique set of challenges for web developers.

Database Languages

Modern database programs, such as Microsoft Access and Oracle, are designed to work with a specialized programming language known as *Structured Query Language (SQL)*. SQL is specifically designed to support the creation, modification, and retrieval of data stored in a database.

Hint

A *database* is an application that is designed to facilitate the storage and retrieval of large amounts of data.

The advantage of working with specialized database programming languages is that they are optimized for interacting with databases and provide extremely efficient code. Typically, database-specific programming languages allow database programmers to create database applications in less time than general-purpose programming languages. A disadvantage of database programming languages is that their use is tied to their respective database and, as such, they do not lend themselves to the development of other types of applications like general programming languages.

Most general programming languages, although not specifically optimized for database application development, do support database access and, as such, are sometimes used in place of database-specific languages. Databases are generally associated with specific operating systems. For example, Microsoft Access only runs on Windows, so any applications developed in conjunction with Microsoft access are restricted to Windows. This limits the portability of database programs.

Finding the Right Programming Language

There is no end of programming languages to choose from. Each programming language has its own particular set of strengths and weaknesses. These languages are applicable to particular programming environments. No one programming language can be used to develop applications that can run on all platforms and operating systems. As such, there is no one best programming language to learn.

Despite this obvious fact, you will find no shortage of individuals ready to argue that their favorite programming language is the best. The truth is that for just about any programming challenge, there are plenty of programming languages to choose from. Ultimately, the choice of languages is less important than the creativity and talent of the programmer who wields it. As a result, a good BASIC programmer can, for example, develop desktop software every bit as good and useful as a C, C++, or Objective-C programmer.

Getting Started with Just BASIC

Just BASIC is a free BASIC programming language. Compared to other BASIC programming languages like Visual Basic, Just BASIC is relatively simple. It does not require that you first learn how to work with a complicated integrated development environment (IDE) or Microsoft's .NET Framework to be able to use it to create standalone Windows applications. Instead, Just BASIC offers a simple editor and a simple BASIC dialect, making it much easier for the first-time programmer to focus on learning the fundamental elements of programming without getting lost in the complexities of other high-end BASIC programming languages.

I selected Just BASIC as this book's programming language because of its relative simplicity compared to most other programming languages. Still, Just BASIC packs plenty of punch and can be used to create Windows desktop applications. In addition to being free, it is backed by a supportive online community of programmers that can help you learn more through online forums.

> **Hint**
>
> Check out Appendix B for a list of online resources where you can go to learn more about Just BASIC, including online forums.

Once you have become comfortable with Just BASIC and are ready, you can make the transition to one of the more advanced BASIC programming languages or perhaps to an entirely different programming language.

Installing Just BASIC

Before you can begin creating new applications using Just BASIC, you must download and install it. To get your free copy, go to www.justbasic.com, as shown in Figure 1.6, and click on the Download tab at the top of the screen. This opens the download page, where you can click on the Download link to download your copy of Just BASIC. At just 2.4MB in size, the download does not take long to complete. When prompted, click on Save to download a copy of Just BASIC's install program to your computer.

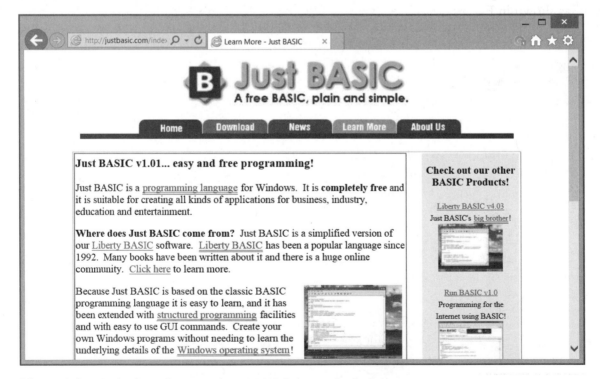

Figure 1.6 Downloading a free copy of Just BASIC from www.justbasic.com.

To begin the installation process, double-click on the installation program. Depending on your version of Microsoft Windows, a User Account Control may appear prompting you to confirm the execution of the Just BASIC install program. By default, if you are installing using a 64-bit version of Windows, the Just BASIC install then prompts you for permission to install Just BASIC in C:\Program Files (x86)\Just BASIC v1.1. Otherwise, you will be prompted to install Just BASIC in C:\Program Files\Just BASIC v1.1. If you are installing Just BASIC on a computer running Windows Vista or later, you do not want to accept the default location. If you do, you will get an error message saying `Runtime Error: "iniFilename" not understood` each time you start Just BASIC. This occurs because Just BASIC needs to be able to write files to its installation directory, but Windows Vista and later versions of Microsoft Windows have protections around files stored within the C:\Program Files (x86) or C:\Program Files directories, resulting in the error. To remedy this situation, create a folder off the root of your computer's disk and name it `Basic`. Once you do this, replace the default install path suggested by Just BASIC's install program with the string C:\Basic Just BASIC v1.01 and click on the Start button.

A dialog appears showing the default installation folder for Just BASIC. During the installation process, a number of files are copied to the Just BASIC folder. Once the installation process is complete, you are prompted to click on OK to close the installation program. Just BASIC then starts, as shown in Figure 1.7.

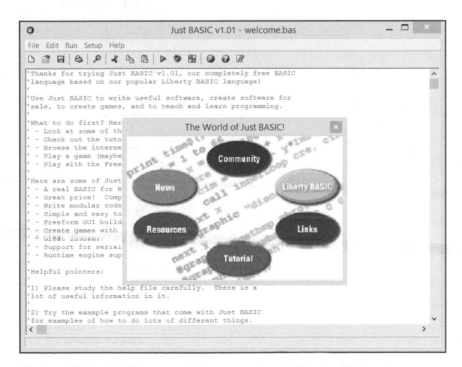

Figure 1.7 Just BASIC automatically starts at the end of its installation process.

As you can see, two windows appear. The smaller window presents a series of links to online resources. For now, just close this window. The second, larger window is Just BASIC's program editor and is the tool you will use to create and test your Just BASIC applications.

Setting Up Just BASIC Help

Just BASIC's help system depends on the Windows Help (WinHlp.exe) program. However, starting with Windows Vista, Microsoft stopped providing this program. If you have installed Just BASIC on a computer running Microsoft Vista or a later version of Windows, you need to install WinHlp.exe to access Just BASIC's help files. The following procedure outlines the steps involved in downloading and installing the Windows Help program.

1. Open the Download Center web page by opening your web browser and loading www.microsoft.com/en-us/download.

2. Type WinHlp32.exe in the search file at the top-right corner of the Download Center web page and press Enter.

3. A list of downloads for the WinHlp32.exe program is displayed. Click on the link representing the program that is appropriate for your version of Microsoft Windows.

4. A page providing detailed information about the version of WinHlp32.exe you have selected is displayed. Click on the Download button.

5. Next, two options are displayed representing 32-bit and 64-bit installation files. Select the option appropriate for your version of Microsoft Windows, and click on Next.

6. Follow the instructions that are then provided to download and install the Windows Help program.

Creating and Executing Your First BASIC Program

Now that you have Just BASIC installed on your computer, let's use it to create a simple computer program. This program will consist of a single program statement that displays a text string message. By developing and executing this program, you will learn the basic mechanics involved in creating any Just BASIC computer program. The steps required to build your first Just BASIC program are outlined here:

1. If Just BASIC is not already running, start it by clicking on Start, All Programs, Just BASIC v1.01 and then Just BASIC v1.01. The Just BASIC Editor appears.

2. To begin creating a new Just BASIC program, click on the File menu and select the New BASIC Source File option. In response, Just BASIC clears out the code editor pane, as shown in Figure 1.8.

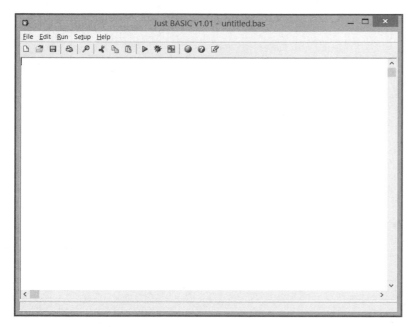

Figure 1.8 Just BASIC applications are created by entering BASIC code statements in the code editor pane.
© 2016 Shoptalk Systems

3. Type `print "Hello World!"` in the code editor pane, as demonstrated in Figure 1.9.

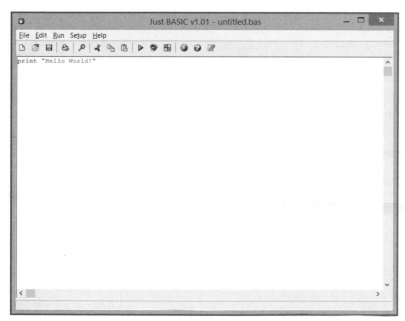

Figure 1.9 Code statements are automatically color-coded by the Just BASIC code editor.
© 2016 Shoptalk Systems

4. Run your new Just BASIC program by clicking on the Run menu and selecting the Run option. In response, Just BASIC compiles your new application and runs it, as shown in Figure 1.10.

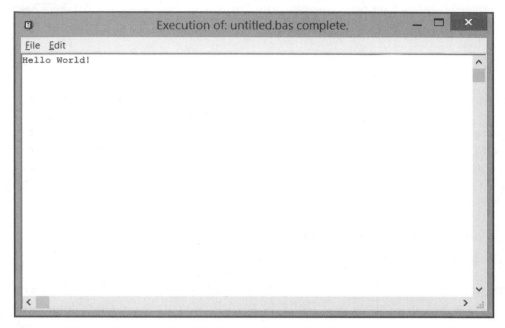

Figure 1.10 By default, every Just BASIC application consists of a default window in which text can be displayed.
© 2016 Shoptalk Systems

That is it. You have just created and executed your first Just BASIC application. In doing so, you keyed in one code statement, which used the print command to display a text string in the application's window. By default, every Just BASIC application automatically displays a default window. In the case of this program, text was displayed on this window using the print command.

Hint

The instructions that you write when developing a computer program are referred to as *statements*. A *program* is a file containing code statements that, when executed, tell the computer to do something. Within this book, the terms *program* and *application* are used interchangeably. When saved to a file, the statements that make up a program are collectively referred to as the program's *source code*.

If you want, you can save your work so that you can load and re-execute it again later by clicking on the code editor's File menu and selecting the Save As option. This displays the Save As dialog, allowing you to specify an application name as well as the location where you want to store your BASIC application.

I suggest that you create a new folder named something like `MyBasicApps` somewhere on your hard drive and that you use it as a repository for all your Just BASIC applications. This will help you keep all your application files organized in one easy-to-find location.

Trick

The Hello World program is admittedly simple, but it does serve as an excellent example of the steps involved in creating and executing a BASIC program. To see how this BASIC program stacks up against the same type of program in other programming languages, visit www.scriptol.com/programming/hello-world.php. Here you will find code examples of similar Hello World programs written in other programming languages, including Assembly, COBOL, Fortran, Visual Basic, C, C++, Java, and JavaScript, just to name a few.

Back to the Knock Knock Joke Game

Now it is time to turn your attention back to the development of this chapter's game project: the Knock Knock Joke game. The creation of this script will reinforce your understanding of the mechanics involved in creating and executing Just BASIC programs. Later, down the road, you will be able to apply this experience when developing and executing programs in other programming languages.

As you follow along with the instructions that outline the steps involved in creating this program, don't worry if you do not understand everything that is going on. It is too early in the book to expect to grasp the meaning and function of the BASIC language statements that make up this game. There will be plenty of time, as you make your way through this book, to learn BASIC.

Designing the Game

Before beginning the development of any new computer program, it is a good idea to spend some time planning the overall design of the application. Taking this approach will not only help to ensure that the end product is a program that looks and works the way you want it to but will also help reduce the possibility of running into problems and errors along the way.

As you saw at the beginning of this chapter, the Knock Knock Joke game executes by displaying prompts in the form of pop-up dialog windows. Default responses are supplied for each part of the jokes to minimize the effort required to complete the game. Each of the game's three jokes is presented in succession, and the game ends once the last of the three jokes has been told. If the user fails to provide the expected responses, the game should display an error message explaining how to correctly formulate the expected response.

As you can see, the Knock Knock Joke game is straightforward. You will create it in six steps, as outlined here:

1. Create a new BASIC file and disable the display of its default window.
2. Display the opening line for the first joke and collect the player's response.
3. Analyze the player's response and respond accordingly.
4. Tell the game's second joke.
5. Tell the game's third joke.
6. Terminate the program's execution.

Creating a Just BASIC File

The first step in the development of the Knock Knock Joke game is to start Just BASIC and to create a new BASIC file. Begin by starting Just BASIC by clicking on Start, All Programs, Just BASIC v1.01, and then select Just BASIC v1.01. Just BASIC starts by displaying two default windows. Dismiss the World of Just BASIC window by clicking on the Close button located in the upper-right corner of the window. Next, create a new BASIC file by clicking on the File menu and selecting the New BASIC Source file. In response, Just BASIC clears out the code editor pane, making it ready to accept the code statements that will make the Knock Knock Joke game.

Even though you have not yet added the code required to create the game, save your BASIC file by clicking on the File menu and then selecting Save As. In response, the Save As dialog appears. Enter KnockKnock.bas as the application's filename, specify the location where you would like to save your new game, and click Save.

At this point, you have created a new empty BASIC file. Let's document the purpose of the Knock Knock game by entering the following code statements into the BASIC file:

```
' ***********************************************************************
'
' Script Name: KnockKnock.bas (The Knock Knock Joke Game)
' Version:     1.0
' Author:      Jerry Lee Ford, Jr.
' Date:        January 1, 2015
'
' Description: This Just BASIC game displays a series of interactive
'              Knock Knock jokes.
'
' ***********************************************************************
```

Each of these statements is actually a comment. In most BASIC programming languages, including Just BASIC, comments begin with the ' character or the REM keyword.

Hint

As the preceding statements demonstrate, comments can be placed on their own line. Comments can also be added to the end of code statements, as demonstrated here:

```
notice "Click on OK to continue." : rem Display a message in a pop-up window
notice "Click on OK to continue." 'Display a message in a pop-up window
```

To use rem to add a comment to the end of a code statement, you must precede the comment with a colon. The colon character is not required when using the apostrophe characters to add a comment to the end of a statement.

You should make liberal use of comments in your program code to provide information about your applications as well as to document the logic implemented by specific code statements. Different programming languages use different characters to represent comments. For example, in C++, the // character is used as the comment character.

Now that you have supplied a little documentation about your new application, add the following statement to the bottom of your BASIC file:

```
nomainwin
```

This statement executes Just BASIC's nomainwin command. This command is unique to Just BASIC. Its purpose is to suppress the display of Just BASIC's default window when a Just BASIC application starts. This statement has been added because the Knock Knock Joke game is designed to display text in pop-up dialogs instead of Just BASIC's default window.

Displaying the Opening Prompt

Now it is time to add the code statements that will display the opening prompt for the first knock knock joke, as shown here:

```
response$ = "Who is there?"

prompt "Knock Knock Joke Game" + chr$(13) + "Knock Knock!"; response$
```

The first statement assigns a text statement to a variable named response$. The contents of this variable will be used to give the player a default response in the pop-up dialog window generated by the second statement. In BASIC, a *string* is a series of zero or more characters surrounded by double quotation marks, and a *variable* is a pointer to a location in memory where a value is stored.

The second statement uses the prompt command to display the first joke's opening prompt in a pop-up dialog window. The player will interact with the game by clicking on the pop-up dialog window's OK button to submit the required response.

Hint

You will learn more about strings and variables in Chapter 4, "Working with Variables and Arrays."

Analyzing Player Input

The next statements that you need to add to your BASIC program are shown next. These statements are responsible for analyzing the response provided by the player and then taking the appropriate actions (either proceeding to tell the rest of the joke or displaying an error message). Because these statements have not been covered yet, I am not going to attempt to explain them in any further detail. For now, just key them in exactly as shown:

```
if response$ = "" then

   notice "Knock Knock Joke Game" + chr$(13) + _
     "Error: You must respond by entering 'Who is there?'"

else

   response$ = "Disease who?"

   prompt "Knock Knock Joke Game" + chr$(13) + "Disease!"; response$

   if response$ = "" then

      notice "Knock Knock Joke Game" + chr$(13) + _
        "Error: You must respond by entering 'Disease who?'"

   else

      notice "Knock Knock Joke Game" + chr$(13) + _
        "Disease jokes seem funny to you?"

   end if

end if
```

At this point, the programming logic required to tell the first joke has been defined.

Telling the Second Joke

The code statements required to tell the game's second joke are listed next. As you can see, except for the text that makes up the second joke, these code statements are identical to the statements that made up the first joke:

```
response$ = "Who is there?"

prompt "Knock Knock Joke Game" + chr$(13) + "Knock Knock!"; response$

if response$ = "" then

   Notice "Knock Knock Joke Game" + chr$(13) + _
     "Error: You must respond by entering 'Who is there?'"

else

   response$ = "Butter who?"

   prompt "Knock Knock Joke Game" + chr$(13) + "Butter!"; response$

   if response$ = "" then

     notice "Knock Knock Joke Game" + chr$(13) + _
       "Error: You must respond by entering 'Butter who?'"

   else

     notice "Knock Knock Joke Game" + chr$(13) + _
       "You butter move on to the next joke."

   end if

end if
```

Telling the Last Joke

The code statements that tell the third joke are provided next. Again, except for the text that makes up the actual joke, these statements are identical to the statements that made up the first and second jokes:

```
response$ = "Who is there?"

prompt "Knock Knock Joke Game" + chr$(13) + "Knock Knock!"; response$

if response$ = "" then

   notice "Knock Knock Joke Game" + chr$(13) + _
     "Error: You must respond by entering 'Who is there?'"

else

   response$ = "Max who?"

   prompt "Knock Knock Joke Game" + chr$(13) + "Max!"; response$

   if response$ = "" then

     notice "Knock Knock Joke Game" + chr$(13) + _
       "Error: You must respond by entering 'Max who?'"

   else

     notice "Knock Knock Joke Game" + chr$(13) + _
       "BASIC, JAVA, C++, it max no difference to me!"

   end if

end if
```

Terminating the Program

You need to add one last statement to the end of your program before calling it a day. This statement consists of a single word.

```
end
```

end is a Just BASIC keyword that identifies the end of your application. Its purpose is to ensure that Just BASIC properly terminates the application before closing any open windows or dialogs. By failing to include this statement in your Just BASIC applications, you run the risk of your applications continuing to run even after the application windows are closed, leaving you without an easy way to terminate them. Including end at the appropriate location in Just BASIC applications is considered a good programming practice.

Trick

If you forget to add the end keyword to one of your Just BASIC applications and find that your application is stuck in a state of limbo with all its application windows closed, you can still terminate it. You accomplish this in Windows 7 by pressing Ctrl+Alt+Delete and then selecting Start Task Manager. You can then select the name of your Just BASIC application from the list of open applications in the Applications property sheet and click on the End Task button. In Windows 8.1, you can terminate a Just BASIC application by pressing Ctrl+Alt+Delete and then selecting Task Manager. You can then select the name of your Just BASIC application from the list of open applications displayed in the Processes property sheet and click on the End Task button.

The Final Result

Okay, that's it. Assuming you followed along carefully and did not make any typing mistakes, your new game should be ready to run. Given the step-by-step approach used to show you how to develop the Knock Knock Joke game, I have gone ahead and provided a complete copy of the application's source code so that you can make sure you keyed in everything correctly and did so in the required order. Also, I have added comments explaining what is going on throughout the source code.

```
' ************************************************************************
'
' Script Name: KnockKnock.bas (The Knock Knock Joke Game)
' Version:      1.0
' Author:       Jerry Lee Ford, Jr.
' Date:         January 1, 2015
'
' Description: This Just BASIC game displays a series of interactive
'              Knock Knock jokes.
'
' ************************************************************************


'Disable the default display of the main window
nomainwin



' ************************************************************************
' Begin telling the first knock knock joke
' ************************************************************************
```

```
'Define the default response for the opening prompt
response$ = "Who is there?"

'Display the opening prompt for the first joke
prompt "Knock Knock Joke Game" + chr$(13) + "Knock Knock!"; response$

'Evaluate the player's response
if response$ = "" then 'No data was entered or the player clicked on Cancel

  'Display an error message
  notice "Knock Knock Joke Game" + chr$(13) + _
    "Error: You must respond by entering 'Who is there?'"

else  'Continue telling the joke

  'Define the default response for the second prompt
  response$ = "Disease who?"


  'Display the follow-up prompt for the first joke
  prompt "Knock Knock Joke Game" + chr$(13) + "Disease!"; response$

  'Evaluate the player's response
  if response$ = "" then   'No data was entered or cancel was clicked

    'Display an error message
    notice "Knock Knock Joke Game" + chr$(13) + _
      "Error: You must respond by entering 'Disease who?'"

  else   'Finish telling the joke

   'Display the joke's punch line
    notice "Knock Knock Joke Game" + chr$(13) + _
      "Disease jokes seem funny to you?"

  end if

end if
```

```
' **********************************************************************
' Begin telling the second knock knock joke
' **********************************************************************

'Define the default response for the opening prompt
response$ = "Who is there?"

'Display the opening prompt for the second joke
prompt "Knock Knock Joke Game" + chr$(13) + "Knock Knock!"; response$

'Evaluate the player's response
if response$ = "" then 'No data was entered or the player clicked on Cancel

  'Display an error message
  Notice "Knock Knock Joke Game" + chr$(13) + _
    "Error: You must respond by entering 'Who is there?'"

else  'Continue telling the joke

  'Define the default response for the second prompt
  response$ = "Butter who?"

  'Display the follow-up prompt for the second joke
  prompt "Knock Knock Joke Game" + chr$(13) + "Butter!"; response$

  'Evaluate the player's response
  if response$ = "" then   'No data was entered or cancel was clicked

    'Display an error message
    notice "Knock Knock Joke Game" + chr$(13) + _
      "Error: You must respond by entering 'Butter who?'"

  else   'Finish telling the joke

    'Display the joke's punch line
    notice "Knock Knock Joke Game" + chr$(13) + _
      "You butter move on to the next joke."

  end if

end if
```

```
' *************************************************************************
' Begin telling the third knock knock joke
' *************************************************************************

'Define the default response for the opening prompt
response$ = "Who is there?"

'Display the opening prompt for the third joke
prompt "Knock Knock Joke Game" + chr$(13) + "Knock Knock!"; response$

'Evaluate the player's response
if response$ = "" then 'No data was entered or the player clicked on Cancel

  'Display an error message
  notice "Knock Knock Joke Game" + chr$(13) + _
    "Error: You must respond by entering 'Who is there?'"

else  'Continue telling the joke

  'Define the default response for the second prompt
  response$ = "Max who?"

  'Display the follow-up prompt for the third joke
  prompt "Knock Knock Joke Game" + chr$(13) + "Max!"; response$

  'Evaluate the player's response
  if response$ = "" then  'No data was entered or cancel was clicked

    'Display an error message
    notice "Knock Knock Joke Game" + chr$(13) + _
      "Error: You must respond by entering 'Max who?'"

  else  'Finish telling the joke

   'Display the joke's punch line
    notice "Knock Knock Joke Game" + chr$(13) + _
      "BASIC, JAVA, C++, it max no difference to me!"

  end if

end if

end
```

Go ahead and execute your copy of the Knock Knock Joke game and put it through its paces. If instead of executing, you get an error, you have made at least one typo somewhere. Hopefully the error message you see will provide you with a clue as to where the error lies. Otherwise, you will need to go back and double-check each statement in the source code to find and eliminate all your typing errors.

Summary

In this chapter, you learned background information that will help you as you work your way through this book. This information includes the introduction of a number of key programming terms. In addition to increasing your programming vocabulary, you learned about different programming languages and how they compare against one another. You also learned about popular BASIC programming languages, including Just BASIC. Finally, you learned how to create and execute your first BASIC program.

Now, before you move on to Chapter 2, "Creating Programs with Just BASIC," I suggest you set aside a few extra minutes to improve the Knock Knock Joke game by addressing the following list of challenges.

Challenges

1. As currently written, the Knock Knock Joke game tells only three jokes. Consider improving the user's experience by adding additional jokes.

2. The error messages displayed by the game when the user fails to provide the expected response are somewhat cryptic. Consider enhancing them to make them easier to understand.

2

Creating Programs with Just BASIC

To work with any programming language, you need access to a set of software tools that facilitate the software development process. These tools include such things as a code editor, a compiler or interpreter, and a source code debugger. This chapter introduces you to these types of resources using tools provided by Just BASIC, demonstrating how these types of tools are employed to develop software applications. In addition, you will receive a thorough overview of Just BASIC's code editor and learn how to configure it to suit your personal preferences and work habits. You will also learn how to create and package standalone applications, which you can then run on computers where Just BASIC is not installed. On top of all this, you will learn how to create your second computer game: the Legend of Mighty Molly.

Specifically, you will learn the following:

- The ins and outs of Just BASIC menu and toolbar commands
- The way to configure Just BASIC editor settings
- The different windows that make up Just BASIC
- The method to create and distribute Just BASIC applications

Project Preview: The Legend of Mighty Molly

In this chapter, you will learn how to create a new game that tells a mad-lib-styled story of the Legend of Mighty Molly. Through the development of this game, you will learn how to interact with the player using the default text window that is automatically generated as part of every Just BASIC application. You will also learn how to clear out text displayed in the window and how to pause program execution to collect player input.

Figure 2.1 shows the game as it appears when it's started.

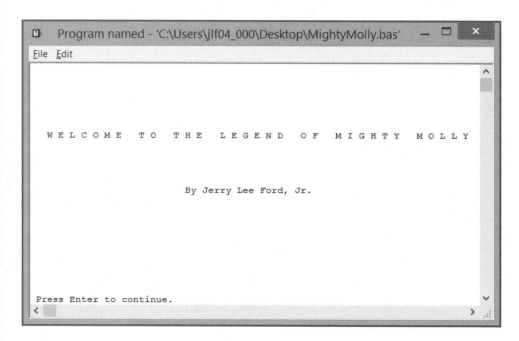

Figure 2.1 The opening screen for the Legend of Mighty Molly.
© 2016 Cengage Learning®

The player must press the Enter key to dismiss the opening welcome screen and advance to the next part of the story. This results in the display of the screen shown in Figure 2.2, which notifies the player that her participation is required to tell the story.

Next, as Figure 2.3 demonstrates, the player is presented with a series of questions. The answers that the player provides are used in the telling of the game's story.

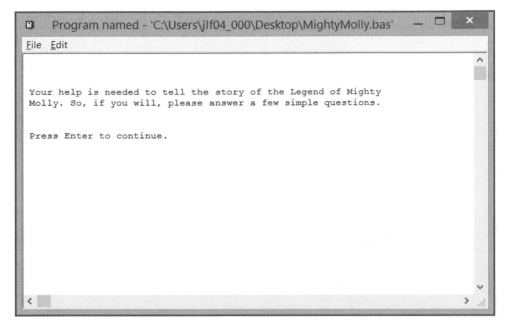

Figure 2.2 The player is given instructions on the interaction required to complete the story.
© 2016 Cengage Learning®

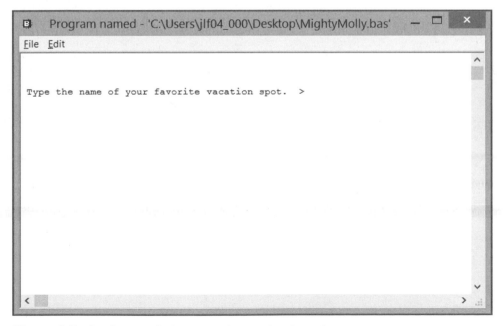

Figure 2.3 The player is asked to respond to a series of questions.
© 2016 Cengage Learning®

Once all questions have been answered, the game notifies the player that it is ready to begin telling the story, as shown in Figure 2.4.

Figure 2.4 The game announces that it is ready to tell its story.
© 2016 Cengage Learning®

Because the story integrates player input, it varies slightly each time it is told. The story is told in four parts. The text for the first part of the story is shown in Figure 2.5.

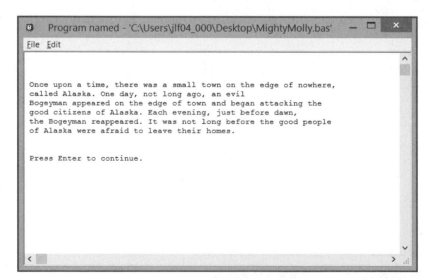

Figure 2.5 The game begins telling the story of the Legend of Mighty Molly.
© 2016 Cengage Learning®

An example of how the second part of the story might look is provided in Figure 2.6.

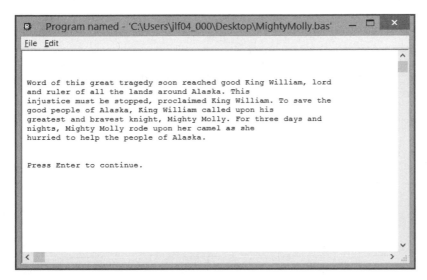

Figure 2.6 The king calls upon Mighty Molly to save the day.
© 2016 Cengage Learning®

The game automatically pauses after each part of the story is displayed, allowing the player to control the pace at which the story unfolds. Figure 2.7 shows an example of how the third part of the story might go.

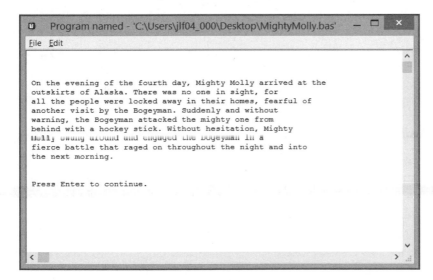

Figure 2.7 Mighty Molly defends the people by fighting the story's antagonist.
© 2016 Cengage Learning®

Finally, the last part of the story is told, as demonstrated in Figure 2.8.

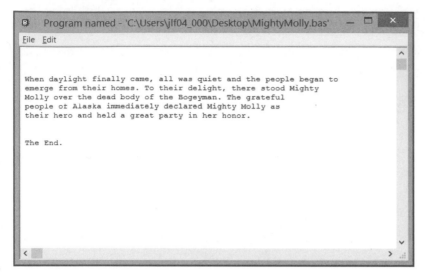

Figure 2.8 Like most stories, the Legend of Mighty Molly has a happy ending.
© 2016 Cengage Learning®

Tools of the Trade

To work with any programming language, a programmer needs access to a number of different software development tools, including the following:

- **Code editor.** Used to enter and save program source code.
- **Compiler or interpreter.** Required to convert program source code into machine language code for execution.
- **Integrated debugger.** Used to locate and analyze errors that occur during the application development process.

Some programming languages come equipped with everything needed to develop software programs. For example, Microsoft Visual C++ provides a complete *integrated development environment (IDE)*. The IDE includes a code editor, compiler, and debugger. In addition, the IDE includes tools that enable Rapid Application Development (RAD) using drag-and-drop *graphical user interface (GUI)* design. Other programming languages, especially scripting languages, require that you provide your own code editor. In the case of Just BASIC, a code editor, compiler, and debugger are provided.

Hint

Just BASIC's distribution package also includes a drag-and-drop GUI forms designer called FreeForm-J. You will learn how to create Just BASIC applications with GUIs in Chapter 3, "Creating Graphical User Interfaces."

Working with Just BASIC

As has already been stated, Just BASIC is a simple and straightforward BASIC dialect that gives programmers the tools they need to develop standalone applications that can be executed on Microsoft Windows. Just BASIC provides programmers with a number of helpful features, including these:

- **Statement color coding.** Just BASIC's code editor automatically color-codes language keywords to make them stand out, which is an especially helpful visual queue for larger programs that can significantly enhance source code readability.
- **Automatic code indentation.** Just BASIC's code editor helps programmers write more legible programs by automatically indenting code statements.
- **Built-in source code debugger.** Just BASIC provides a debugging facility that allows programmers to pause program execution so they can check on the status of program variables and trace program execution flow on a line-by-line basis.
- **GUI forms editor.** Included as part of the Just BASIC distribution is a form generator that enables the drag-and-drop design of GUIs.
- **Built-in sprite engine.** Just BASIC's sprite engine provides facilities for adding animated graphical effects to Windows applications.
- **Support for playing audio files.** Just BASIC gives programmers the ability to play audio files and MIDI music.

Each time Just BASIC is started, two windows are displayed: The World of Just BASIC! window and the code editor window. The code editor window offers access to everything you need to create and test Just BASIC programs. The World of Just BASIC! window includes access to a host of Just BASIC resources.

The World of Just BASIC! Window

The World of Just BASIC! window, shown in Figure 2.9, is automatically displayed each time you start Just BASIC.

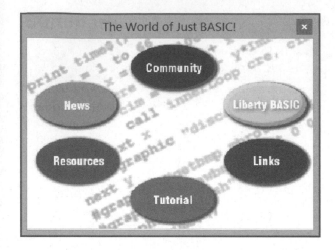

Figure 2.9 The World of Just BASIC! window provides single-click access to a number of helpful programming resources.

© 2016 Cengage Learning®

This window consists of six graphical links that provide access to the following resources:

- Community
- Liberty BASIC
- Links
- Tutorial
- Resources
- News

Each of these links is explained in detail in the sections that follow.

Community

The Community link offers access to the Community web page located on the Just BASIC website, as shown in Figure 2.10. From here, programmers can access the Just BASIC Message Forum. This forum provides an online location for Just BASIC programmers to congregate and share information with one another and is a great source of information and help when you run into programming problems that you are unable to figure out on your own.

Liberty BASIC

The Liberty BASIC link provides access to information about Liberty BASIC, which is posted at the Just BASIC website, as shown in Figure 2.11. Liberty BASIC is the commercial upgrade to Just BASIC.

Figure 2.10 The Just BASIC website's Community page provides access to the Just BASIC Message Forum.

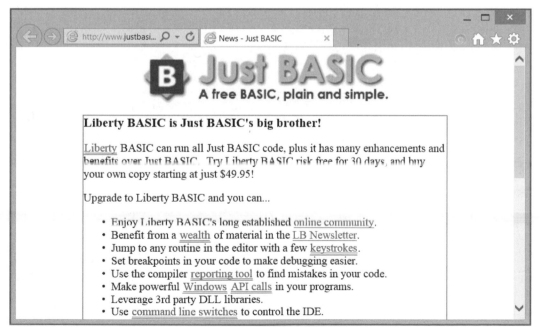

Figure 2.11 Liberty BASIC is the commercial upgrade to Just BASIC.

Liberty BASIC supports Just BASIC code 100 percent. In addition, it provides a number of features not found in Just BASIC, including the following:

- Additional debugging features
- Improved sprite commands
- The ability to access *input/output (I/O)* ports
- Additional commands for performing string and file operations

Links

The Links link offers access to a small collection of online Just BASIC websites and resources, as shown in Figure 2.12.

Figure 2.12 Accessing additional online Just BASIC resources.
© 2016 Shoptalk Systems

Tutorial

The Tutorial link has quick access to Just BASIC's help system. As shown in Figure 2.13, Just BASIC's help system includes a six-week tutorial as well as the ability to search for Just BASIC information using search and find options.

Figure 2.13 Access to help is also provided from the Just BASIC code editor's menu system.
© 2016 Shoptalk Systems

Resources

The Resources link gives you easy access to a number of websites (as demonstrated in Figure 2.14) where you can interact with other Just BASIC programmers as well as find sample programs.

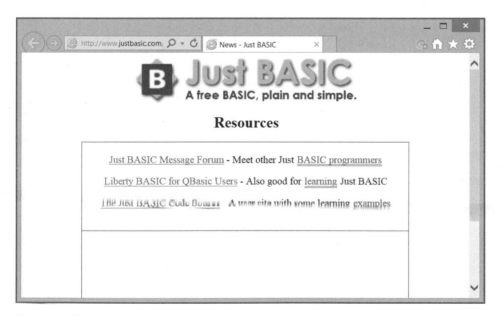

Figure 2.14 Use the Resources link to locate websites where you can go to find sample code developed by other programmers.
© 2016 Shoptalk Systems

News

Click on the News link to find current information about what is going on with Just BASIC, as demonstrated in Figure 2.15.

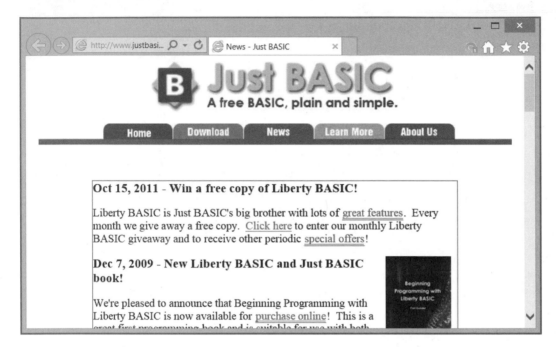

Figure 2.15 Viewing Just BASIC news.
© 2016 Shoptalk Systems

The Code Editor Window

The code editor window is where you will spend most of your time when developing Just BASIC applications. As shown in Figure 2.16, Just BASIC's code editor is organized into four main parts.

Like any good text editor, the code editor provides slider controls on the right and bottom of the editor window that are enabled whenever the amount of source code exceeds the window's visible area.

By default, the code editor automatically opens and displays a basic program named welcome.bas each time it is started. This program consists of a large collection of comments that have instruction designed to help new Just BASIC programmers get started. If you scroll down to the bottom of this file, you will find the following code statements:

```
nomainwin
run "winhlp32 justbasic.hlp"
end
```

Menu bar

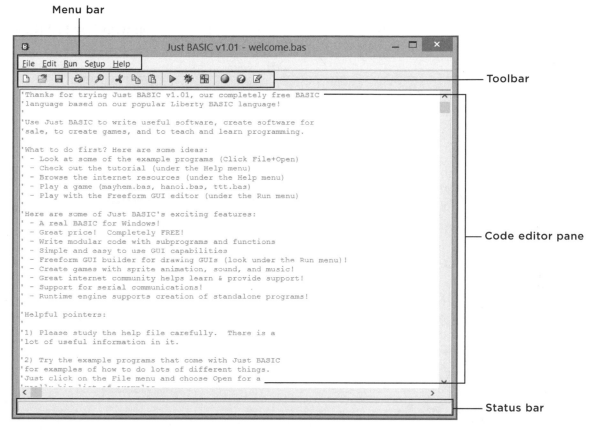

Toolbar

Code editor pane

Status bar

Figure 2.16 Just BASIC's code editor window.
© 2016 Shoptalk Systems

When executed, this program opens Just BASIC's help system. The first statement executes the nomainwin command, which suppresses the display of the application's default text window.

Hint

As you may remember, a default text window is automatically created for every Just BASIC program. This window is named mainwin. You can use this window, as demonstrated later In the Legend of Mighty Molly story, to display text and interact with users.

The second statement executes the run command and passes it two arguments for processing. You use the run command to execute external programs. In this example, the first argument being passed to the run command is winhelp32, which is the name of the program to be executed.

Winhlp32 is a Windows Help File viewer, which you were given instructions on how to install in Chapter 1, "Introduction to Programming." The second argument passed to the run command is justbasic.hlp, which is the name of Just BASIC's help file.

Hint

An *argument* is a piece of data passed to a program for processing.

The last statement executes the end command, which ensures that the program terminates in a clean manner. If you want, you can run this program by opening the Run menu and clicking on the Run command. Many Just BASIC programmers find that having Just BASIC automatically load the welcome.bas program each time it starts is a nuisance and configure Just BASIC to prevent this behavior from happening. You will learn how to do this later in the chapter in the section titled "Configuring Just BASIC Preferences."

Hint

The end **statement forces the clean termination of an application, ensuring that any open files and windows are properly closed.**

Just BASIC's Menu System

The Just BASIC code editor gives programmers access to numerous commands through its menu system, located at the top of the editor window. As Figure 2.17 shows, the File menu provides access to commands that allow you to create new BASIC programs, open existing programs, and save and print their contents. In addition, a listing of recently edited programs is maintained, allowing you to easily open them again.

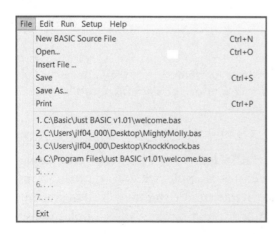

Figure 2.17 The File menu provides commands for creating and opening BASIC programs.
© 2016 Shoptalk Systems

The Edit menu, shown in Figure 2.18, contains commands that allow you to Copy, Cut, and Paste code statements as well as to select or clear out code currently typed into the editor. The Edit menu also provides access to Find and Replace commands, allowing you to perform code searches and to make mass code changes.

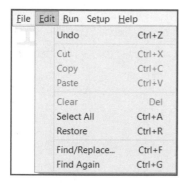

Figure 2.18 Accessing commands located on the Just BASIC Edit menu.
© 2016 Shoptalk Systems

The Run menu, shown in Figure 2.19, contains commands that allow you to run your Just BASIC programs. The Run command runs your program normally, and the Debug command runs programs in debug mode, enabling you to track down and fix program errors. The Run menu also has a Kill command that lets you forcibly terminate the execution of any Just BASIC applications that are currently running.

Hint

Instruction on how to kill Just BASIC programs is provided later in this chapter.

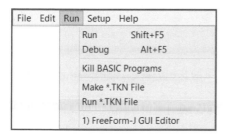

Figure 2.19 The Run menu provides access to commands that execute BASIC programs.
© 2016 Shoptalk Systems

As Figure 2.19 shows, the Run menu also provides access to a pair of commands that allow you to make and run *.TKN files. A *.TKN file is a *token* file providing the basis for creating Just BASIC applications that can run as standalone applications and is the key to creating Just BASIC applications that you can then distribute to other computers. You'll learn the specific steps involved in creating standalone applications later in this chapter in the section titled "Building Standalone Applications."

One additional command provided by the Run menu starts the FreeForm-J GUI Editor. *FreeForm-J* is an external utility that you can use when laying out GUIs. FreeForm-J assists in designing graphical windows interfaces using drag and drop to add and organize interface elements such as text boxes and button controls. You will learn how to work with FreeForm-J in Chapter 3.

The Setup menu, shown in Figure 2.20, provides access to windows that you can use to modify Just BASIC configuration settings. You can make changes to these settings to customize Just BASIC's configuration to suit your own personal preferences. You'll find a detailed discussion of how to configure Just BASIC later in this chapter.

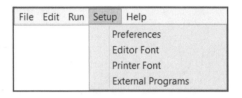

Figure 2.20 The Setup menu provides access to windows that control Just BASIC's configuration settings.
© 2016 Shoptalk Systems

Just BASIC's last menu is its Help menu. As shown in Figure 2.21, it provides access to Just BASIC's help systems and to a Just BASIC tutorial. You can also access Just BASIC's release notes and online news and links from this menu.

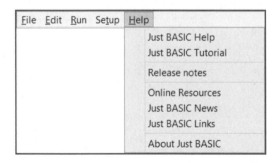

Figure 2.21 Just BASIC provides access to extensive help information and resources.
© 2016 Shoptalk Systems

Just BASIC's Toolbar

Just BASIC's toolbar, shown in Figure 2.22, has single-click access to a number of commonly used editor commands.

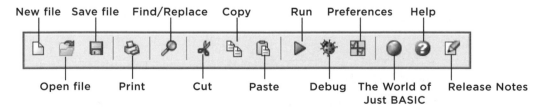

Figure 2.22 The Just BASIC toolbar provides single-click access to commonly used commands.
© 2016 Shoptalk Systems

TABLE 2.1 JUST BASIC'S TOOLBAR SHORTCUTS		
Toolbar Command	**Menu Equivalent**	**Keyboard Shortcut**
New File	File, New BASIC File	Alt+F+N
Open File	File, Open	Alt+F+O
Save File	File, Save	Alt+F+S
Print	File, Print	Alt+F+P
Find/Replace	Edit, Find/Replace	Ctrl+F
Cut	Edit, Cut	Ctrl+X
Copy	Edit, Copy	Ctrl+C
Paste	Edit, Paste	Ctrl+V
Run	Run, Run	Shift+F5
Debug	Run, Debug	Alt+F5
Preferences	Setup, Preferences	Alt+T+P
Help	Help, Just BASIC Help	Alt+H+L
Release Notes	Help, Release Notes	Alt+H+P

© 2016 Shoptalk Systems

Configuring Just BASIC Preferences

Like many programming languages, you can customize the look and operation of Just BASIC. This is accomplished through its Preferences window, shown in Figure 2.23. You access the Preferences window by clicking on Just BASIC's Setup menu and selecting Preferences or by clicking on the Preferences button on the Just BASIC toolbar.

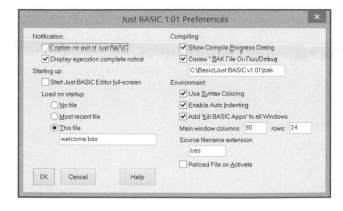

Figure 2.23 Configuring Just BASIC preference settings.
© 2016 Shoptalk Systems

Just BASIC Preferences are organized into the following major categories:

- Notification
- Starting up
- Compiling
- Environment

Notification Settings

Just BASIC's notification settings allow you to specify how much information and interaction you want when working with the code editor. Either of the following options can be configured:

- **Confirm on Exit of Just BASIC.** Instructs Just BASIC to display a prompt asking for confirmation before closing the Just BASIC code editor window.
- **Display Execution Complete Notice.** Instructs Just BASIC to display a message in the title bar of a program's main window indicating when program execution has completed. This option is enabled by default.

Startup Settings

Just BASIC's startup configuration settings give you control over the initial appearance of the code editor window as well as the ability to specify which, if any, BASIC file should be automatically located into the code editor at startup. Either of the following options can be configured:

- **Start Just BASIC Editor full-screen.** Instructs Just BASIC to open the code editor window in full screen mode, filling the entire display area.
- **Load on Startup.** Controls which BASIC file, if any, is automatically loaded at startup.

The Load on Startup option can be useful when you're working on a BASIC application that requires a considerable amount of time to complete or when working on an application that must be frequently modified. This option allows you to choose from any of the following three options:

- **No File.** Instructs Just BASIC to start without loading a BASIC file.
- **Most Recent File.** Instructs Just BASIC to load the most recently edited program at startup.
- **This File.** Instructs Just BASIC to load the specified file.

As mentioned earlier in this chapter, Just BASIC automatically displays the welcome.bas file each time it is started. You can alter this behavior by specifying No File as the setting for the Load on Startup option.

Compiler Settings

Just BASIC lets you configure two compiler settings, both of which are enabled by default. The Show Compile Progress Dialog setting instructs Just BASIC to display a graphic representation of the compile process whenever you compile a program. Although it's often barely noticeable for small programs, this option can be useful for larger applications with a longer compile time, allowing the programmer to cancel the compilation at any time during the process.

The Create *.BAK File on Run/Debug option allows you to instruct Just BASIC to maintain a backup copy of any Just BASIC application every time you run it from within the code editor. Just BASIC automatically saves backup files in its installation folder. The obvious advantage of this option is that it allows you to recover the previous version of any Just BASIC application in case something goes wrong with the most recent version. If you need it, all you have to do is navigate to the specified backup folder and retrieve the appropriate backup file. Just rename its file extension from .bak to .bas, and you can begin working with it.

> **Hint**
>
> You were advised in **Chapter 1** to create a directory named Basic at the root of your computer's disk drive and to use that directory as your installation folder.

Environmental Settings

The next set of configuration settings that you can modify are the environmental settings. In total, there are six environment settings that you can configure, as outlined here:

- **Use Syntax Coloring.** When enabled, this option instructs Just BASIC to apply different colors to language keywords that make up code statements.
- **Enable Auto Indenting.** When enabled, this option instructs Just BASIC to repeat the previous level of indentation each time the Enter key is pressed when keying in code statements.
- **Add 'Kill BASIC Apps' to All Windows.** When enabled, this option instructs Just BASIC to add a special Kill BASIC Apps menu item to each Just BASIC window, which you can use to forcibly terminate any active Just BASIC application.
- **Main Window Columns.** Specifies the default window size for the default main window of any Just BASIC program. The default values define a text window that is 80 columns wide and 24 rows tall.
- **Source Filename Extension.** Defines the default filename extension for Just BASIC programs. The default file extension is .BAS.
- **Reload File on Activate.** When enabled, this configuration option supports the execution of Just BASIC applications being edited outside of the Just BASIC code editor.

Trick

The Reload File on Activate environmental configuration setting deserves a little extra explanation. Its purpose is to allow you to open the same file twice: once in the Just BASIC code editor and a second time in a third-party editor of your choice. This allows you to write and modify your application's source code using your favorite editor and, if the Reload File on Activate setting has been enabled, switch over to Just BASIC and run your application. Just BASIC automatically reloads a fresh copy of your application running it in order, ensuring that the most current version is executed.

Other Configuration Options

The Just BASIC Setup menu also lets you configure editor and printer font sizes for all text. Just BASIC uses the Courier New font with a Regular style font size of 9 as the default for the code editor. Just BASIC's default for printed text is Courier New, Regular style font with a font size of 10.

The Setup menu also gives you the ability to configure Just BASIC to add entries for external programs to its Run menu. This is accomplished by clicking on the Setup menu's External Programs menu item, which displays the Setup External Programs window shown in Figure 2.24.

Figure 2.24 Adding entries to external programs under the Just BASIC Run menu.
© 2016 Shoptalk Systems

As you can see, there is an entry for the FreeForm-J GUI Editor by default, thus making it easy to start this external program from within the Just BASIC code editor. Using the Setup External Programs window, you can add entries for other software programs. For example, you might want to add an entry for an alternative editor or a graphics drawing program. To do so, click on the New button, type a descriptive name for the program being added, click on the Browse button, specify the name and path of the program, and click on Open. When you click on Close to dismiss the Setup External Programs window, a prompt appears informing you that you must stop and restart Just BASIC for your modifications to become effective.

Working with Applications

You have already learned how to use Just BASIC to create and execute new Windows desktop applications. In the sections that follow, you will learn how to reopen saved Just BASIC programs and how to kill the execution of a Just BASIC program that did not end properly on its own.

Trick

Unlike many other programming language IDEs, Just BASIC's code editor only allows you to edit one BASIC program at a time. However, you can start up as many different instances of Just BASIC at a time as you want and edit multiple applications that way.

Opening and Saving Programs

You can reopen and edit any Just BASIC program by clicking on the File menu and selecting the Open menu item. In response, the Open File window is displayed, as shown in Figure 2.25.

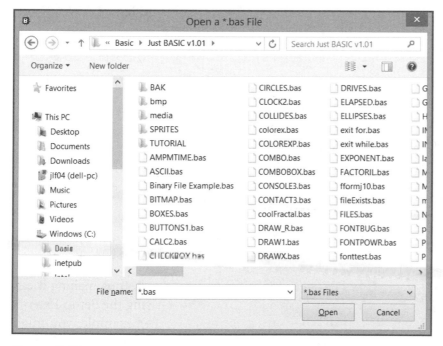

Figure 2.25 Opening a BASIC file using Just BASIC.

Using the Open File window, locate and select the BASIC file you want to edit and click on the Open button. Just BASIC opens the file and displays its contents in the code editor pane. At this point, you may edit the program or run it by clicking on the Run button. When Just BASIC's Run command is executed, be it from the Run menu or by clicking on the Run button on the toolbar, it takes a few moments for your program to begin executing. In the background, Just BASIC must first compile your program's source code into machine code. Once this task has been completed, Just BASIC runs your compiled program.

Hint

You can also run your BASIC application by pressing the Shift and the F5 key simultaneously.

Trick

You may have noticed that when the Open File window was first displayed, it showed the contents of the Just BASIC folder. This folder contains dozens of sample programs supplied as part of Just BASIC's distribution package. These programs are generally small and demonstrate how to perform a host of different tasks using various Just BASIC programming features. You can learn much from studying these examples. For example, if you were to select Lander.bas, you'd open a Just BASIC drawing application that when executed looks like the application shown in Figure 2.26.

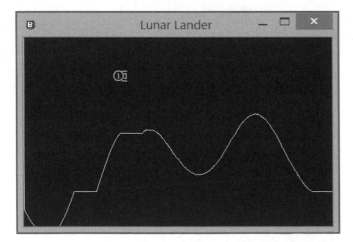

Figure 2.26 Executing the Lander.bas program supplied with Just BASIC.
© 2016 Shoptalk Systems

Killing Programs

Just BASIC provides a Kill command to assist you if you execute a Just BASIC program that fails to terminate properly. To execute this command, click on the Run menu and select the Kill BASIC Programs option. In response, Just BASIC displays a context menu that lists all currently running Just BASIC programs, as demonstrated in Figure 2.27.

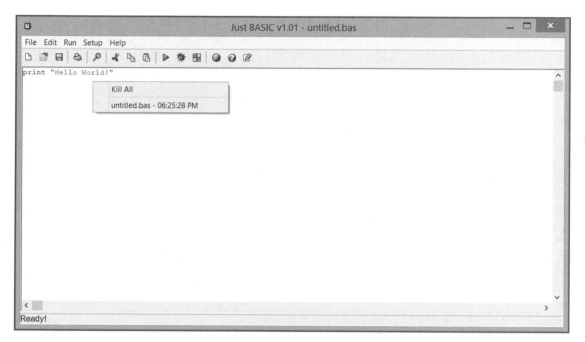

Figure 2.27 Killing a Just BASIC program that has failed to properly terminate.
© 2016 Shoptalk Systems

To forcibly terminate a Just BASIC application, click on its name. Also, take note that also included in the context menu is a Kill All option. Selecting this option forces the termination of all currently running Just BASIC programs.

Hint

Remember to add the end command to the end of your Just BASIC programs. This command instructs Just BASIC to close any open resources prior to terminating an application and helps prevent applications from getting hung up.

Other Just BASIC Components

Just BASIC's code editor is the only tool that you need to develop and test Just BASIC programs. However, like many modern programming languages, Just BASIC gives programmers additional tools that assist in the development of software applications. These programs include an external Just BASIC application called FreeForm-J and Just BASIC's built-in Debugger window.

Designing Forms

Using commands provided by Just BASIC, you can programmatically generate a window's GUI from code. However, the FreeForm-J program, supplied as part of Just BASIC's distribution, lets you lay out GUIs by dragging and dropping interface elements onto windows, as demonstrated in Figure 2.28.

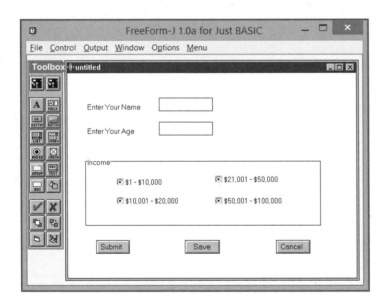

Figure 2.28 FreeFrom-J is an external program supplied with Just BASIC that assists in the development of GUIs.
© 2016 Shoptalk Systems

FreeForm-J is started by clicking on the FreeForm-J entry located on the Run menu. Once you have used FreeForm-J to design a window's layout, you can generate the underlying source code required to re-create the interface. You can then add this code to your Just BASIC application to enable it to generate the interface. Step-by-step instructions for using FreeForm-J are provided in Chapter 3.

> **Trick**
>
> FreeForm-J is actually a software program written using Just BASIC. Its source code is shipped with Just BASIC and can be found in the same folder as Just BASIC's other sample programs. If you want, you can modify and customize FreeForm-J to suit your own particular needs.

The Just BASIC Debugger

Every programmer experiences errors when developing software programs. Programmers commonly refer to such errors as *bugs*. With proper design and testing, programmers can eliminate most program bugs. Unfortunately, some program errors are harder to track down and fix than others. To assist you in performing this difficult task, most programming languages provide some sort of debugging program or utility. Just BASIC is no exception, supplying programmers with access to its own GUI debugger program.

You can start Just BASIC's debugger by opening the Run menu and selecting the Debug menu item or by clicking on the toolbar button that looks like a small beetle bug. Once started, the debugger window appears, as demonstrated in Figure 2.29.

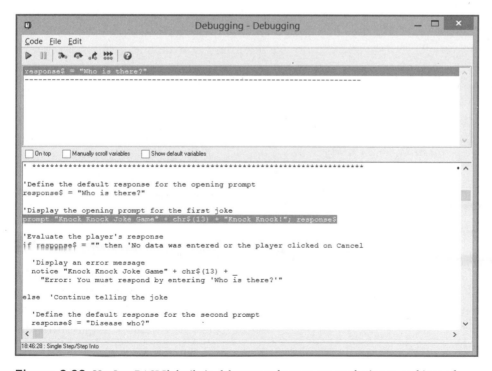

Figure 2.29 Use Just BASIC's built-in debugger to keep an eye on the inner workings of a Just BASIC application as it executes.
© 2016 Shoptalk Systems

Using the debugger, you can track the internal execution of any Just BASIC program on a line-by-line basis. In addition, you can keep an eye on the value of data as the application collects and processes it. By providing you with a fine-tuned, internal view of your application's execution, application debuggers help you search for and find the needle in the haystack that is causing problems in your application. Step-by-step instructions for using Just BASIC's internal debugger are provided in Chapter 11, "Debugging Your Applications."

Building Standalone Applications

Many programming languages, like Microsoft C++ and Visual Basic, generate a single executable file with an .exe file extension when you compile your application. To share your application, you have to distribute this executable file to your customers and users. However, to create stand-alone Just BASIC applications, you need to create a tokenized version of your application.

Creating a Tokenized File

To create a tokenized copy of an application file, you must load the application into the code editor and then select the Make *.TKN File menu item located on the Run menu. Just BASIC responds by opening the Save *.TKN File As window, as shown in Figure 2.30. Just BASIC generates a filename for the tokenized file based on the current name of the BASIC file. If you want, you can change this name before clicking on Save to generate a tokenized copy of the application file.

Trick

Tokenized files run faster than nontokenized files. Therefore, you might want to generate tokenized files for Just BASIC programs that you intend to run often within the Just BASIC code editor or that you plan to add to Just BASIC's Run menu.

Once you have saved your tokenized file, you can run it within the Just BASIC code editor by clicking on the Run *.TKN File option located on the Run menu. In response, Just BASIC displays the Run a *.TKN file window, as demonstrated in Figure 2.31.

Once loaded, the tokenized application immediately begins executing. If you have added an entry to Just BASIC's Run menu for the tokenized file, you can run it at any time by clicking on the Run menu and selecting it.

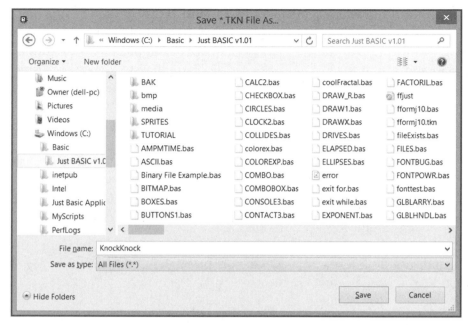

Figure 2.30 Saving a tokenized version of a Just BASIC program.
© 2016 Shoptalk Systems

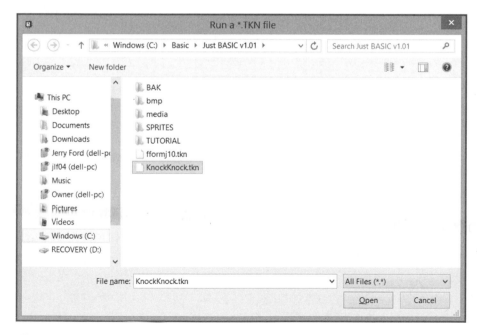

Figure 2.31 Running the tokenized version of a Just BASIC program.
© 2016 Shoptalk Systems

Distributing Your Just BASIC Applications

To distribute copies of your Just BASIC applications, you need to perform the following tasks:

- Generate a tokenized file.
- Make a copy of Just BASIC's runtime file and rename it to match the name assigned to the tokenized file.
- Collect any additional files required to support the execution of your application.

Once you have finished creating and testing your Just BASIC application, you need to create a tokenized copy of your application file to distribute and run the application on another computer where Just BASIC may not be installed. For example, you might take the Knock Knock Joke game created in Chapter 1 and create a tokenized version of that file called knockknock.tkn.

The next step in preparing to distribute your application is to make a copy of Just BASIC's runtime file, JBRUN101.exe, and rename it to match the name of your tokenized file. In the case of the Knock Knock Joke game, you would assign knockknock.exe as the new name for the copy of Just BASIC's runtime file.

To execute a Just BASIC program as a standalone application on other computers, you also need to assemble copies of the following Just BASIC system files:

- VBAS31W.SLL
- VGUI31W.SLL
- VOFLR31W.SLL
- VTHK31W.DLL
- VTK1631W.DLL
- VTK3231W.DLL
- VVM31W.DLL
- VVMT31W.DLL

You will find the files located in Just BASIC's installation folder.

The last step in assembling your standalone application is to assemble a disk, CD-ROM, DVD, or other type of package that contains the tokenized file, the renamed copy of Just BASIC's runtime file, and the Just BASIC systems files listed earlier. Once you have finished putting together your package, as demonstrated in Figure 2.32, you are ready to begin distributing your application to your friends, users, and customers. Of course, if your application uses any other external files, such as a text or graphics file, you need to add them to your distribution package as well.

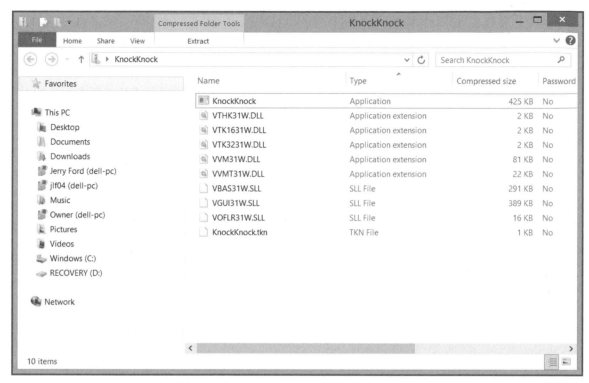

Figure 2.32 The distribution files for the Knock Knock Joke game.
© 2016 Shoptalk Systems

Trick

One convenient and simple way to distribute your Just BASIC application is to create a Zip file containing your tokenized Just BASIC file along with the other files needed to run it as a standalone program. This way, all that your users and customers need to do to run your program is to unzip it into a folder on their computer. WinZip also provides a self-extraction feature that allows you to create a Zip file that unpacks itself when the user opens it, allowing you to make things even easier for your users.

Another alternative that you may want to investigate is freeware and shareware software distribution programs that automate the software distribution and installation process. Examples of these types of programs include Setup2Go (www.dev4pc.com/) and Agentix Installer (www.aginstaller.com).

Back to the Legend of Mighty Molly

Now it is time to turn your attention back to the development of this chapter's game project, the Legend of Mighty Molly. In this game, data collected from the player is used in the creation of a mad-lib styled story. Unlike the Knock Knock Joke game, which used pop-up dialogs to interact with the player, this game uses the text window supplied as part of every Just BASIC application to collect and display information.

Designing the Game

The design of the Legend of Mighty Molly game is pretty straightforward. The game relies mainly on the `print`, `input`, and `cls` commands to control the data collection process and display the game's story.

As you learned in Chapter 1, you can use the `print` command to display text strings on the mainwin window. The `input` command displays a text message prompt and collects the user's response as input to your program. The `cls` command clears out any text displayed in mainwin.

Hint

The syntax for the `input` command is shown here:

```
input #Handle  "String";  VariableName
```

#Handle is an optional argument that, when used, specifies a filename or device. *String* is an optional placeholder representing a string that can be displayed. *VariableName* is the name of a variable that will be used to store any input the user enters before pressing the Enter key.

The Legend of Mighty Molly game is created in eight steps, as outlined here:

1. Create a new BASIC file and document its purpose.
2. Display the game's opening welcome screen.
3. Provide instructions to the player.
4. Display the game's first question and collect the player's input.
5. Display the rest of the game's questions.
6. Tell the first part of the story.
7. Tell the rest of the story.
8. Clear the screen and prepare the game for termination.

Creating a Just BASIC File Script

You'll begin the development of the Legend of Mighty Molly game by starting Just BASIC and creating a new BASIC file. Next, you'll document the purpose of the game by adding the following code statements:

```
' ********************************************************************
'
' Script Name: MightyMolly.bas (The Legend of Mighty Molly)
' Version:     1.0
' Author:      Jerry Lee Ford, Jr.
' Date:        January 10, 2015
'
' Description: This Just BASIC game displays a mad-lib styled story in
'                 which the player input is used to tell a humorous story.
'
' ********************************************************************
```

Before continuing, save your new Just BASIC file, assigning it a name of MightyMolly.bas.

Displaying a Welcome Screen

Now you'll add the code statements that are responsible for displaying a welcome screen for the game by adding the following statements to the program:

```
print
print
print
print
print
print
print "   W E L C O M E   T O   T H E   L E G E N D   O F   M I G H T Y" _
     + "   M O L L Y"
print
print
print
print
print "                          By Jerry Lee Ford, Jr."
print
print
print
print
```

```
print
print
print
print
print
input " Press Enter to continue."; input$
```

The last statement uses the input command to pause the execution of the application until the player presses the Enter key.

Hint

Note that the input$ variable is automatically assigned an empty string ("") as its value when the player presses the Enter key. The program does not use the value assigned to input$. It has been included only because the syntax of the input command requires a variable assignment.

Providing Game Instructions

As straightforward as this game may be, it is still a good idea to provide the player with a little direction at the beginning of the game. To do so, add the following statements to the end of your program:

```
cls

print
print
print
print " Your help is needed to tell the story of the Legend of Mighty"
print " Molly. So, if you will, please answer a few simple questions."
print
print
input " Press Enter to continue."; input$
```

As you can see, the cls command clears the screen, and then the game's instructions are presented using a series of print commands followed by the input command to pause program execution until the player is ready to continue.

Prompting the Player for Input

It is now time to begin prompting the player to provide the game with the data needed to tell its story. The code statements responsible for displaying the game's first question are shown here:

```
cls

print
print
print
input " Type the name of your favorite vacation spot.  > "; location$
```

The input command is once again used to pause the execution of the program and wait for the player to key in her input and then press the Enter key. The input the player provides is then stored in a variable named location$ so that the program can display its value later.

Collecting Additional Player Input

The next set of statements to be added to your program is shown next. These statements are responsible for collecting the three remaining pieces of information the game needs to tell its story. Note that separate variables are used to store each of the three inputs the player provides. Once the program has everything it needs, it announces that it is ready to tell its story:

```
cls

print
print
print
input " Name something that scared you as a child.  > "; creature$

cls

print
print
print
input " Name a piece of sports equipment.  > "; weapon$

cls

print
print
print
input " Name a popular four-legged animal.  > "; vehicle$

cls

print
print
print
input " Excellent answers. Please press Enter to begin the story."; input$
```

Beginning the Story

The next set of statements clears the screen and displays the first part of the game's story. The input command pauses the program until the player has finished reading:

```
cls

print
print
print
print " Once upon a time, there was a small town on the edge of nowhere,"
print " called " + location$ + ". One day, not long ago, an evil "
print " " + creature$ + " appeared on the edge of town and began attacking"
print " the good citizens of " + location$ + ". Each evening, just before"
print " dawn, the " + creature$ + " reappeared. It was not long before the"
print " good people of " + location$ + " were afraid to leave their homes."
print
print
input " Press Enter to continue."; input$
```

Telling the Rest of the Story

The code statements shown next finish telling the story by dividing its display into three parts, each of which is displayed a screen at a time:

```
cls

print
print
print
print " Word of this great tragedy soon reached good King William, lord"
print " and ruler of all the lands around " + location$ + ". This"
print " injustice must be stopped, proclaimed King William. To save the"
print " good people of " + location$ + ", King William called upon his"
print " greatest and bravest knight, Mighty Molly. For three days and"
print " nights, Mighty Molly rode upon her " + vehicle$ + " as she"
print " hurried to help the people of " + location$ + "."
print
print
input " Press Enter to continue."; input$

cls
```

```
print
print
print
print " On the evening of the fourth day, Mighty Molly arrived at the"
print " outskirts of " + location$ + ". There was no one in sight, for"
print " all the people were locked away in their homes, fearful of"
print " another visit by the " + creature$ + ". Suddenly and without"
print " warning, the " + creature$ + " attacked the mighty one from"
print " behind with a " + weapon$ + ". Without hesitation, Mighty"
print " Molly swung around and engaged the " + creature$  + " in a"
print " fierce battle that raged on throughout the night and into"
print " the next morning."
print
print
input " Press Enter to continue."; input$

cls

print
print
print
print " When daylight finally came, all was quiet and the people began to"
print " emerge from their homes. To their delight, there stood Mighty"
print " Molly over the dead body of the " + creature$ + ". The grateful"
print " people of " + location$ + " immediately declared Mighty Molly as"
print " their hero and held a great party in her honor."
print
print
input " The End."; input$
```

Preparing to End the Program

Now that the game's story has been told, it is time for the program to terminate. Before doing so, clear the screen with the cls command and then add the end command to the end of the program to ensure that the program is ready for termination:

```
cls

end
```

Hint

Although the game used the end command to identify the logical end of the program, the program does not actually terminate until the player closes the application window. In Chapter 3, you will learn how to associate the end command with a window's closing to better coordinate the execution of the command with the actual end of the program.

The Final Result

Okay, that's all there is to it. Assuming that you did not make typos as you keyed in the code for the application, your new game should be ready to run. However, before you run it, take a few minutes to look it over. Take note of the sequential manner in which the program code executes, beginning with the first statement and then processing each statement that follows until the last statement is executed. In future chapters, you will learn how to create programs that make use of loops, conditional logic, and subroutines to create more complex programming logic that can change the order in which statements are executed.

Summary

In this chapter, you learned about the different types of software tools programmers use to develop new applications. In addition, you learned the ins and outs of working with the Just BASIC code editor. You learned how to work with Just BASIC's code editor to configure its configuration settings. You also learned how to create and package standalone applications.

Before moving on to Chapter 3, why don't you set aside a little time to improve the Legend of Mighty Molly by tackling the following list of challenges.

Challenges

1. As it is currently written, this program is lacking in internal documentation that helps explain what is going on. Consider rectifying this situation by embedding comments at key locations throughout the program file.

2. Consider increasing the length of the story and collecting additional user input to make the story line even more dynamic.

3. Create a ZIP file distribution package for the Legend of Mighty Molly and use it to share your new program with your friends.

3

Creating Graphical User Interfaces

One of the most important features of any Windows desktop application is its *graphical user interface (GUI)*. As such, it is important that your application windows be well organized and intuitive. In this chapter, you will learn about the fundamental building blocks of Windows application GUIs. This will include learning how to create different types of windows and work with different types of interface controls like buttons, textboxes, and comboboxes. You will learn how to link interface controls to program code through the development of event handlers. You will also learn how to programmatically interact with interface controls and set properties like color and font type, and how to enable and disable access to controls. Beyond all this, you will learn how to create your next game: the BASIC Crazy 8 Ball game.

Specifically, you will learn the following:

- The different types of application windows supported by Just BASIC
- How to open and close windows and to set different windows properties such as color and font type
- How to programmatically generate different interface controls
- How to set up control event handlers
- How to work with FreeForm-J so you can design GUIs

Project Preview: The BASIC Crazy 8 Ball Game

This chapter's game project is the BASIC Crazy 8 Ball game. This game emulates the children's crazy 8 ball toy by displaying random answers to player questions. The creation of this game requires you to design a GUI that consists of multiple windows using button, statictext, and textbox controls. In addition to giving you experience in developing GUIs, the development of this game introduces you to event-driven programming, in which program code is associated with individual windows and controls and executed based on the manner in which the player interacts with the game.

When it's started, the BASIC Crazy 8 Ball game displays a window that includes a welcome message and two button controls, as shown in Figure 3.1. If the player clicks on the Quit button, the game ends. If the player clicks on the Play button, gameplay continues.

Figure 3.1 The opening window for the BASIC Crazy 8 Ball game.
© 2016 Cengage Learning®

To ask the game a question, the player types her question in the text box field that is shown and clicks on the Ask button, as shown in Figure 3.2.

The player must enter a question for the game to generate an answer. If the player clicks on the Ask button without typing anything, an error message is displayed, as demonstrated in Figure 3.3.

To play the game, the player asks the game a series of questions that must be worded in such a way as to work with yes/no-styled answers, as demonstrated in Figure 3.4.

In response to each question, the game displays a randomly generated answer of YES, NO, or MAYBE, as demonstrated in Figure 3.5.

Figure 3.2 The player is prompted to ask a question.
© 2016 Cengage Learning®

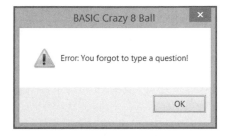

Figure 3.3 An error message is displayed if the player fails to ask a question.
© 2016 Cengage Learning®

Figure 3.4 The player's questions need to support yes/no answers.
© 2016 Cengage Learning®

Figure 3.5 The game provides an answer to the player's question.
© 2016 Cengage Learning®

Mainwin

As you have already seen, Just BASIC automatically adds a text window, referred to as mainwin, to every new application, as demonstrated in Figure 3.6. Once displayed, your application can write text to this window using `print` commands and collect user data using the `input` command.

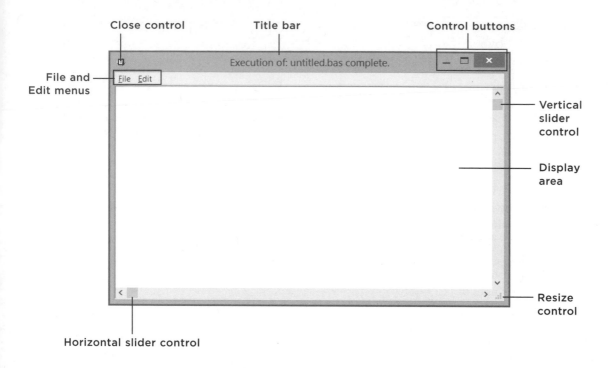

Figure 3.6 Every Just BASIC application is automatically assigned a default text window.
© 2016 Shoptalk Systems

As Figure 3.6 shows, this window offers programmers an abundance of built-in features that provide the basis upon which you can build a text-based Windows desktop application. With no work on your part, Just BASIC automatically generates a text window that you can resize, maximize, minimize, and close. The File and Edit menus come with all the menu commands that you would expect from any Windows application, including Open, Save, Cut, Copy, and Paste. This functionality enables the user to open, display, modify, and save the contents of any text file. However, not all Windows applications are text based. Most are GUI based. Therefore, if desired, you can suppress the display of the mainwin by adding the nomainwin command to the beginning of your Just BASIC applications.

If necessary, you can specify the initial size of mainwin by specifying the number of columns and rows using the mainwin statement, which has the following syntax:

```
mainwin Columns Rows
```

Columns is a placeholder representing the number of columns the window should have, and *Rows* is a placeholder representing the height of the window in terms of the number of rows displayed.

Using the previous command, you can instruct Just BASIC to modify the default size of the mainwin window by adding a statement similar to the following to the beginning of any Just BASIC application:

```
mainwin 40 20
```

Once opened, you work with the mainwin window by sending it commands. One commonly used command is print, which, as you have seen, you can use to display text on mainwin.

Hint

The syntax of the print statement is outlined next. It consists of the keyword print followed by an optional reference to a handle, which when specified identifies the window or control to which the print command is directed. Next comes an optional comma, which is then followed by one or more expressions representing the text to be displayed. If more than one expression is provided, semicolons are used to separate them, and the text strings are displayed one after another.

```
print #handle, expression1 ; expression2 ; expression3…
```

The print command has many uses. In addition to displaying text on text windows and on interface controls that accept text, it can send commands to windows and controls to control their actions. In the following example, a text string is displayed on an application mainwin window:

```
print "Welcome to my Just BASIC application!"
```

Other commands that you can use when working with mainwin include input and cls. You use the input command to prompt the user to provide input and the cls command to clear out the window's display area.

Hint

The syntax of the input command is outlined here:

```
input #handle "string"; variablename
```

It consists of the keyword input followed by an optional reference to a window name (for example, #handle) and a string that is to be displayed. The display string is followed by a semicolon and then the name of a variable, which temporarily stores the input the user provides.

In the following example, the input command displays a prompt asking the user to enter her name. Because there is no explicit reference to a particular window, the prompt is displayed on the application's mainwin window:

```
input "What is your name? "; username$
```

GUI Application Development

Modern programming languages, such as Visual Basic and C++, support desktop application development through windows-based applications. These applications generate GUIs, which display information and interact with users through controls displayed on application windows. Examples of window controls include buttons, textboxes, checkboxes, and listboxes.

Just BASIC is no different. It allows programmers to generate different types of windows and populate those windows with an assortment of interface controls.

Working with Application Windows

Different operating systems support different types of application windows, each of which is designed to suit a specific purpose or situation. Just BASIC supports four types of windows, listed next. Just BASIC applications may consist of any number of these windows:

- **Window.** A regular window as used in most applications. This type of window can contain interface controls and supports optional features such as resizing and menus.
- **Text.** A window designed specifically for displaying text. Text windows always display a menu bar containing File and Edit menus but cannot contain other controls.
- **Graphics.** A window designed to display graphics and sprite animation. Only limited support is included for controls. Window resizing is optional.
- **Dialog.** A special pop-up window designed to collect user information. This window can contain other controls but cannot display menus.

Hint

You can commonly find each of these types of windows on applications that run on Microsoft, Linux, and UNIX operating systems. Other operating systems, such as Mac OS X, support additional types of windows not found elsewhere. For example, Mac OS X supports sheet windows, from which another attached window is displayed using animation that makes it look as if the additional window drops down from the parent window's title bar. Mac OS X also supports drawer windows, in which a child window is displayed using animation that makes it look like the window is sliding out from underneath its parent window.

You saw an example of how to work with various dialog windows back in Chapter 1, "Introduction to Programming," when you created the Knock Knock Joke game. In Chapter 2, "Creating Programs with Just BASIC," you learned how to work with text windows to tell the Legend of Mighty Molly. In this chapter, you learn how to work with the graphics window so you can build desktop applications that interact with users through controls. A graphics window, such as the one shown in Figure 3.7, can spice up applications by displaying interesting backgrounds. Graphics windows also provide the foundation upon which animation is performed. Later, in Chapter 9, "Working with Sound and Graphics," you learn more about the graphics window.

Figure 3.7 An example of a graphics window displaying an image.
© 2016 Cengage Learning®

Regular Windows

Most applications use regular windows, as shown in Figure 3.8. These windows can contain any number of interface controls. By default, a regular window contains a title bar and control buttons located in the upper-right corner that allow you to minimize, maximize, and close the window. You can also resize regular windows.

Figure 3.8 A regular window can contain any type of interface control.
© 2016 Shoptalk Systems

Text Windows

Text windows are highly specialized. They cannot contain other controls; they can only be used to display and collect text data and allow text to be modified and saved. The mainwin window, supplied as part of every Just BASIC application, is an example of a text window.

Graphics Windows

Graphics windows are another special form of window designed to display graphics images and to support the execution of sprites. Although some controls are capable of working on graphics windows, they are not intended for this purpose.

Hint

A *sprite* is an image that is integrated into a larger background scene and forms the basis of computer animation.

Dialog Windows

Just BASIC provides dialog windows so you can interact with users. Dialog windows, also referred to as pop-up dialogs, can optionally be set up to run as application modal. An *application modal* window is a window that prevents other application windows from being accessed while it is open. When this is the case, you can't access any other application windows until you close the dialog window. Dialog windows, therefore, are useful when you require information from the user that must be collected before the application can continue running.

Like most programming languages, Just BASIC supports a number of different types of dialog windows. These variations are listed and explained here:

- **Notice.** Displays a text string message and waits for the user to click on OK.
- **Confirm.** Displays a text string message and waits for the user to click on either Yes or No.
- **Prompt.** Displays a text string message and waits for the user to type in a response before clicking on OK (or alternatively on Cancel).
- **Filedialog.** Displays a dialog window that allows the user to either specify a file to be opened or the name and location of a file to be saved.

You will learn more about dialog windows, including how to generate them and use them to collect user input, later in this chapter.

Window Variations

Just BASIC supports a number of variations of each of the previously listed windows. For example, an application using a text window can open it in window or in full-screen mode. Alternatively, a text window can be generated so that it does or does not support scrollbars. Alterations to application windows are specified using style suffixes. A list of these suffixes is supplied in Table 3.1.

TABLE 3.1 WINDOW STYLE SUFFIXES SUPPORTED BY JUST BASIC

Suffix	Description
_fs	Opens a window in full screen
_nf	Opens a window without a frame, preventing it from being resized
_nsb	Prevents the display of window scrollbars
_ins	Inserts an inset text editor
_modal	Prevents other application windows from being accessed while the window is open

Not all windows support all the different variations shown in Table 3.1. In some cases, Just BASIC allows programmers to combine two or more suffixes. Table 3.2 provides a listing of the various combinations of features supported by each window type.

TABLE 3.2 STYLE SUFFIXES SUPPORTED BY DIFFERENT WINDOWS

Window	Supported Suffix	Window	Supported Suffix
window	_nf	dialog	_nf
text	_fs		_fs
	_nsb		_modal
	_nsb_ins		_nf_modal
graphics	_fs		_nf_fs
	_nsb		
	_fs_nsb		
	_nf_nsb		

> **Hint**
>
> Over the years, most users have become accustomed to having applications look and act a certain way. Failure to provide applications that look and feel intuitive can lead to disappointment. Therefore, it is important for programmers to give serious attention to the development of their application's user interface. A programmer might build the world's best application only to find that no one wants to use it because its user interface is hard to figure out. One way of approaching this challenge is to spend a little time studying how the user interfaces of popular applications have been constructed. Another option is to check out the User Interface Design and Development page at http://msdn2.microsoft.com/en-us/library/aa286531.aspx.

Opening and Closing Windows

With the exception of the mainwin window, you must explicitly open any other window that you want to add to your Just BASIC applications. To display a new application window, you must use the open command. The syntax of the open command is outlined here:

```
open device for purpose as #handle [LEN = n]
```

device is a parameter representing the resources to be opened. When you use it to open a window, you supply a caption to be displayed in the window's title bar as this parameter. *purpose* is a parameter that represents the type of window to be opened (text, window, graphics, or dialog), and *#handle* is a parameter that specifies a handler (or reference) by which the windows can be identified. Handle names must begin with the # character and can only be made up of letters and numbers. Special characters and blank spaces are not allowed.

> **Hint**
>
> The open command is versatile. You can use it to communicate with hardware devices and open a file or application window. This chapter limits discussion of this command to just the opening of application windows.

An example of how to use the open command to open a new application window is shown here:

```
open "Sample Window" for window as #main
```

When you open a window, you must specify its type (window, text, graphics, dialog). Here, a new application window is displayed. The text string "Sample Window" is displayed in its title bar. The window has been opened as a regular window and has been assigned a handle of #main.

As with any programming language, you must remember to add programming logic to your application to close any open resources, including windows, before allowing the applications to terminate. In the case of open windows, this means using the close command, which has the following syntax:

```
close #handle
```

#handle identifies the handle of a previously opened window. Thus, you can use the following statement to close a window named #main:

```
close #main
```

To get a better understanding of how to work with and control application windows, consider the following example:

```
nomainwin

open "Sample Window" for text as #main

print #main, "Welcome to my Just BASIC application."
print #main, "!trapclose [terminate]"

wait

[terminate]

  close #main
  end
```

In this small Just BASIC program, the display of the default text window has been suppressed. Next, a new text window is opened and assigned a handle of #main. The next statement uses the print command to display a text string on the window. The statement after that uses the print statement in a new way. This time the print statement has been used to pass a command, instead of a text string, to the window. Just BASIC knows that a command is being passed because the text enclosed inside the double quotation marks begins with the ! character. The word that follows the ! command is trapclose. This instructs Just BASIC that whenever the window receives instruction to close, such as when the user clicks on the Close button in the upper-right corner of the text window, it should jump to the location within the program code labeled [terminate]. The wait statement is then executed, causing the program to pause execution and wait for the user input.

Trap

You must precede any command passed to a windows or interface control with the ! character if that window or control accepts text. For example, windows of type text and interface controls like the button and text box controls, discussed later in this chapter, display text that is passed to them using the `print` command unless that text is preceded by the ! character, in which case Just BASIC interprets the string passed by the `print` statement as a command that must be executed. If, on the other hand, the window or control that you are working with does not display text, which would be the case with a window of type `window` or a control like the `bmpbutton` control, then including the ! character is optional. However, rather than using the ! in some situations and not in others, it's recommend that you use it anytime you want to use the `print` command to pass a command to a control or window.

The code statement that follows the [terminate] label, also referred to as a switch label, is the event handler for the window's close event. An *event* is an action, generally initiated by the user. For applications to communicate with the users, there must be a way of linking or associating program code with different parts of the user interface. For example, when the user clicks on a given button control, certain code statements should be executed; when a different button is clicked, a different set of code statements should be executed. This connection between interface controls and application code statements is established by defining event handlers.

Event Programming

Events occur when the user does something such as clicking on a button control, keying data into a text box control, or closing an open window. Like other programming languages, Just BASIC gives programmers a means of defining specific programming logic and associating it with specific events. Different types of events are associated with different types of windows and controls. Button controls, for example, recognize click events. Windows, on the other hand, recognize close events. Other controls respond to other types of events.

One way to set up a window or interface control to work with an event is to add a label to it as part of its definition. If the event for the window or interface control occurs, the program jumps to the location within the program where that label has been placed and executes any program statements that it finds. In the case of the previous example, this meant jumping to the [terminate] switch label and executing the `close` and `end` commands. This ensures that any time the user closes the application window, Just BASIC makes sure that the application terminates cleanly by closing any open resources; in this case, this is the window itself.

> **Hint**
>
> You can also implement event programming using functions in place of labels. You will learn how to do this in Chapter 7, "Improving Program Organization with Functions and Subroutines."

Specifying Windows Size and Location

By default, Just BASIC determines the initial size of application windows. In addition, if not otherwise specified, Microsoft Windows determines the initial location where windows are displayed. However, by setting any combination of the following four special variables, you can specify the size and initial display location for any application window:

- **WindowHeight.** Sets the height of the window in pixels.
- **WindowWidth.** Sets the width of the window in pixels.
- **UpperLeftX.** Specifies the location of the upper-left corner of the window in relation to the left side of the display area.
- **UpperLeftY.** Specifies the location of the upper-left corner of the window in relation to the top of the display area.

To see how you might set these variables to control the display of an application window, consider the following example:

```
nomainwin

UpperLeftX = 1
UpperLeftY = 1

WindowWidth = 200
WindowHeight = 200

open "Sample Window" for window as #main

wait
```

Here, a window of type `window` is opened that is 200 pixels wide by 200 pixels tall. When it's initially opened, there is just one pixel between the top and left side of the window and the edge of the display area.

Hint

A *pixel* (picture element) is the smallest addressable area that can be written to on the screen or the window. Computer displays are measured in terms of the number of pixels displayed.

Trick

Just BASIC gives programmers access to two special variables that retrieve the current width and height of the display area. These variables are named `DisplayWidth` and `DisplayHeight`, and you can use them when calculating the desired value of `WindowWidth` and `WindowHeight`. For example, you might create a window that fills most but not all of the display area, as demonstrated here:

```
nomainwin

UpperLeftX = 1
UpperLeftY = 1

WindowWidth = DisplayWidth - 200
WindowHeight = DisplayHeight - 200

open "Sample Window" for window as #main

wait
```

Note that you must set the size of an application window prior to opening it.

Trap

`UpperLeftX`, `UpperLeftY`, `WindowWidth`, `WindowHeight`, `DisplayWidth`, and `DisplayHeight` are all case sensitive and thus must be spelled exactly as shown here. Otherwise, Just BASIC does not recognize them, and your results are not as expected.

Setting Foreground and Background Colors

Like most programming languages, Just BASIC applications by default assign colors consistent with the Windows operating system's currently assigned color scheme. However, if you prefer, you can also change the foreground and background colors used in the display of application windows by setting the value of the `BackgroundColor$` and `ForegroundColor$` special variables.

Hint

Foreground color refers to the color used to display text, and *background color* refers to the color of the window's background on which controls and text are displayed. The background color setting also affects the display of the groupbox, statictext, radiobutton, and checkbox controls.

Just BASIC allows you to set the value of both the `BackgroundColor$` and `ForegroundColor$` special variables to any of the following colors:

- Black
- Blue
- Brown
- Buttonface (represents the current default color scheme)
- Cyan
- Dark blue
- Dark cyan
- Dark gray
- Dark green
- Dark pink
- Dark red
- Green
- Light gray (same as pale gray)
- Pale gray (same as light gray)
- Pink
- Red
- White
- Yellow

To get a better understanding of how the specification of the `BackgroundColor$` and `ForegroundColor$` special variables affects the display of application windows, consider the following example:

```
nomainwin

WindowWidth = 400
WindowHeight = 400
```

```
BackgroundColor$ = "darkred"
ForegroundColor$ = "yellow"

statictext #main.static, "Yellow on Darkred", 20, 20, 100, 50

open "Sample Window" for window as #main

wait
```

Here, a window that is 400 pixels wide by 400 pixels high is displayed with a dark red background, and any text that is displayed appears in yellow. Figure 3.9 shows the window in black and white.

Figure 3.9 Setting window background and foreground color.
© 2016 Cengage Learning®

Trap

`BackgroundColor$` **and** `ForegroundColor$` **are case sensitive and thus must be spelled exactly as shown here. Otherwise, Just BASIC does not recognize them, and your results are not as expected.**

Setting Font Attributes

Just BASIC also gives you control over the type and size of the text font used to display text strings on windows. In addition, Just BASIC gives you control over other font properties, including these:

- Bold
- Italic
- Strikeout
- Underscore

Setting the font type and size for a window, by default, affects all text displayed on that window, including the font type and size of text displayed on window controls. Font size and type can be configured using the syntax outlined here:

```
print #handle, "font fonttype pointsize [italic, bold, strikeout, underscore]"
```

Using this syntax, font type is specified by supplying a value in place of *fonttype*, and font size is specified using point size. You may also include any of four optional modifiers that affect font appearance. For example, the following statement establishes a font type of Arial font size 14.

Hint

A point is 1/72 of an inch.

```
nomainwin

statictext #main.static, "Font demo", 20, 20, 200, 50
open "Sample Window" for window as #main
print #main, "font Arial 14"

wait
```

Similarly, this next example establishes a font type of Courier New with a font size of 24 using bold:

```
nomainwin

statictext #main.static, "Font demo", 20, 20, 200, 50
open "Sample Window" for window as #main
print #main, "font Courier_New 24 bold"

wait
```

Hint

When specifying a font type whose name consists of multiple words, use the _ character to substitute for blank space when keying in the font name. For example, instead of Times New Roman, you must type Times_New_Roman. If the font you specify is not installed on the computer, Just BASIC selects the closest available match.

Adding Controls to Windows

Most desktop application user interfaces consist of a collection of different interface controls like buttons and text boxes. As the following list shows, Just BASIC allows programmers to add a number of different graphical interface controls to application windows:

- Button
- Bmpbutton
- Checkbox
- Radiobutton
- Statictext
- Textbox
- Texteditor
- Listbox
- Combobox
- Groupbox
- Graphicbox

By adding instances of these types of controls to application windows, you can create complex application GUIs. Each control has its own particular syntax that you must use when adding the code required to generate an instance of the control on an application window. Alternatively, you can use the FreeForm-J program, supplied with Just BASIC, to visually design your application windows and then generate the required code statements needed to re-create the window's user interface for you.

> **Hint**
>
> As impressive as the list of controls provided by Just BASIC is, the collection of controls is small compared to the list of controls provided by many other programming languages. For example, programming languages like Microsoft C++ supply programmers with access to dozens of different controls. Examples of controls not supplied by Just BASIC include the progress bar, HTML Viewer, database, and toolbar controls.

Reviewing Just BASIC Controls

Desktop applications are made up of windows that display data and interact with users through the use of controls placed on top of those windows. Just BASIC includes a number of predefined interface controls. Each of these controls is designed to provide a different type of functionality to your applications. A brief overview of these controls and their functionality is provided in the sections that follow. As you work your way through the sample game application presented in this book, you will get a chance to see working examples of a number of these controls.

Button Controls

The button control displays a graphical button that users can click to send a command to a program. Button controls display a text string and are activated by clicking on them. You can programmatically add buttons to windows using the following syntax:

```
button #handle.ext, "caption", [label | subroutine] , corner, x, y [, width, height]
```

handle must refer to the handle of the window on which the control will be displayed, and *.ext* is an optional extension that uniquely identifies the control, allowing it to be programmatically referenced later in the program. *caption* represents the button control's caption. *label* and *subroutine* are mutually exclusive and optional, meaning that you can supply one or neither but never both. When supplied, Just BASIC jumps to the specified label or subroutine and begins executing its code statements. You will learn more about how to work with labels later in this chapter and learn how to work with subroutines in Chapter 7. *corner* specifies the corner of the window used to anchor the button control. Possible choices include UL, UR, LL, and LR. *x* and *y* specify the location of the button, in pixels, relative to the specified corner, and *width* and *height* are optional parameters that specify the dimensions of the button (in pixels). If omitted, Just BASIC makes the button just large enough to display its caption text.

Hint

UL refers to the upper-left corner of the window. UR refers to the upper-right corner of the window. LL refers to the lower-left corner of the window, and LR refers to the lower-right corner of the window.

Button controls are typically used to send commands to applications. For example, the following code statements generate a window that displays a button control with a caption of Exit:

```
nomainwin

button #main.button1, "Exit", [terminate], UL, 130, 150, 60, 40
open "Sample Window" for window as #main

wait

[terminate]
```

```
notice "Thanks for using my application!"
close #main
end
```

When executed, this program displays a window with a button control that is 60 pixels wide by 40 pixels tall, roughly in the center of the window, as shown in Figure 3.10. When clicked, the button control's click event executes. As a result, the program jumps to the [terminate] label and executes the code that follows that label, which in this example displays a pop-up window thanking the user for using the application before closing the window and terminating the program's execution.

Figure 3.10 Button controls provide single-click access to application commands.
© 2016 Shoptalk Systems

Bmpbutton Controls

The bmpbutton control is similar to the button control—the only difference being that the bmpbutton control displays an image instead of a text string. Bmpbuttons let users execute a program command. You can programmatically add bmpbuttons to windows using the following syntax:

bmpbutton #handle.ext, filename, [label | subroutine], corner, x, y

As you can see, the syntax for the bmpbutton control is similar to that of the button control. The only differences are that you cannot specify a display string, and you must supply the full or relative path of the bitmap image file to be displayed. You cannot set the width and height of bmpbutton controls either. The size of a bmpbutton control is determined by the size of the image itself.

The following example is a modified copy of the previous example, replacing the button control with a bmpbutton control:

```
nomainwin

bmpbutton #main.button1, "bmp\xoutbttn.bmp", [terminate], UL, 140, 150
open "Sample Window" for window as #main

wait

[terminate]
  notice "Thanks for using my application!"
  close #main
  end
```

As you can see, the location of the bmpbutton control is specified as "bmp\xoutbttn.bmp". This is an example of a relative path specification; the location of a file is specified based on its location to the current working directory. In this example, the location of the xoutbttn.bmp bitmap image is found by looking in a subdirectory of the current working directory named bmp for the image file. When executed, this example displays the window containing the bmpbutton shown in Figure 3.11.

 Figure 3.11 An example of a typical bmpbutton control.
© 2016 Shoptalk Systems

Hint

Just BASIC supplies you with access to a number of bitmap images that you can find in the BMP folder located inside the Just BASIC installation folder.

Checkbox Controls

The checkbox control gives the user a choice between either of two options. Check boxes include a text string that describes their function or value and can be set to either of two states: set or reset (cleared). When set, a check box control displays a square filled with a graphic checkmark. When cleared, a check box is displayed as an empty square. Check boxes are often used to collect user preferences or to enable or disable certain application functions. You can add a check box to an application window using the following syntax:

```
checkbox #handle.ext, "caption", setHandler, resetHandler, x, y, width, height
```

As you can see, the syntax for the checkbox control is similar to that of the button control. The only differences between the two controls are that you can specify two event handlers that will be executed when the user sets or clears the checkbox control, and the width and height parameters are required.

To better understand how to work with the checkbox control, take a look at the following example. Here a window is opened that contains a checkbox and a button control. Clicking on the button control when it is in a cleared state causes the execution of the code statements located under the [set] switch label. When this occurs, a checkmark is displayed on the checkbox control. Clicking on the button control when it is in a set state causes the execution of the code statements located under the [reset] switch label. When this occurs, the checkmark is removed from the checkbox control. Lastly, when the button control is clicked, the current state of the checkbox control is displayed in a pop-up dialog window.

Hint

Note the use of the `goto` command as the last statement under the `[set]` and `[reset]` switch labels. The `goto` command tells Just BASIC to jump to the specified switch label and execute any statements found there. In most computer programming languages, use of the `goto` command is considered to be a poor programming practice. Instead, most programming languages use functions and subroutines to group collections of code statements that can be called upon to execute and, once done, return to the code statement that called on them. Just BASIC also supports the use of functions and subroutines. However, the `goto` command is also commonly used, as evidenced in Just BASIC's online help documentation. You'll read about the use of labels in this chapter because of their historical value and because of Just BASIC's support for them. However, the next chapter relies exclusively on subroutines and functions in place of labels. You'll find a detailed discussion of both subroutines and functions in Chapter 7.

```
nomainwin

checkbox #main.checkbox1, "Enable Sound", [set], [reset], 106, 50, 130, 20
button #main, "Get Checkbox Value", [get_checkbox_value], UL, 65, 150
open "Checkbox test" for window as #main
print #main, "trapclose [terminate]"

[pause]
  wait

[set]
  print #main.checkbox1, "set"
  goto [pause]

[reset]
  print #main.checkbox1, "reset"
  goto [pause]

[get_checkbox_value]
  print #main.checkbox1, "value? cbstate$"
  notice "The checkbox control is currently set to "; cbstate$
  goto [pause]

[terminate]
  close #main
  end
```

When executed, this example displays the window shown in Figure 3.12.

Figure 3.12 An example of a checkbox control.
© 2016 Cengage Learning®

Hint

Take note of the last print statement in bold in the preceding example. It retrieves the current value of the checkbox control and assigns it to the cbstate$ variable.

Radiobutton Controls

The radiobutton control is used in groups of two or more as a means of giving users mutually exclusive choices. Radiobutton controls display a text label just to the right of the control. When selected, a radiobutton control's circular image is filled in, and all other radiobutton controls are cleared.

Trick

All radiobutton controls that are placed on a window are automatically treated as a group, allowing only one radiobutton control to be selected at a time. However, by placing radiobutton controls inside separate groupbox controls, you can define a separate set of radiobutton controls.

You can add a radiobutton control to an application window using the following syntax:

```
radiobutton #handle.ext, "caption", setHandler, resetHandler, x, y, width, height
```

As you can see, the syntax for the radiobutton control is the same as that used by the checkbox control. To better understand how to work with the radiobutton control, take a look at the following example.

Here a window is opened that contains three radiobutton controls:

```
nomainwin

statictext #main.statictext "Please specify your age:", 60, 60, 120, 20
radiobutton #main.low, "17 or under", [warning], [nil], 60, 85, 130, 20
radiobutton #main.medium, "18 - 65", [reminder], [nil], 60, 115, 130, 20
radiobutton #main.high, "66 or older", [disclaim], [nil], 60, 145, 130, 20
textbox #main.textbox, 30, 280, 250, 20

open "Age Confirmation" for window as #main
print #main, "trapclose [terminate]"
print #main.low, "set"

[warning]
  #main.textbox, "You must be at least 18 years of age to continue."
  wait

[reminder]
  #main.textbox, "Please have your credit card ready to proceed."
  wait

[disclaim]
  #main.textbox, "Warning! This site is not for the faint of heart!"
  wait

[nil]
  wait

[terminate]
  close #main
  end
```

When executed, this example displays the window shown in Figure 3.13. Each time a different radiobutton control is selected, the message displayed in the textbox control is updated.

As with the checkbox control, Just BASIC lets you retrieve a radiobutton control's value (set or reset), as demonstrated here:

```
print #main.low, "value? rbstate$"
```

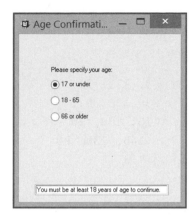

Figure 3.13 An example of a group of radiobutton controls.
© 2016 Cengage Learning®

Here, the value of the radiobutton control with a handle of #main.low is retrieved and assigned to a variable named rbstate$.

Statictext Controls

A statictext control is used to display a text string on a window. Statictext controls are typically used to display descriptive information about other controls and to offer users instructions and other helpful information. You can add a statictext control to an application window using the following syntax:

```
statictext #handle.ext, "caption", x, y, width, height
```

As you can see, the syntax for the statictext control is straightforward. To better understand how to work with the statictext control, look at the following example. Here, a window is opened that displays the opening line of a story using the statictext control:

```
nomainwin

statictext #main.Statictext "Once upon a time…", 40, 60, 210, 30
open "The Three Little Pigs" for window as #main
print #main, "font Garamond 12 bold"

wait

[terminate]
  close #main
  end
```

When executed, this example displays the window shown in Figure 3.14.

Figure 3.14 An example of a statictext control used to display text on a window.
© 2016 Cengage Learning®

Textbox Controls

The textbox control is a single-line input field that you can use to collect small amounts of text input the user provides. You can also use the textbox control to display text. Finally, you can add a textbox control to an application window using the following syntax:

```
textbox #handle.ext, x, y, width, height
```

To see how to add an instance of the textbox control to a window, take a look at the following example:

```
nomainwin

statictext #main.statictext "Please type your name:", 20, 30, 110, 30
textbox #main.Textbox, 20, 60, 200, 20

open "Textbox Control Demo" for window as #main

print #main, "trapclose [terminate]"

wait

[terminate]
  close #main
  end
```

Here, a textbox control that is 200 pixels long and 20 pixels high has been added to an application window, as demonstrated in Figure 3.15.

Figure 3.15 An example of a textbox control being used to collect user input.
© 2016 Cengage Learning®

When the textbox control is executed, the user can type text into it. You can programmatically retrieve any text keyed by the user into a textbox control using the following syntax:

```
print #handle.ext, "!contents? input$";
```

Here, the text the user enters is stored in a variable named `input$`.

Texteditor Controls

The texteditor control provides a multiline text field that you can use to display text or to collect the user's text input. Using the texteditor control, programmers can create text-editing applications like Windows Notepad or FreeForm-J.

Scrollbars located on the right and bottom of the texteditor control allow users to edit text that exceeds the visible display area of the control. The texteditor control allows text to be displayed in different fonts and sizes. It also supports numerous text-editing capabilities such as the ability to copy, cut, and paste a selected portion of text as well as the ability to select all displayed text.

You can add a texteditor control to an application window using the following syntax:

```
texteditor #handle.ext, x, y, width, height
```

To see an example of how to add an instance of the texteditor control to a window, take a look at the following example:

```
nomainwin

texteditor #main.texteditor, 20, 20, 270, 250

open "Texteditor Control Demo" for window_nf as #main

print #main, "trapclose [terminate]"

wait

[terminate]
  close #main
  end
```

Here, a texteditor control that is 270 pixels long and 250 pixels high has been added to an application window, as demonstrated in Figure 3.16.

Figure 3.16 An example of the texteditor control in action.
© 2016 Cengage Learning®

When the texteditor control is executed, the user can type text into it. You can programmatically retrieve any text keyed by the user into a texteditor control using the following syntax:

```
print #handle.ext, "!contents? input$";
```

As with the textbox control, this statement takes any text the user enters and assign it to a variable named input$.

Listbox Controls

The listbox control displays a list of items from which the user can make a selection. Once it's selected, you can navigate the list of items using the keyboard's up and down keys. If the list of items stored in the listbox is greater than what can be displayed, scrollbars are automatically added to the listbox control. You can add a listbox control to an application window using the following syntax:

```
listbox #handle.ext, array$(), [label | subroutine], x, y, width, height
```

The listbox control is populated by associating an array with it through the *array$()* parameter. To better understand how to work with the listbox control, take a look at the following example:

```
nomainwin

names$(0) = "Mary"
names$(1) = "William"
names$(2) = "Molly"
names$(3) = "Alexander"
names$(4) = "Jerry"
names$(5) = "Bridget"
names$(6) = "Lazlo"
names$(7) = "Dolly"
names$(8) = "Mike"
names$(9) = "Mark"
names$(10) = "Nick"

statictext #main.statictext "Select a name:", 30, 30, 80, 20
listbox #main.listbox, names$(), [doubleclick], 30, 60, 100, 140
button #main.button, "OK", [displaychoice], UL, 60, 220, 40, 30
open "Listbox Control Demo" for window as #main
print #main, "trapclose [terminate]"

wait

[doubleclick]
  wait

[displaychoice]
  print #main.listbox, "selection? selected$"
  notice "You selected: "; selected$

[terminate]
  close #main
  end
```

> **Hint**
>
> This example creates an *array*, which is an indexed list of values, and uses it to populate the contents of the combobox control. You will learn all about arrays in Chapter 4, "Working with Variables and Arrays."

When executed, this previous example displays the window shown in Figure 3.17.

Figure 3.17 An example of the listbox control preloaded with items.
© 2016 Cengage Learning®

Combobox Controls

The combobox control includes features provided by the listbox and textbox controls. You use the combobox control to present users with a list of options from which to select, similar to a listbox control. Alternatively, users can type in their own entry, similar to a textbox control. Comboboxes are often used when space is limited and there is insufficient room available to display both listbox and textbox controls. You can add a combobox control to an application window using the following syntax:

```
combobox #handle.ext, array$(), [label | subroutine], x, y, width, height
```

The combobox control is populated by associating an array with it. To get a better understanding of how to create and populate a combobox control with items, take a look at the following sample program:

```
nomainwin

names$(0) = "Mary"
names$(1) = "William"
names$(2) = "Molly"
names$(3) = "Alexander"
names$(4) = "Jerry"
```

```
names$(5) = "Bridget"
names$(6) = "Lazlo"
names$(7) = "Dolly"
names$(8) = "Mike"
names$(9) = "Mark"
names$(10) = "Nick"

statictext #main.statictext "Select a name:", 30, 30, 80, 20
combobox #main.combobox, names$(), [select], 30, 60, 100, 140
button #main.button, "OK", [displaychoice], UL, 60, 240, 40, 30

open "Combobox Control Demo" for window as #main

print #main, "trapclose [terminate]"

wait

[select]
  wait

[displaychoice]
  print #main.combobox, "selection? selected$"
  notice "You selected: "; selected$

[terminate]
  close #main
  end
```

When executed, this example displays a window with a combobox and a button control. Clicking on the combobox control's down arrow displays a list of items, as shown in Figure 3.18.

Figure 3.18 An example of a combobox control loaded with items.
© 2016 Cengage Learning®

Groupbox Controls

The groupbox control is used to group controls on a window. A groupbox control consists of a box with a label displayed in the upper-left corner. You can use groupbox controls to visually organize other controls. However, groupbox controls are typically used to group radiobutton controls, allowing different groups of radiobutton controls to operate independently of each other.

You can add a groupbox control to an application window using the following syntax:

```
groupbox #handle.ext, "caption", x, y, width, height
```

As you can see, the syntax for the groupbox control is straightforward. To better understand how to work with the groupbox control, take a look at the following example:

```
nomainwin

groupbox #main, "Please specify your age:", 40, 60, 200, 120

radiobutton #main.low, "17 or under", [warning], [nil], 60, 85, 130, 20
radiobutton #main.medium, "18 through 65", [reminder], [nil], 60, 115, 130, 20
radiobutton #main.high, "66 or older", [disclaimer], [nil], 60, 145, 130, 20
textbox #main.textbox, 30, 280, 250, 20

open "Age Confirmation" for window as #main
print #main, "trapclose [terminate]"
print #main.low, "set"

[warning]
  #main.textbox, "You must be at least 18 years of age to continue."
  wait

[reminder]
  #main.textbox, "Please have your credit card ready to proceed."
  wait

[disclaimer]
  #main.textbox, "Warning! This site is not for the faint of heart!"
  wait

[nil]
  wait

[terminate]
  close #main
  end
```

This example is almost identical to the one presented earlier when the radiobutton control was introduced. The only difference is that instead of preceding the list of radiobutton controls with a statictext control, the controls are organized and presented inside a groupbox control, as shown in Figure 3.19. As such, each of these three radiobutton control functions is part of a group. Any other radiobutton control that might be added to the application window outside of the group-box control are treated as part of a separate group.

Figure 3.19 An example of the groupbox control used to group a list of radiobutton controls.
© 2016 Cengage Learning®

Graphicbox Controls

The graphicbox control gives programmers the ability to display bitmap images. Alternatively, the graphicbox control also allows programmers to draw shapes such as squares, circles, and text characters.

You can add a graphicbox control to an application window using the following syntax:

```
graphicbox #handle.ext, x, y, width, height
```

As you can see, the syntax for the graphicbox control is straightforward. Once it's added, you can use it to display graphics and draw graphic shapes using graphics commands. To better understand how to work with the graphicbox control, take a look at the following example:

```
nomainwin

graphicbox #handle.gbox, 30, 30, 200, 200
open "Drawing" for window as #handle

print #handle.gbox, "home"          'Center the pen
print #handle.gbox, "down"          'Ready to draw

print #handle.gbox, "fill yellow"   'Fill the graphics area yellow
```

```
print #handle.gbox, "circle 80"      'Draw a circle
print #handle.gbox, "flush"          'Make the graphics stick

wait
```

In this example, a graphicbox control is added to a window that is 200 pixels wide by 200 pixels high. A series of `print` commands is then executed that locate the center of the control, prepare it for drawing, fill in the background color with yellow, and then draw a circle with a radius of 80 pixels, as shown in Figure 3.20. Finally, the `flush` command is executed, ensuring that the image is not overwritten if the window is covered or temporarily minimized. You will learn more about graphics commands later in Chapter 9.

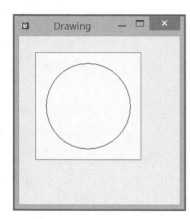

Figure 3.20 An example of the graphicbox control used to draw a circle on a yellow background.
© 2016 Cengage Learning®

Setting Control Focus

When the user clicks on an interface control, such as a textbox control, that control is said to have focus. This means that any keyboard input is sent to the control. Therefore, a textbox or texteditor control with focus accepts as input any text the user keys in. Likewise, a control such as button that has focus responds if the user presses the Enter key, which is equivalent to clicking on the control using the mouse. You can programmatically assign focus to a given control using the `setfocus` command, as demonstrated here:

```
print #main.textbox, "!setfocus"
```

Here, focus is set to a textbox control whose handle is `#main.textbox` on a window whose handle is `#main`. Because the textbox control accepts text input, you must precede the `setfocus` command with the `!` character to prevent the command from being displayed as a string in the control instead of being executed.

Enabling and Disabling Controls

If necessary, you can manage the availability of a control by enabling and disabling it during program execution. A disabled control is visible on the application window but is grayed out and cannot be accessed. You might want to disable a control that saves a file until the application opens a file. Once it's opened, you can enable the control, and when the file is closed, you might want to again disable the control.

To disable a control, all you have to do is pass the `disable` command to it, as demonstrated here:

```
print #main.button "!disable"
```

Here, a button control is disabled. The button control accepts text input passed to it from the `print` command as its caption. Adding the `!` character to the beginning of the `disable` command instructs Just BASIC to instead execute the `disable` command. As you might guess, you can enable any control using the `enable` command, as demonstrated here:

```
Print #main.button "!enable"
```

Specifying the Control Font and Color

Earlier in the chapter, you learned how to use the `font` command to specify the font type and size for an application window and its controls. Just BASIC allows you to override this font setting on a control-by-control basis. You accomplish this by using the `print` command to send the `font` command to a specific control by referencing that control's handler, as demonstrated here:

```
print #main.button, "!font Arial 14"
```

Here, the button control's font type has been set to Arial size 14. This statement only sets the font type and size for the specified control and has no effect on the rest of the window or on any other controls that have been added to the window.

Earlier in the chapter, you also learned how to set a window's background and foreground colors by modifying the value of the `BackgroundColor$` and `ForegroundColor$` special variables. If you want, you can change the background color assigned to the textbox, combobox, listbox, and texteditor controls by assigning a color to the following special variables:

- `ComboboxColor$`
- `ListboxColor$`
- `TextboxColor$`
- `TexteditorColor$`

For example, the following statement sets the background color of any textbox controls to yellow (regardless of what the window's background color may be set to):

```
TextboxColor$ = "yellow"
```

Building Application Menus

Menus are drop-down lists located at the top of the window, just underneath the window's title bar. Menus consist of menu items. The user interacts with menus by clicking on them and then selecting the appropriate menu item, which in turn sends a command to the application. Menus are defined using the menu command, which has the following syntax:

```
menu #handle, "title", "menuitem1", [label | subroutine], [|], _
  ["menuitem2", [ label | subroutine] ]
```

title sets the name of the menu (File, View, Settings, Help, and so on). *menuitem* specifies the name of a menu item (Open, Save, Close, Exit, and so on). You can add as many menu items as necessary to a menu. You can also include an optional | character between menu items to insert a separator line. A separator line helps you visually organize related groups of menu items, as demonstrated in Figure 3.21.

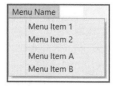

Figure 3.21 A separator line can help visually organize menu items into logical groupings.
© 2016 Cengage Learning®

Hint

In Just BASIC, menus are added to application windows programmatically via code statements. Other programming languages like Visual Basic give programmers the option of creating application menus visually. For example, Visual Basic provides an interface control that facilitates the addition of application menus.

You can set up accelerator keys for menus and menu items by inserting the & character at the appropriate location in the *title* or *menuitem* name. When inserted, the character following the & character becomes the menu or menu item's accelerator key. You can easily identify accelerator keys when the application is run because they are underlined. Accelerator keys are activated by holding down the Alt key and then pressing the specified accelerator key (for example Alt+P to print or Alt+S to save). Using accelerator keys, users can access menus and menu items using only the keyboard.

Just like window interface controls, you must define any menus prior to opening the windows that will contain them. For a better understanding of how to add menus to your Just BASIC applications, consider the following example:

```
nomainwin

menu #main, "&File", "&Open", [openfile], |, "&Save", [savefile], _
   "&Save As", [saveas], |, "&Exit", [terminate]
menu #main, "&Help", "App&lication Help", [apphelp], |, "&About My Application", _
   [aboutapp]

open "Menu Demonstration" for Window as #main

wait
```

Hint

To create desktop applications that meet the needs and expectations of today's users, your Windows applications need to follow certain standards. In regards to menus, this means using familiar titles when naming menus (File, View, Help, and so on). Users also expect to have the option of using accelerator keys. You should follow standard conventions when assigning accelerator keys to menus and menu items. Otherwise, users become confused. For example, the accelerator key for File menu items like Open should be the letter O, whereas the accelerator key for the Help menu is always the letter H.

Here, two menus have been added to the window: File and Help. The File menu has been assigned an accelerator key of Alt+F, and the Help menu has an accelerator key of Alt+H. The File menu contains four menu items, each of which has been configured to call upon a different label, and the Help menu contains two menu items. If executed, the previous example produces the menus shown in Figure 3.22.

Figure 3.22 An example of a window application with two menus.
© 2016 Cengage Learning®

Hint

Any windows to which you add a textbox or texteditor control automatically inherit an Edit menu. By default, the Edit menu appears to the right of any other menus that you may have added to a window. If you want, you may specify the location of the Edit menu using the menu command, as demonstrated here:

```
menu #main, "&File", "&Open", [openfile]
menu #main, "edit"
menu #main, "&Help", "App&lication Help", [apphelp]
```

You must specify the menu command for the Edit menu exactly as shown here. Do not include the & character or attempt to specify or modify the contents of the Edit menu; otherwise, things do not work properly.

Building Interfaces with FreeForm-J

FreeForm-J is a Just BASIC application supplied as part of Just BASIC's distribution package. FreeForm-J assists Just BASIC programmers in visually designing GUIs. It allows programmers to add instances of controls to a window and then move and resize them and modify their properties. FreeForm-J also facilitates the creation of menus and can be used to specify a window's title bar, type, and handle and color scheme. Once you have used FreeForm-J to design an application window, you can instruct it to generate the program code required to regenerate the window for you. You can then copy and paste this code into your Just BASIC application.

Designing an Application Window

Most modern Windows programming languages that support desktop application development provide a Rapid Application Development (RAD) window development capability, allowing programmers to design application windows using prebuilt controls that are dragged and dropped onto windows. For example, Visual Basic Express 2013 gives programmers an assortment of controls that can be dragged and dropped onto the application windows and then rearranged and resized as necessary, as demonstrated in Figure 3.23.

Just BASIC only supports the generation of application windows from code. However, an application named FreeForm-J, written in Just BASIC, is shipped with the programming language and goes a long way toward providing Just BASIC with a visual application window development tool.

To start FreeForm-J, click on Just BASIC's Run menu and select the FreeForm-J GUI Editor menu item. FreeForm-J automatically opens a new blank application window when you start, as demonstrated in Figure 3.24.

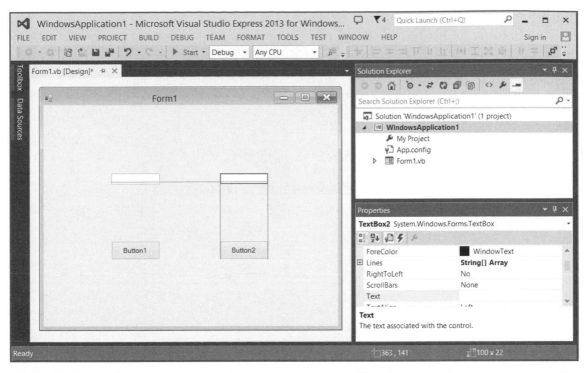

Figure 3.23 Visual Basic Express 2013 assists programmers by providing alignment indicators that automatically appear as programmers use drag and drop to build application windows.

Source: Microsoft Corporation

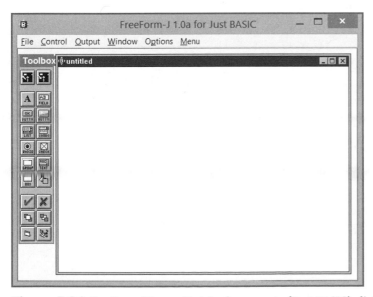

Figure 3.24 FreeForm-J is provided for free as part of Just BASIC's distribution package.

© 2016 Shoptalk Systems

To design an application window using FreeForm-J, you click on an image representing a Just BASIC control from the Toolbox pane. In response, FreeForm-J places an instance of that control on the application window and opens a property window that displays a list of properties associated with that control, as demonstrated in Figure 3.25. In some cases, such as when a button control is added, you are first prompted to provide some additional information such as the name of the caption to be displayed on the control.

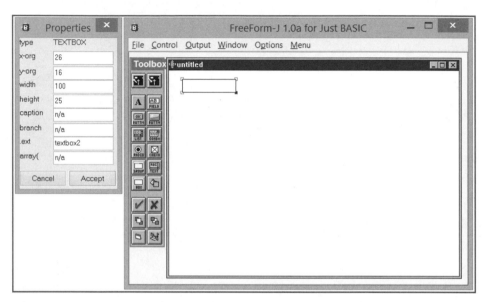

Figure 3.25 A textbox control has been added to the application window.
© 2016 Shoptalk Systems

Once the control is added, you can make changes to it. For example, using the resize button handlers that appear when you click on the control, you can change the size of the control. You can also drag it to a different location on the window. Finally, you can modify the control by making changes to the text fields displayed in the control's Properties window.

You can set the window's title bar string or change the window's type, handle, and color scheme by opening FreeForm-J's Window menu and selecting the appropriate menu option, as shown in Figure 3.26. Each of the menu items opens a pop-up window that lets you specify the appropriate window setting.

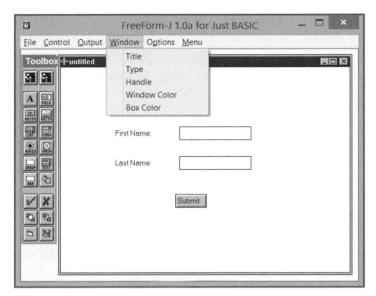

Figure 3.26 Using FreeForm-J to configure window properties.
© 2016 Shoptalk Systems

Using FreeForm-J to Build Window Menus

FreeForm-J also assists programmers in developing application menus. To do so, just click on the Add a Menu option on FreeForm-J's Menu menu. In response, the Add a Menu window is displayed. To add a menu to the application window, enter a name for it in the Enter New Menu Name field and click on Accept. You may include the & character to assign an accelerator key to the menu, as demonstrated in Figure 3.27.

Figure 3.27 Adding a menu to a Just BASIC application window.
© 2016 Shoptalk Systems

You can add as many menus as you want to the application window. Once you have finished adding all the menus needed on the application window, you can edit each menu to assign its menu items. You do this by clicking on the Edit Menus option located on the Menu menu. This opens the Edit Menus window, as shown in Figure 3.28.

Figure 3.28 The Edit Menus window lets programmers visually design application menus.
© 2016 Shoptalk Systems

To edit a menu, select it from the list of menus that you have added to the window and then click on the New Item button. This opens the Menu Item Properties window, which prompts you to supply a name and label for the menu item, as demonstrated in Figure 3.29.

Figure 3.29 Adding a menu item for the selected menu.
© 2016 Shoptalk Systems

Using FreeForm-J to Generate Source Code

Once you have completed the design of your new application window, you can tell FreeForm-J to generate the code statements required to programmatically regenerate the window for you by clicking on the Output menu and selecting either the Produce Code or Produce Code + Outline menu items. Selecting the Produce Code menu item instructs FreeForm-J to generate and display the source code required to re-create the application window, as demonstrated in Figure 3.30.

Selecting the Produce Code + Outline menu item instructs FreeForm-J to not only provide the program code required to regenerate the application window but include labels as part of the program code, as demonstrated in Figure 3.31.

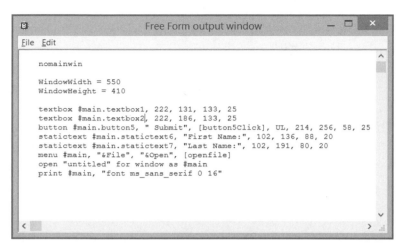

Figure 3.30 Instructing FreeForm-J to provide you with the program code required to regenerate the newly designed application window.
© 2016 Shoptalk Systems

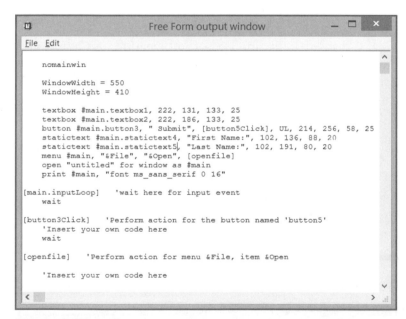

Figure 3.31 FreeForm-J can also generate labels for each control that requires them.
© 2016 Shoptalk Systems

Once you have designed an application window, have everything looking like you want it to, and have generated the program code required to regenerate it, you can copy the program code and paste it into your Just BASIC application. This saves you the time and effort required to otherwise programmatically develop the source code to create the application window yourself.

Taking Advantage of Built-In Dialogs

It is not always necessary to add new windows to your Just BASIC applications in order to interact with the user. Like many programming languages, such as Visual Basic and VBScript, Just BASIC gives programmers access to a number of prebuilt dialogs that can be used to communicate with users and to collect small amounts of information. These dialogs include the following:

- Notice
- Confirm
- Prompt
- Filedialog

By taking advantage of these dialog windows, you can reduce the number of windows your application needs and simplify your program code.

Notice

You use the `notice` command to display pop-up dialogs that display a text string and an OK button. Programmers can use this dialog to display small amounts of information and pause program execution until the user closes the dialog. To display a Notice dialog, you use the `notice` command, which has the following syntax:

```
notice "string"
```

To see the `notice` command in action, look at the following example:

```
notice "Your report is ready."
```

When executed, this statement produces the pop-up dialog shown in Figure 3.32.

Figure 3.32 Using the notice command to display a short message.
© 2016 Cengage Learning®

Trick

If you insert the carriage return character (chr$(13)) between two strings, as demonstrated next, you can display a message in the title bar of a Notice dialog:

```
notice "Reminder!" + chr$(13) + "Your report is ready."
```

In this example, the string "Reminder!" is displayed in the Notice dialog's title bar, and the second string is displayed as a message inside the dialog. If you add three or more carriage return character-separated strings to a notice command, Just BASIC displays the first string in the dialog's title bar, and the rest of the strings are displayed as a multiline message. You can also use the carriage return character to display title bar messages and to display multiline messages when working with the confirm and prompt commands.

Confirm

The Confirm dialog is similar to the Notice dialog. However, the Confirm dialog displays two buttons, Yes and No, allowing programmers to display a question and to collect either of two answers. The Confirm dialog is generated using the confirm command, which has the following syntax:

```
confirm "string"; response$
```

response$ is used to collect the user's input. To see the confirm command in action, look at the following example:

```
confirm "Would you like to continue?"; response$
```

When executed, this statement produces the pop-up dialog shown in Figure 3.33.

Figure 3.33 Using the Confirm dialog to prompt the user to pick between two choices.
© 2010 Cengage Learning®

Prompt

The Prompt dialog displays a pop-up dialog that prompts the user to enter a small amount of text. This dialog displays two buttons: OK and Cancel. The Prompt dialog is generated using the prompt command, which has the following syntax:

```
prompt "string"; response$
```

*response$* is used to collect the user's input. If the user clicks on the Cancel button without entering input, an empty string ("") is returned. If you assign a value to the response$ variable prior to displaying a Prompt dialog, the value of response$ is displayed as the default response inside the pop-up dialog, allowing the user to accept this value by clicking on the OK button.

To see the prompt command in action, look at the following example:

```
prompt "Enter your age:"; response$
```

When executed, this statement produces the pop-up dialog shown in Figure 3.34.

Figure 3.34 Prompting the user to provide a small amount of input using the Prompt dialog.
© 2016 Cengage Learning®

Filedialog

The Filedialog dialog is used to display the Windows Common Filedialog window. This window lets you navigate the Windows file system to either locate a file or specify the name and location where a file should be saved. The Filedialog dialog is generated using the filedialog command, which has the following syntax:

```
filedialog "title", "template", response$
```

title represents a string to be displayed in the dialog's title bar. *template* is a string that identifies the type of file to be opened. For example, specifying "*.txt" tells the application to only show files with a .txt file extension. You can set the dialog to display more than one file type by setting template equal to two or more file extensions separated by semicolons ("*.txt; *.doc; *.wtf"). *response$* represents the name of a variable to be used to store the full file and path name of the file.

The following example demonstrates how to use the Filedialog window to allow the user to select a file to be opened:

```
filedialog "Select a File to Open", "*.txt", filename$
```

When executed, this statement produces the pop-up dialog shown in Figure 3.35, and the name of the file the user selects is stored in a variable named filename$.

If you include the word "save" somewhere in the string representing the title bar message, the save style of the dialog will be displayed instead, as demonstrated here:

```
filedialog "Save Your File", "*.txt", filename$
```

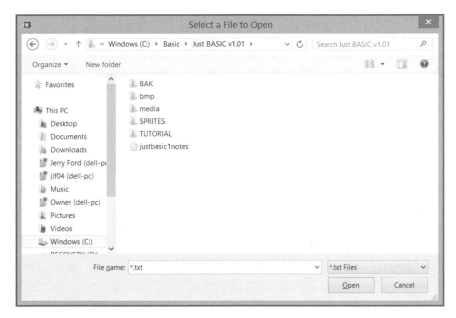

Figure 3.35 Using the Filedialog to locate a file to open.
© 2016 Shoptalk Systems

When executed, this statement produces the pop-up dialog shown in Figure 3.36, allowing the user to specify the directory to be used to store its file output (for example, the data stored in the `filename$` variable).

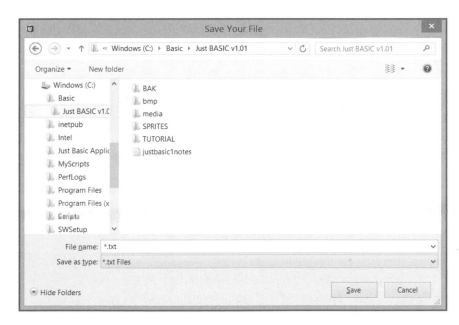

Figure 3.36 Using the Filedialog to specify the name and path of a file to be saved.
© 2016 Shoptalk Systems

Back to the BASIC Crazy 8 Ball Game

Okay, now it's time to turn your attention back to the development of this chapter's game project, the BASIC Crazy 8 Ball game. The development of this game gives you firsthand experience with GUI development. Rather than develop the game's GUI windows using FreeForm-J, the instructions provided focus on the programmatic development of those windows. This approach gives you a better understanding of the programming logic required to build application interfaces. It also encourages your appreciation for programming languages like Visual Basic and Visual C++ should you decide to switch over to them down the road. Later, once you feel you have a solid understanding of the mechanics involved in GUI development, you can take advantage of FreeForm-J if you want to speed up window development.

Designing the Game

The design of the BASIC Crazy 8 Ball game follows the same patterns used in previous chapters to develop chapter projects. The BASIC Crazy 8 Ball game is created in seven steps, as outlined here:

1. Create a new BASIC file and document its purpose.
2. Display the game's opening welcome screen.
3. Initiate gameplay.
4. Close the game if the user decides not to play.
5. Collect the player's question.
6. Generate an answer.
7. Close the game when the player finishes asking questions.

Creating a Just BASIC File Script

The first step in the creation of the BASIC Crazy 8 Ball game is to create a new BASIC file and add the following statements to it so you can provide a little information about the game and its author:

```
' ***************************************************************************
'
' Script Name: Crazy8Ball.bas (The BASIC Crazy 8 Ball Game)
' Version:     1.0
' Author:      Jerry Lee Ford, Jr.
' Date:        January 20, 2015
'
' Description: This Just BASIC game imitates a Crazy 8 fortune telling
'              ball
'
' ***************************************************************************
```

Displaying a Welcome Screen

The next step in the development of the game is to display a window that welcomes the player to the game and prompts the player to begin gameplay. This is achieved by adding the following statements to the end of the program file:

```
nomainwin    'Suppress the display of the default text window


WindowWidth = 500   'Set the width of all application windows to 500 pixels
WindowHeight = 400 'Set the height of all application windows to 400 pixels


BackgroundColor$ = "Black"    'Set the window's background color to black
ForegroundColor$ = "Yellow"   'Set the window's foreground color to yellow


'Use variables to store text strings displayed in the window
IntroMsg1$ = "W E L C O M E    T O    T H E    C R A Z Y    8    B A L L"
IntroMsg2$ = "F O R T U N E    T E L L I N G    G A M E"
IntroMsg3$ = "Copyright 2015"
IntroMsg4$ = "Jerry Lee Ford, Jr,"


'Define the format of statictext controls displayed on the window
statictext #main.statictext, IntroMsg1$, 120, 50, 300, 14
statictext #main.statictext, IntroMsg2$, 147, 80, 300, 14
statictext #main.statictext, IntroMsg3$, 210, 160, 300, 14
statictext #main.statictext, IntroMsg4$, 204, 190, 300, 14


'Define the format of button controls displayed on the window
button #main.button "  Play   ", [PrepareGame], UL, 174, 300
button #main.button "  Quit   ", [CloseMain], UL, 260, 300


'Open the window with no frame and a handle of #main
open "BASIC Crazy 8 Ball" for window_nf as #main


'Pause the application to wait for the player's instruction
Wait
```

As you can see, the first statement executes the nomainwin command to prevent the display of the mainwin window. The next two statements set the value of WindowWidth and WindowHeight to 500 and 400, respectively, thus determining the size of the application window. Next, the values of BackgroundColor$ and ForegroundColor$ are set to black and yellow, respectively. The next set of statements assigns text strings to a series of variables, which are used in the four statements that follow. These statements add statictext controls to the window to display the text that introduces the game to the player. The two statements that follow add two button controls to the window: one labeled Play and the other labeled Quit. When the application is run, clicking on the Play button executes the code statements located after the [PrepareGame] label, and clicking on the Quit button executes the code statements located after the [CloseMain] label. The next statement displays the application window using the open command. Finally, the last statement executes the wait command, pausing the application to wait for the player to click on one of the button controls.

Initiating Gameplay

The next step in the development of the BASIC Crazy 8 Ball game is to add the code statements associated with the [PrepareGame] label, shown next, to the end of the program:

```
'This static handle is executed when the player clicks on the button
'control labeled Play located on the #main window. It closes the
'#main window and initiates gameplay by switching to the [PlayGame]
'static handler
[PrepareGame]

  close #main     'Close the #main window
  goto [PlayGame]    'Switch to the [PlayGame] static handler
```

The code statements located under the [PrepareGame] label execute when the player clicks on the button control labeled Play. The first statement closes the opening window using the close command, passing it the window's handle. The second statement used the goto command to execute the code statements associated with the [PlayGame] label.

Controlling Game Termination from the Welcome Screen

Now it is time to add the code statements for the [CloseMain] label, which are shown next, to the end of the program file. These statements are responsible for terminating the application if the player clicks on the button control labeled Quit.

```
'This static handle is executed when the player clicks on the button
'control labeled Quit. It closes the #main window and then terminates
'the execution of the game
[CloseMain]

  close #main
  end
```

The first statement closes the application window, and the second statement executes the end command, which stops the application's execution.

Prompting the Player to Ask a Question

Now it is time to add the code statements for the [PlayGame] label, shown next, to the end of the program file. When executed, the code statements that follow the [PlayGame] label are responsible for displaying an application window that collects the player's question:

```
'When executed, this static handler displays a window that collects the
'player's question.
[PlayGame]

  BackgroundColor$ = "White"    'Set the window's background color to white
  ForegroundColor$ = "Black"    'Set the window's foreground color to black

  'Use variables to store text strings displayed in the window
  Instructions1$ = "Type your question in the entry field provided below"
  Instructions2$ = "and click on the Ask button to have your fortune told!"

  'Define the format of statictext controls displayed on the window
  statictext #play.statictext, Instructions1$, 120, 50, 300, 14
  statictext #play.statictext, Instructions2$, 116, 80, 300, 14

  'Define the format of button controls displayed on the window
  button #play.button " Ask    ", [AskQuestion], UL, 174, 300
  button #play.button "  Quit  ", [ClosePlay], UL, 260, 300
  textbox #play.textbox 30, 140, 430, 25

  'Open the window with no frame and a handle of #play
  open "BASIC Crazy 8 Ball" for window_nf as #play

  'Set focus to the textbox control
  print #play.textbox, "!setfocus"

  'Pause the application to wait for the player's instruction
  wait
```

The first two statements set the background and foreground color of the new window. The next two statements assign a text string to two variables. Two statictext controls are then added to the window, displaying the values assigned to Instructions1$ and Instructions2$. Next, two button controls labeled Ask and Quit are added to the window. When clicked, the button control labeled Ask causes statement execution to jump to the [AskQuestion] label. Likewise, if the button control labeled Quit is clicked, the statement following the [ClosePlay] label is executed.

Next, a textbox control is added to collect the player's input. Finally, the open command is used to display the application window, focus is assigned to the textbox control, and the wait command is executed, pausing the application until the player does something.

Generating Answers

Next, you'll add the code statements associated with the [AskQuestion] label, shown next, to the end of the BASIC file. These statements are responsible for generating and displaying an answer to the player's question.

```
'This static handler is called from the #play window when the player clicks
'on the Ask button. Its job is to process the player's input and respond
'appropriately.
[AskQuestion]

  'Retrieve the text string stored in the textbox control
  print #play.textbox, "!contents?"
  'Assign the text string to a variable named question$
  input #play.textbox, question$

  close #play     'Close the #play window

  'Displays an error message in the event the player did not enter anything
  if question$ = "" then

    'Display an error message in a popup dialog
    notice "BASIC Crazy 8 Ball" + chr$(13) + _
      "Error: You forgot to type a question!"

    'Switch back to the [PlayGame] handle to allow the player to ask a new
    'question
    goto [PlayGame]

  else  'Generate a random answer to the player's question

    'Use the rnd() function to retrieve a random number between 1 and 3 and
    'assign the result to a variable named RandomNumber
    RandomNumber = int(rnd(1)*3) + 1
```

```
'Select an answer based on the value assigned to the RandomNumber
'variable
if RandomNumber = 1 then answer$ = "YES"
if RandomNumber = 2 then answer$ = "MAYBE"
if RandomNumber = 3 then answer$ = "NO"

'Display the answer to the player's question in a popup dialog
notice "BASIC Crazy 8 Ball" + chr$(13) + "The answer is " + _
  answer$ + "."

'Switch back to the [PlayGame] handle to allow the player to ask a new
'question
goto [PlayGame]

end if
```

The first statement following the [AskQuestion] label retrieves the contents of the textbox control, and the statement that follows places a copy of the data that is retrieved into a variable named question$. Next, the window containing the player's question is closed. The rest of the code statements located under this label are wrapped inside if…then…else code blocks. The if…then…else statements are used to implement conditional logic, which you will learn about in Chapter 5, "Making Decisions with Conditional Logic." The logic contained in these statements first checks to see if the player keyed in a question before clicking on the Ask button, displaying an error message if this is the case. Assuming that the player provided input, a random number between 1 and 3 is generated and, based on the number that is selected, a value of YES, MAYBE, or NO is selected and displayed as the answer to the player's question.

Hint

To generate the game's random number, two built in Just BASIC functions are used: int() and rnd(). A *function* is a collection of code statements that can be called on and executed as a unit. The int() function takes a number as input and returns an integer. The rnd() function returns a random number between 0 and 1. Therefore, the statement

```
RandomNumber = int(rnd(1)*3) + 1
```

uses the rnd() function to generate a number between 0 and 1, multiplies that number by 3, and then adds 1. The result is a number between 1.0 and 3.99. The int() function then processes this value, resulting in a value of 1, 2, or 3. This value is then assigned to the RandomNumber variable.

The notice command displays messages in a pop-up dialog window. In addition, the goto command is used to jump the program back to the [PlayGame] label, thus preparing the game to redisplay the #play window and allowing the player to ask another question.

Terminating Gameplay

The final set of statements to be added to the end of the BASIC file are those associated with the [ClosePlay] label. These statements arc shown here:

```
'This static handle is executed when the player clicks on the button
'control labeled Quit. It closes the #play window and then terminates
'the execution of the game
[ClosePlay]

  close #play
  end
```

When called, these statements close the application window and then terminate application execution by running the end command.

The Final Result

That's it. Assuming that you have not made any typos when keying in the source code for the game, everything should be ready. So go ahead and run the game a few times to see if everything works as expected. When testing the game, make sure that you try every feature by taking the time to click on every control and window button. Also, try submitting a question without actually typing anything to make sure that the game correctly informs you that an error has occurred.

Summary

In this chapter you learned how to create graphical user interfaces for Windows applications. This included learning how to create different types of application windows as well as how to add different interface controls, such as button and textbox controls, to application windows. You learned how to implement event-driven programming in order to associate specific code statements with specific windows and interface controls. You learned how to set window and control properties such as font size and type and foreground and background color. On top of all this, you also learned how to work with FreeForm-J in order to visually create graphical user interfaces and to generate source code that goes along with them.

Before moving on to Chapter 4, why don't you set aside some time to improve the BASIC Crazy 8 Ball game by tackling the following list of challenges.

Challenges

1. As currently written, the instructions provided by the game are a little sparse. Consider adding additional text to give the player a better set of instructions. You might also want to make the text displayed in the game's pop-up dialogs a little more user friendly.

2. As designed, the BASIC Crazy 8 Ball game has only three possible answers from which to draw. Consider expanding the range of answers available to the game. For example, you might want to add answers such as NEVER, ABSOLUTELY, or THAT'S NOT GOING TO HAPPEN.

3. Create a distribution package for your game and use it to install the game on another Windows computer and make sure that it still runs (for example, that you have not forgotten to include one or more required supporting Just BASIC files).

Learning How to Write Basic Programs

Working with Variables and Arrays

All computer programs process some kind of data. This data may be embedded inside the program, or the user may supply it—from external files or from the computer itself. Regardless of where it originates, programmers need a means of storing and later retrieving data used during application execution. You have already seen examples of how this works in the game programs you've created in this book. In this chapter, you will learn how the retrieval and storage of data in computer memory really works, both in Just BASIC and other programming languages. In addition, you will learn how to create your next computer application, the Ask Genie game.

Specifically, you will learn the following:

- How to store and retrieve individual pieces of data in variables
- How to store groups of data using arrays
- The rules to follow when naming variables and arrays
- How some programming languages use constants
- The different types of data that can be stored
- How to convert numbers to strings and vice versa

Project Preview: The Ask Genie Game

In this chapter, you will learn how to create a new computer game called Ask Genie. Tabethia is a good genie who lives in a small lamp. She does not like to be disturbed and won't respond if you rub her lamp. However, she has one weakness: she cannot bear to be asked the same request three times in a row.

The game begins by welcoming the player and providing a little background information, as shown in Figure 4.1.

The player must click on the Play button to continue, displaying the screen shown in Figure 4.2. A list of questions that can be asked of Tabethia is provided in a listbox control located at the lower-left corner of the window. Once a question has been selected, Tabethia's answer is displayed in a texteditor control located in the lower-right corner of the window.

Figure 4.1 By specifying different font sizes, you can emphasize different text elements.
© 2016 Cengage Learning®

Figure 4.2 To ask Tabethia a question, the player must double-click on one of the questions shown in the listbox control.
© 2016 Cengage Learning®

The trick to winning the game is to remember that Tabethia will answer any question asked of her three times in a row. If the player forgets this fact, a hint can be displayed by clicking on the Hint button. In response, the pop-up dialog shown in Figure 4.3 is displayed.

If the player insists on seeing the hint (by clicking on the Yes button), the pop-up dialog shown in Figure 4.4 is displayed.

Once asked the same question three times in a row, Tabethia gives up and grants the player's every wish, as shown in Figure 4.5.

Figure 4.3 The player is discouraged from asking for help.
© 2016 Cengage Learning®

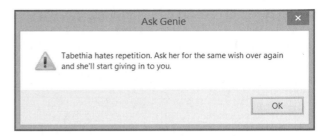

Figure 4.4 A clue is provided to help remind the player of Tabethia's weakness.
© 2016 Cengage Learning®

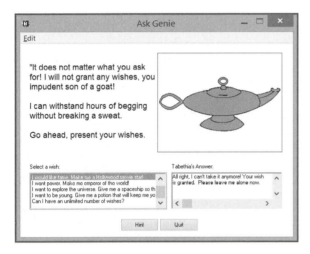

Figure 4.5 After promising to grant the player's wish, Tabethia asks to be left undisturbed.
© 2016 Cengage Learning®

Working with Program Data

All computer programs process data in some manner. *Data* is information that your application collects, stores, processes, and modifies during execution. This data may be embedded within the programs. For example, you might create a word guessing game in which you embed a dozen words used to play the game in the program code. Data can also be retrieved from the computer on which your programs run. For example, a program that processes financial transactions may depend on the system clock to generate date/time stamps for each record that is generated. That same final program will also depend on data input from other sources. For example, it might look for data files stored on your computer, or it might allow users to key input into a graphical user interface.

Any data your computer programs use must be stored in computer memory. The location in memory where a particular piece of data is stored is referred to as an *address*. To retrieve a piece of data and work with it again later in a program, the program must reference the address where the data is stored. Some programming languages, including assembly languages and C++, allow programmers to directly manipulate specific memory addresses. This requires extra care on the part of the programmer because any error can have disastrous consequences, potentially corrupting other programs' data or even causing the computer to crash. This is why most programming languages insulate programmers from the complexities of dealing directly with memory addresses.

Most programming languages, including Just BASIC, allow you to store individual pieces of data in variables. Rather than allow you to access specific memory addresses, these languages allow you to refer to a variable by name and then manage the storage and retrieval process for you. You have seen many examples of this in applications that you have already developed.

Exploring Different Ways of Storing Data

Programming languages offer different ways of storing and retrieving data. One way to store data within a program is to hard-code it as a literal value, as demonstrated here:

```
print "I am 42 years old."
```

Here, a numeric value of 42 has been embedded within a text string. Although it's certainly useful as a means of displaying static information, using data in this manner is limited. You cannot, for example, alter this value or use it to perform calculations.

In addition to supporting literal values, all programming languages let you store individual pieces of data in variables and groups of related data in arrays. In addition, most programming languages support the use of constants to store data whose value is known at development time and does not change during program execution. Each of these data storage options has its own unique characteristics and is suited to specific situations. Which ones you use will depend on the programming language you are using as well as the type of data you are working with.

Defining Constants

A *constant* is a descriptive name assigned to a known value that does not change throughout the execution of a program. Programmers use constants when the data an application uses is known in advance and not subject to change. For example, a mathematical application might store the value of pi (3.14) in a constant at the beginning of the program and then reference it in various locations throughout the rest of the application. Because pi is a numeric constant and is not subject to change, it is a good candidate for assignment to a constant.

By assigning a value to a constant, as opposed to a variable, you eliminate the possibility of accidentally modifying it when the application is run. In addition, constants generally require less memory than variables, making programs slightly more efficient in terms of resources consumed. Simpler BASIC dialects, including Just BASIC, do not support the use of constants. However, more robust BASIC dialects, like Visual Basic, do.

Trick

To define a constant in programming languages such as Visual Basic and C++, you use the const keyword:

```
const defaultScore As Integer = 100
```

Here, a constant named defaultScore has been defined as an integer and assigned a value of 100. Because you can assign a descriptive name to a constant, the program code is easier to understand. For example, you might use the preceding statement to set the default score assigned to players at the beginning of a computer game. By referencing this descriptive name, you help to document your document whenever this value is used. This is a lot more meaningful than simply embedding the number 100 over and over again in different code statements. In addition, code maintenance is simplified through the use of constants. In this scenario, all a programmer would have to do to change the default score is modify this value one time in the const declaration statement.

Many programming languages, such as Visual Basic, also give programmers access to a collection of predefined constants. For example, instead of controlling the display of text using carriage returns by inserting Chr$(13) into strings as is done in Just BASIC, Visual Basic lets programmers reference built-in constants like ControlChars.Cr (carriage return) and ControlChars.CrLf (carriage return and line feed).

Declaring Variables

Any time you have a piece of data to keep track of and modify, such as the value of a player's score during gameplay, you need to store it in a variable. A *variable* is a pointer to a location in memory (address) where a value is stored. In most programming languages, including Just BASIC, a value (string or numeric) is assigned to a variable using the equals operator (=), as demonstrated here:

```
initialScore = 0
confirmMsg$ = "Are you sure you want to quit?"
```

The first statement shown creates a variable named initialScore and assigns it a numeric value of 0. The second statement creates a string variable named confirmMsg$ and assigns a text string of "Are you sure you want to quit?" to it. In addition to allowing you to create your own variables, many programming languages provide programmers with access to special variables. A *special variable* is one that is predefined by the programming languages and can be referenced at any time during program execution. Table 4.1 is a listing of Just BASIC special variables.

TABLE 4.1 JUST BASIC SPECIAL VARIABLES		
BackgroundColor$	Joy1x	ListboxColor$
ComboboxColor$	Joy1y	Platform$
CommandLine$	Joy1z	PrinterFont$
DefaultDir$	Joy1button1	TextboxColor$
DisplayHeight	Joy1button2	TexteditorColor$
DisplayWidth	Joy2x	Version$
Drives$	Joy2y	WindowHeight
Err	Joy2z	WindowWidth
Err$	Joy2button1	UpperLeftX
ForegroundColor$	Joy2button2	UpperRightY

You may remember from Chapter 3, "Creating Graphical User Interfaces," that special variables like BackgroundColor$, ListboxColor$, ComboboxColor$, TextboxColor$, TexteditorColor$, and ForegroundColor$ let you specify the colors used when rendering windows and controls and that DisplayHeight, DisplayWidth, WindowHeight, and WindowWidth can be used to affect the size of application windows.

Creating Arrays

Variables are generally all that you need to effectively define and manipulate a few pieces of data at a time. However, some applications involve the manipulation and storage of a large amount of related information. For these applications, arrays are typically used to handle data storage. An *array* is an index list of data stored and managed as a unit. Data stored in an array is accessed by specifying the name of the array and the index position of the data to be stored or retrieved.

Suppose you want to create an online contact list for all your friends and associates. One way of doing this is to save a list of contacts and their phone numbers in a text file and then write a program that opens that file and reads this list into an array. Once the information is loaded into an array, you can use data stored in the array to populate a combobox or listbox control.

Just BASIC has support for single-dimension and double-dimension arrays. A single-dimension array is a list of data, such as usernames. A two-dimensional array is like a table or an Excel spreadsheet with rows and columns. Other programming languages like Visual Basic and C++ support arrays with even more dimensions.

Other Data Storage Options

Although Just BASIC support for data manipulation is limited to variables and one- or two-dimensional arrays, other programming languages offer additional ways of storing and retrieving data. For example, Perl allows programmers to define hashes, sometimes referred to as *associated arrays*, in which data is stored in key-value pairs, and each data element stored in a hash is assigned a unique key. You can then retrieve data from the hash by referencing its associated key.

Other programming languages, like Visual Basic and C++, support the use of structures. Structures allow programmers to define a collection of related variables stored within an array. This allows loosely related data such as customer names, phone numbers, and addresses to be stored together and referenced individually or as a group. Object-oriented programming languages, like C++ and Visual Basic, also allow programmers to store data using custom classes, which can be used as a template to create objects where data can be stored.

In short, different programming languages support different data storage and retrieval options over and above variables and arrays. Still, variables and arrays are by far the most commonly used means of storing and manipulating data. As such, Just BASIC supplies an excellent platform from which to experience and learn to work with both.

Working with Different Types of Data

A key concept to understand when developing computer programs is that types of data are treated differently. For example, various types of numbers require different amounts of storage in memory. Similarly, you can do certain things to some types of data that you cannot do to others. As an example, consider numbers and strings. You can add, subtract, multiply, and divide numbers. You cannot do the same with strings. However, you can concatenate strings together to create larger strings. Simpler programming languages like Just BASIC support two types of values: string and numeric. More industrial-strength programming languages like Visual Basic support a much broader range of data types. For example, the following list shows just a portion of the different data types that Visual Basic supports.

- Boolean   A value of True or False
- Date   A value representing date and time
- Decimal   A numerical value up to 79,228,162,514,264,337,593,543,950,335
- Double   A numeric value in the range of −1.79769313486231570E+308 to −4.94065645841246544E-324 for negative numbers and 4.94065645841246544E-324 to 1.79769313486231570E+308 for positive numbers
- Integer   A numeric value in the range of −32,768 to 32,767
- Long   A numeric value in the range of −2,147,483,648 to 2,147,483,647

- Single   A numeric value in the range of −3.402823E+38 to −1.401298E-45 for negative numbers and 1.401298E-45 to 3.4028235E+E38 for positive numbers
- String   A string value in the range of up to two billion characters

In programming languages that support different data types, specifying the appropriate data type associated with a variable or array is important because it impacts the amount of memory dedicated to storing different variables. In addition, data type definitions restrict the types of operations that can be performed on values.

As has been stated, Just BASIC only supports string and numeric data types. In Just BASIC, as in most programming languages, a string is anything enclosed within matching double quotation marks. In Just BASIC, strings can contain up to 2,000,000 characters. Just BASIC also distinguishes between two types of numbers: integer and floating point (for example, numbers containing decimals).

Trick

Although Just BASIC does not support date and time data types, it does give programmers access to two built-in functions that retrieve date and time data from the computer in the form of a number or a string. Depending on how the Date$() function is used, it returns either a string or a numeric value, as demonstrated here:

```
print date$()              'Returns January 15, 2015 as a string
print date$("mm/dd/yyyy")  'Returns 01/15/2015 as a string
print date$("mm/dd/yy")    'Returns 01/15/15 as a string
print date$("yyyy/mm/dd")  'Returns 2015/01/15 as a string
print date$("days")        'Returns 99999 (days since Jan. 1, 1901) as a number
```

Depending on how the Time$() function is used, it returns either a string or a numeric value, as demonstrated here:

```
print time$()                'Returns "12:55:04" as a string
print time$("seconds")       'Returns 28456 as a number (seconds past midnight)
print time$("milliseconds")  'Returns 99999999 as a number
                             '(milliseconds past midnight)
```

Learning How to Work with Variables

As has been already stated, variables allow you to store individual pieces of data during program execution. Some programming languages, such as C, require that you formally declare a variable and its type before allowing you to assign data to it or work with it. Other programming languages, such as Just BASIC and JavaScript, let you create variables on the fly, without declaring them in advance or specifying data. Still other programming languages, such as Visual Basic, allow you to enable or disable the requirement to explicitly define variables before using them.

Trick

By default, Visual Basic allows for variable creation on the fly just like Just BASIC. However, by adding the following statement at the beginning of a Visual Basic program, you can instruct Visual Basic to enforce strict variable declaration:

```
Option Explicit
```

Declaring Variables

Just BASIC does not require programmers to declare variables prior to their use, instead allowing variables to be created and used on the fly. Although this brings about flexibility, it also tolerates sloppy programming and errors. Therefore, it is important that you take great care to check the spelling of all your variable names. Otherwise, a small typo can lead to errors. Consider the following example:

```
round1Score = 10
round2Score = 20

totalScore = round1Score + Round2Score
print totalScore
```

In this example, the intention was to take the values assigned to round1Score and round2Score, add them together, and assign the result to totalScore. However, instead of assigning a value of 30 to totalScore, this example assigned a value of 10. The reason for this unexpected turn of events was the change in spelling of the round2Score variable in the third statement. If you look carefully, you will see that the first character of this variable name has been capitalized. Just BASIC is a case-sensitive programming language, meaning that variable names in different case are viewed as being different variables.

Storing Data in Variables

Like most programming languages, if you do not assign an initial value to a variable, Just BASIC will assign a default value for you. By default, numeric values are assigned a value of 0. String variables, on the other hand, are assigned an empty string, equivalent to "". If you do not want these defaults, you need to make sure that you assign an initial value to your variables.

In most programming languages, including Just BASIC, the = operator is used to assign data to variables, as demonstrated here:

```
name$ = "William"
age = 8
```

However, some languages differ. For example, AppleScript uses the keyword "To" to assign a value to a variable.

Understanding Scope

One important concept for you to understand is variable scope. Scope defines the area within a program where a variable can be accessed. Just BASIC supports two levels of variable scope:

- **Local.** Local variables are ones that are only accessible from within the function or subroutine in which they were created. (*Functions* and *subroutines* are blocks of code that perform a specific task. Both are covered in Chapter 7, "Improving Program Organization with Functions and Subroutines."
- **Global.** Variables accessible throughout the program.

Hint

Some programming languages, like Visual Basic, support additional levels of scope, giving programmers additional degrees of control over variable access.

Working with Local Variables

A local variable can only be accessed within the scope in which it has been created. For example, a variable used inside a subroutine can only be accessed from within that subroutine. By default, variables used outside of functions and subroutines in Just BASIC programs are not visible inside functions and subroutines. Likewise, a variable used inside a function or subroutine is not accessible outside of that function or subroutine. The following example demonstrates how to create a local variable within a subroutine:

```
sub TestSub
  msg$ = "Hi!"
  notice msg$
end sub
```

A local variable only exists within the scope in which it is created. If two subroutines are added to the same program and both contain a reference to variables named msg$, Just BASIC treats each instance of that variable in both subroutines as being entirely different variables. If you want both subroutines to be able to access the same variable, you must declare that variable as being global, as explained in the next section.

Working with Global Variables

Variables declared as global can be accessed from anywhere within a Just BASIC program.

Hint

Special variables, such as `BackgroundColor$`, `ForegroundColor$`, `DisplayHeight`, `DisplayWidth`, `WindowHeight`, and `WindowWidth`, are always global; they're accessible from anywhere in your Just BASIC programs.

To declare a variable as global, you use the `global` command, which has the following syntax:

```
global variable1, variable2,... variableN
```

As you can see, you can declare any number of variables as being global by specifying a comma-separated list of variable names. For example, the following statements declare a variable named `totalScore` as being global and then assign a value to that variable:

```
global totalScore
totalScore = 0
```

Trick

In general, it is a good idea to limit the scope of your variables whenever possible. This conserves memory and eliminates the possibility of accidentally changing a variable's value from a different location within your application (which can happen when using global variables).

Variable Naming Rules

All programming languages impose certain rules on programmers when it comes to naming variables. Some programming languages are case sensitive, meaning that they will view two identically named variables with differing case as being different. Other programming languages are case insensitive, meaning that they ignore case and consider any identically named variables to be the same. Some programming languages prohibit the use of certain characters in variable names. Failure to follow variable naming rules will result in errors.

Just BASIC variable names can be of any length. However, you will want to keep them reasonably short and descriptive. Just BASIC variable names are case sensitive. In Just BASIC, variables named `userage` and `USERAGE` represent two different variables.

The following list outlines a few rules that you must follow when assigning names to Just BASIC variables:

- Variable names must begin with a letter.
- Variable names can only contain letters, numbers, and the dot (.) and dollar sign ($) characters.
- String variable names must end with the $ character.
- Variable names cannot include blank spaces.
- Variable names cannot be reserved words.

Converting Variables

In many programming languages, specifying a variable data type is required. These languages are said to be strongly typed. Programming languages like Just BASIC, which allow you to create variables without formally declaring them or specifying their data type, are considered to be loosely typed.

From time to time, you may find that you need to convert data from one data type to another. Just BASIC gives you access to conversation functions that you can use to convert data from one type to another. These operators include the following:

- `val()`
- `str$()`

Converting from String to Numeric Values

Using the `val()` function, you can convert a string that contains a number into a numeric value. If the string being analyzed cannot be evaluated to a number, a value of 0 is returned. The `val()` function has the following syntax:

`val(expression)`

expression can be a literal string or a variable. To get a better understanding of how the val() function works, take a look at the following example:

```
apples$ = "25"
oranges = 5

apples = val(apples$)
fruit = apples + oranges

print "You have "; fruit; " pieces of fruit."
```

Here, a string variable named apples$ has been assigned a string value of 25 and a numeric variable named oranges has been assigned a value of 5. Next, the val() function is used to convert the string value assigned to apples$ to its numeric equivalent. The numeric values of apples and oranges are then added together and the results assigned to a variable named fruit, whose value is then displayed.

Converting from Numeric to String Values

Using the str$() function, you can convert a numeric value into its string equivalent. The str$() function has the following syntax:

```
str$(expression)
```

To get a better understanding of how the str$() function works, take a look at the following example:

```
oranges = 20
oranges$ = str$(oranges)
print "You have " + oranges$ + " oranges"      'error
```

Here, a numeric variable named oranges is assigned a value of 20. Next, the str$() function is used to convert the numeric value assigned to oranges to a string value of "20", which is then assigned to oranges$. This value is then displayed as part of a concatenated string in the last statement.

Hint

Concatenation is the process of joining two or more strings to create a new string. Different programming languages use different concatenation characters. For example, in Visual Basic, the & character is used to concatenate strings. Just BASIC, on the other hand, uses the + character to perform concatenation.

Trick

Strings are created by enclosing text within a pair of matching double-quotation marks. If you need to include a double-quotation mark within a string, you might be tempted to try something like the following:

```
print "Tom told Bob to "run" but he wouldn't."
```

However, Just BASIC will flag this statement as a syntax error. The workaround for this situation in Just BASIC is to use the chr$() function, as demonstrated here:

```
print "Tom told Bob to " + chr$(34) + "run" + chr$(34) + " but he wouldn't."
```

As you can see, chr$(34) evaluates to a value of a double quote, thus allowing you to insert double quotation marks within your text strings.

Other programming languages provide different ways of inserting special characters into text strings. For example, when displaying a text string in a Perl script, you can precede any character that you want to be interpreted literally with the \ character.

Working with Numeric Variables

Unlike string variables, Just BASIC does not allow you to add a $ as the last character in a numeric variable's name. Just BASIC numeric variables can store both integers and double-precision floating-point numbers, as demonstrated here:

```
x = 2     'Integer
y = 1.99 'Floating point number
```

Trap

If you attempt to add the $ character to the end of a numeric variable name, Just BASIC will generate a *Type Mismatch* error.

Like many programming languages, Just BASIC gives programmers access to a host of built-in functions, which can be used in conjunction with numeric data. The following list, which should look familiar to any Visual Basic programmer, shows the numeric functions that Just BASIC provides:

- **ABS().** Returns the absolute value of a number
- **SQR().** Returns the square root of a number
- **EXP().** Returns the exponent of a number

- **LOG()**. Returns the natural log of a number
- **INT()**. Returns the integer portion of a number
- **RND()**. Returns a random number between 0 and 1

By using built-in numeric functions, you save yourself the trouble of having to develop your own programming logic to perform the same types of calculations, thus simplifying your program code. All that you have to do to use these functions is enclose a numeric value within the numeric function's parentheses, as demonstrated here:

```
playerScore = 10.5
playerScore = int(playerScore)  'value is now 10
```

Here, a floating-point number, 10.5, is converted to an integer using the int() function.

Functions That Manipulate Strings

Most programming languages also provide built-in functions that you can use to manipulate text strings. In the case of Just BASIC, you will find functions that you can use to search strings, extract portions of strings, or convert characters from lower- to uppercase or vice versa. The following list, which again should look familiar to any Visual Basic programmer, shows the complete collection of Just BASIC's string functions:

- **InStr()**. Performs a search, looking for one string within another string, specifying the starting character location of the string if found
- **Left$()**. Returns a specified number of characters from a string, sometimes referred to as a substring, starting from the left side of the string
- **Len()**. Returns a value showing the number of characters in a string
- **Lower$()**. Returns a string that has been converted to all lowercase
- **Mid$()**. Extracts a specific number of characters from a string (if found), beginning at the specified character position
- **Right$()**. Returns a specified number of characters from a string, sometimes referred to as a substring, starting from the right side of the string
- **Space$()**. Returns a string made up of a specified number of characters
- **Trim$()**. Removes leading blank spaces from the beginning and the end of a string
- **Upper$()**. Returns a string that has been converted to all uppercase

To see an example of a number of these string manipulation functions in action, take a look at the following example:

```
storyText$ = "   Once upon a time…"
storyText$ = trim$(storyText$) 'Returns "Once upon a time…"
```

```
storyText$ = upper$(storyText$) 'Returns "ONCE UPON A TIME…"
storyText$ = lower$(storyText$) 'Returns "once upon a time…"
x = len(storyText$) 'X equals 17
```

Here, a variable named `storyText$` is assigned a text string that includes three blank spaces followed by four words and three period characters. The second statement uses the `trim$()` function to reassign a string with no leading or trailing spaces back to `storyText$`. The third statement uses the `upper$()` function to reassign an all-uppercase string to `storyText$`. The fourth statement converts the string assigned to `storyText$` to all lowercase characters. Finally, the last statement uses the `len()` function to return a numeric value representing the number of characters of the value assigned to `storyText$`.

Storing Data in Arrays

As handy as variables are for storing individual pieces of data, they lose some value when you need to create programs that must handle large amounts of data. In most cases, the data processed by an application is closely related. For example, an address book application might need to manage a list of names. One way to handle the storage and retrieval of related data is through arrays. An *array* is an indexed list of data. Just BASIC arrays are zero-based, meaning that the first element stored in an array is assigned an index number of 0, the second element in the array has an index position of 1, and so on.

Virtually every major programming language supports the use of arrays. Although many programming languages, like Visual Basic, support the creation of arrays with numerous dimensions, Just BASIC's support for arrays is limited to single- and double-dimension arrays. As with variables, you can use arrays to store string and numeric data.

Creating an Array

You can create small, single-dimension arrays of fewer than ten elements by simply assigning nine or fewer elements to a like-named array, as demonstrated here:

```
names$(0) = "Alexander"
names$(1) = "William"
names$(2) = "Molly"
names$(3) = "Jerry"
names$(4) = "Mary"
```

Here I've created an array containing five elements. For arrays with ten or more elements, Just BASIC requires that you use the `dim` command to first declare the array. This command has the following syntax:

```
dim ArrayName(dimensions)
```

dimensions is a comma-separated list of values, representing the different dimensions of an array. Just BASIC arrays can have either one or two dimensions. The following statement demonstrates how to define an array that can store up to 20 elements:

```
dim names$(20)
```

Once the array has been defined, you can begin assigning data to it, as shown here:

```
names$(0) = "Alexander"
names$(1) = "William"
names$(2) = "Molly"
names$(3) = "Jerry"
names$(4) = "Mary"
.

.

names$(19) = "Mike"
```

Hint

Just like variables, Just BASIC requires that you add a $ character to the end of array names that will be used to store string data.

Retrieving Data from an Array

Once you have created an array and populated it with data, you can reference elements stored there by specifying the name of the array followed by the index number of the element to be retrieved, as shown here:

```
notice names$(4)
```

Here, the fifth element stored in an array named names$() is retrieved and displayed in a pop-up dialog.

Hint

Referencing array contents an element at a time is okay for small arrays, but for arrays that contain dozens, hundreds, or thousands of elements; it is just not practical. Instead, you will want to set up a loop to process all the contents of the array. Loops are covered in Chapter 6, "Using Loops to Process Data."

Resizing an Array

You can resize any Just BASIC array using the `redim` statement. Using this statement, you can change the size of an array:

```
redim userNames$(9)
```

Here, the size of the `userNames$()` array is changed so that it can hold ten elements (0–9).

Two-dimensional arrays can also be resized, as demonstrated here:

```
redim addressBook$(9, 9)
```

Here a two-dimensional array has been resized so that it can hold 20 elements of data.

Trap

There is one major drawback to using the `redim` statement to resize arrays in Just BASIC. Any data already stored in the arrays is automatically deleted. Other programming languages, such as Visual Basic, allow you to retain data stored in arrays when resizing them.

Reserved Words

Every programming language has a list of reserved words—sometimes referred to as *keywords*—that have special meaning to the language. These reserved words can only be used as documented by the programming languages in accordance with specific syntax requirements. An example of a Just BASIC reserved word is button. As you know, button is the name of a Just BASIC interface control. Because it is a reserved word, you can only use it when defining a button control on a user interface. If you attempt to use it as the name of a variable or array, you will run into problems.

Table 4.2 is a listing of Just BASIC's reserved words. Take a few minutes to scan it. You may want to bookmark this page and refer back to it any time you are thinking about assigning a name to a variable or array that you think might sound like a reserved word, just to make sure it's not.

Hint

Just BASIC also considers built-in functions and variables to be reserved words. Just BASIC's collection of built-in functions includes the following: ABS(), ACS(), ASC(), ASN(), ATN(), CHR$(), COS(), DATE$(), EOF(), EXP(), INPUT$(), INSTR(), INT(), LEFT$(), LEN(), LOF(), LOG(), LOWER$(), MIDIPOS(), MID$(), MKDIR(), NOT(), RIGHT$(), RMDIR(), RND(), SIN(), SPACE$(), SQR(), STR$(), TAB(), TAN(), TIME$(), TRIM$(), TXCOUNT(), UPPER$(), USING(), VAL(), and WORD$().

TABLE 4.2 JUST BASIC RESERVED WORDS

And	Data	Gosub	Maphandle	Put	Sub
Append	Dialog	Goto	Menu	Radiobutton	Text
As	Dim	Graphicbox	Name	Random	Textbox
Beep	Do	Graphics	Next	Randomize	Texteditor
Bmpbutton	Dump	Groupbox	Nomainwin	Read	Then
Bmpsave	Else	If	None	Readjoystick	Timer
Boolean	End	Input	Notice	Redim	Unloadbmp
Button	Error	Kill	On	Rem	Until
Byref	Exit	Let	Oncomerror	Restore	Wait
Call	Field	Line	Open	Return	Wend
Case	Filedialog	Listbox	Or	Run	While
Checkbox	Files	Loadbmp	Output	Scan	Window
Close	For	Long	Playmidi	Select	Word
Cls	Function	Loop	Playwave	Statictext	Xor
Combobox	Get	Lprint	Print	Stop	
Confirm	Global	Mainwin	Prompt	Stopmidi	

Hint

Just BASIC's collection of built-in variables includes the following: BackgroundColor$, ComboboxColor$, CommandLine$, DefaultDir$, DisplayHeight, DisplayWidth, Drives$, Err, Err$, ForegroundColor$, Joy1x, Joy1y, Joy1z, Joy1button1, Joy1button2, Joy2x, Joy2y, Joy2z, Joy2button1, Joy2button2, ListboxColor$, Platform$, PrinterFont$, TextboxColor$, TexteditorColor$, UpperLeftX, UpperLeftY, Version$, WindowHeight, and WindowWidth.

Back to the Ask Genie Game

Okay, let's turn our attention back to the development of this book's next game project, the Ask Genie game. In this game you will get additional hands-on experience working with variables and arrays. You will also get the chance to work with the listbox and texteditor controls.

Designing the Game

The design of the Ask Genie game is relatively straightforward. The Ask Genie game will be created in eight steps, as outlined here:

1. Create a new BASIC file and document its purpose.
2. Display a welcome screen.
3. Start gameplay.
4. Close the #main window.
5. Accept player questions.
6. Generate answers to questions.
7. Provide the player with a hint.
8. Terminate gameplay.

The applications that you are developing in this book are getting more complicated as you move from chapter to chapter. In the previous chapter, you learned how to use labels as a way to organize groups of statements that you could call upon from anywhere within a program. In this chapter's game project, you will use subroutines instead.

Hint

A *subroutine* is a collection of related statements that are called and executed as a unit. Once it's executed, a subroutine returns processing control back to the statement that called on it to execute. More information about subroutines and how to work with them is available in Chapter 7.

Creating a Just BASIC File Script

As with all the previous Just BASIC applications that you have worked on in this book, let's begin by adding a few comment statements to the beginning of the program file in order to document the overall purpose of the application and provide a little information about its author:

```
' *********************************************************************
'
' Script Name: AskGenie.bas (The Ask Genie Game)
' Version:     1.0
' Author:      Jerry Lee Ford, Jr.
' Date:        January 20, 2015
'
' Description: In this Just BASIC game the player is challenged to
```

```
'              convince Tabethia, a powerful but somewhat temperamental
'              genie, to grant wishes.
'
' ************************************************************************
```

Because this application does not use a text window, let's also add the following statement to the end of the program file to instruct Just BASIC not to generate the default mainwin window.

```
nomainwin    'Suppress the display of the default text window
```

Welcoming the Player

The Ask Genie game will begin by displaying a welcome screen that introduces the game and gives the player a little background information. Add the following code statements to the end of the program file to generate this window and manage its interaction with the player.

Hint

Even though you may be tempted not to key in the comment statements that are provided as part of the code statements shown next, go ahead and do so. These statements provide detailed step-by-step documentation of every code statement and make the program code easier to read and understand.

```
'Define two global variables to keep track of player wishes
global previousSelection$, consecutiveWishes

WindowWidth = 600   'Set the width of the application windows to 600 pixels
WindowHeight = 480  'Set the height of the application windows to 480 pixels

BackgroundColor$ = "white"    'Set the window's background color to white
ForegroundColor$ = "black"    'Set the window's foreground color to black

'Use variables to store text strings displayed in the window

IntroMsg1$ = "A S K   G E N I E"
IntroMsg2$ = "Copyright 2015"
IntroMsg3$ = "Welcome to the Ask Genie game. In this game, the " _
    + "objective is to get the game's genie, Tabethia, to grant your " _
    + "wishes. She will resist you. Your task is to wear her down " _
    + "until she is willing to cooperate and grant any wish that " _
    + "you present to her."
```

```
'Define the format of statictext controls displayed on the window
statictext #main.statictext1, IntroMsg1$, 160, 50, 330, 32
statictext #main.statictext2, IntroMsg2$, 380, 90, 300, 14
statictext #main.statictext3, IntroMsg3$, 100, 180, 400, 110

'Define the format of button controls displayed on the window
button #main.button "  Play  ", PrepareGame, UL, 220, 360
button #main.button "  Quit  ", CloseMain, UL, 305, 360

'Open the window with no frame and a handle of #main
open "Ask Genie" for window_nf as #main

'Set the font type, size, and properties for each of the static controls
print #main.statictext1, "!font Arial 22 bold"
print #main.statictext2, "!font Arial 8"
print #main.statictext3, "!font Arial 11"

'Pause the application to wait for the player's instruction
wait
```

The first code statement just shown declares two global variables: previousSelection$ and consecutiveWishes. These variables will be used to keep track of the player's last wish (so that it can be compared against her current wish) and to keep count of the number of times in a row that the most recently asked wish has been requested.

The next four statements set the width and height of the application window as well as its foreground and background colors. The next three statements assign text strings to three string variables. The value of these variables is then displayed in three static text controls that follow. Next, two button controls are defined: one labeled Play and the other labeled Quit. A subroutine named PrepareGame is called whenever the player clicks on the button labeled Play, and a subroutine named CloseMain is called when the player clicks on the Quit button.

The open command is then used to open a window with a handle of #main. Next, three print statements are executed, specifying different font type, size, and property characteristics for each of the window's statictext controls. Finally, the wait command is executed, pausing the game to wait for the player's input.

Starting Gameplay

The code statements that make up the PrepareGame subroutine are shown next and should be added to the end of the program file. This subroutine is called and executed whenever the player clicks on the button labeled Play located on the #main window:

```
'This subroutine is called when the Play button is clicked and is
'responsible for starting gameplay
sub PrepareGame handle$

  close #main      'Close the #main window
  call PlayGame    'Switch to the [PlayGame] static handle

end sub
```

As you can see, this subroutine begins with the keyword sub followed by the name assigned to the subroutine (PrepareGame) and then a parameter named handle$. This parameter represents the name of the control that has called the subroutine.

The subroutine itself consists of two statements. The first statement closes the #main window, and the second statement uses the call command to execute a subroutine named PlayGame. The PlayGame subroutine is responsible for collecting player guesses and determining Tabethia's responses.

Closing the Opening Window

The code statements that make up the CloseMain subroutine are shown next and should be added to the end of the program file. This subroutine is called whenever the player clicks on the Quit button located on the #main window. It consists of a single statement that uses the close command to close the #main window:

```
'When called, this subroutine closes the application's #main window
sub CloseMain handle$

  close #main

end sub
```

Accepting Player Input

The PlayGame subroutine, shown next, is responsible for displaying the #play window, which is where the game is actually played. It lists wishes from which the player can select and displays responses provided on behalf of Tabethia:

```
'This subroutine accepts player wishes and displays Tabethia's responses
sub PlayGame

  WindowWidth = 600   'Set the width of the window to 600 pixels
  WindowHeight = 480  'Set the height of the window to 480 pixels
```

```
BackgroundColor$ = "White"     'Set the window's background color to white
ForegroundColor$ = "Black"     'Set the window's foreground color to black

'The following array contains a list of wishes that the player can ask
'Tabethia to answer
wishes$(0) = "Can I have a million dollars?"
wishes$(1) = "I would like fame. Make me a Hollywood movie star!"
wishes$(2) = "I want power. Make me emperor of the world!"
wishes$(3) = "I want to explore the universe. Give me a spaceship " _
    + "so that I can blast off."
wishes$(4) = "I want to be young. Give me a potion that will keep " _
    + "me young forever."
wishes$(5) = "Can I have an unlimited number of wishes?"

loadbmp "copyimage", "C:\images\lamp.bmp" 'Load the specified bitmap
                                          'file into memory

'Add a graphicbox control to the #play window
graphicbox #play.gbox, 300, 20, 270, 216

'Use variables to store text strings displayed in the window
Instructions1$ = chr$(34) + "It does not matter what you ask for! I " _
    + "will not grant any wishes, you impudent son of a goat!" + chr$(13) _
    + chr$(13) + "I can withstand hours of begging without" _
    + " breaking a sweat." + chr$(13) +  chr$(13) + "Go ahead, present" _
    + " your wishes. But it won't do you any good." + chr$(34)
Instructions2$ = "Select a wish:"
Instructions3$ = "Tabethia's Answer:"

'Define the format of statictext controls displayed on the window
statictext #play.statictext4 Instructions1$, 20, 40, 280, 170
statictext #play.statictext5 Instructions2$, 20, 260, 280, 14
statictext #play.statictext6 Instructions3$, 330, 260, 280, 14

'Add a listbox control to the #play window and load the contents of
'the wishes$() array into it
listbox #play.listbox, wishes$(), doubleClick, 20, 280, 300, 80

'Define the format of button controls displayed on the window
button #play.button1 "  Hint  ", GetHint, UL, 220, 380
button #play.button2 "  Quit  ", ClosePlay, UL, 305, 380
```

```
'Add a texteditor control to the #play window (used to display Tabethia's
'responses)
texteditor #play.texteditor, 330, 280, 240, 80

'Open the window with no frame and a handle of #play
open "Ask Genie" for window_nf as #play

'Set the font type and size for the specified statictext control
print #play.statictext4, "!font Arial 11"

'Use the flush command to prevent the contents of the graphicbox control
'from being overwritten when the window is first generated
print #play.gbox, "flush"

'Display the pre-loaded bitmap image in the graphicbox control
print #play.gbox, "drawbmp copyimage 1 1"

'Use the flush command to prevent the contents of the graphicbox control
'from being overwritten if the user opens or moves another window on top
'of the #play window
print #play.gbox, "flush"

'Pause the application to wait for the player's instruction
wait
```

```
end sub
```

The first four statements set the window's width, height, background, and foreground colors. An array named wishes$() is then created and populated with six items. Each item represents a question that the player can select. The loadbmp command is then used to load a bitmap image into memory. This image will be used at the end of the subroutine to display a picture of a magic genie's lamp on the application window. Next, a series of three string variables are created and then used by three statictext controls to display text.

Hint

You will find a copy of the lamp.bmp image file along with the source code for the Ask Genie game on this book's companion website (www.cengageptr.com/downloads).

Next, a listbox control is added to the #play window. The elements stored in the wishes$() array are loaded into this control. To select one of the wishes listed in the control (to ask Tabethia a question), the player must double-click on it. When this occurs, the doubleClick subroutine is called. Next, two button controls and a texteditor control are added to the window, which is then opened. A series of print statements follow that set font size and type and display the bitmap image previously loaded into computer memory. To display the bitmap image, the drawbmp command is used. In addition, the flush command is used. This command prevents the bitmap image from disappearing if the player opens or moves another window on top of the bitmap image.

Hint

loadbmp, drawbmp, **and** flush **are examples of graphics commands. You will learn more about how to work with graphics in Chapter 9, "Working with Sound and Graphics."**

Answering Player Questions

The doubleClick subroutine, shown next, is responsible for keeping track of each wish asked by the player and generating answers on behalf of Tabethia:

```
'This subroutine processes player wishes and generates Tabethia's
'responses
sub doubleClick handle$

  'Retrieve the wish selected by the player
  #play.listbox "selection? choice$"

  'check to see if this is the first time in a row that this wish has
  'been asked
  if previousSelection$ <> choice$ then

    print #play.texteditor, "!cls"  'Clear the texteditor control

    'Display the specified response
    print #play.texteditor, "Stop submitting wishes. I will not grant them!"

    consecutiveWishes = 1   'Reset the variable used to keep track of
                            'consecutively asked wishes to 1

  else  'The wish has been asked at least twice in a row

    print #play.texteditor, "!cls"  'Clear the texteditor control
    'Display the specified answer
```

```
    print #play.texteditor, "Your requests are making my head hurt. " _
      + chr$(13) + "I beg you to stop!"
    consecutiveWishes = consecutiveWishes + 1   'Increment the variable
                                                'used to keep track of
                                                'consecutively asked
                                                'wishes by 1


    if consecutiveWishes = 3 then   'The player has asked the same wish
                                    '3 times in a row


      print #play.texteditor, "!cls"   'Clear the texteditor control


      'Display the specified answer
      print #play.texteditor, "All right, I can't take it anymore! Your " _
        + "wish " + chr$(13) + "is granted.  Please leave me alone now."


    end if


  end if


  previousSelection$ = choice$   'Save the player's choice so that it can
                                 'be compared against when the player
                                 'makes a new request


  wait


end sub
```

The first statement in this subroutine determines which listbox entry the player selected and assigns its value to a variable named choice$. Next, an if…else…end if code block executes. It is responsible for analyzing the value of previousSelection$ and choice$ to see if they are different. If their values are not equal, this is the first time in a row that the player has asked for this wish. If these two variables' values are equal, the wish has been asked at least twice in a row. If this is the case, the value of consecutiveWishes is checked to see if it is equal to 3, in which case it is time for Tabethia to break down and grant the wish. If this is only the second time in a row that the same wish has been asked, Tabethia instead responds by telling the player that her head is beginning to hurt (indicating that the player's line of questioning is starting to have an effect). Tabethia's answers are displayed inside the texteditor control using play statements.

> **Hint**
>
> You will learn all about if...else...end if code blocks in Chapter 5, "Making Decisions with Conditional Logic."

Providing the Player with a Hint

If, after playing for a while, the player cannot figure out how to get Tabethia to relent and grant wishes, she can get a hint by clicking on the button labeled Hint (located on the #play window). When this happens, the code statements located inside the GetHint subroutine are executed. The code statements for this subroutine are shown here and should be added to the end of the program file:

```
'This subroutine is called when the player clicks on the Hint button
sub GetHint handle$

  'Get confirmation before displaying a hint
  confirm "Hints are for wimps! Are you sure you want one?"; answer$

  if answer$ = "yes" then   'The player clicked on Yes

    'Display the hint
    notice "Ask Genie" + chr$(13) + "Tabethia hates repetition. Ask " _
      + "her for the same wish over again and she'll start giving in " _
      + "to you."

  end if

end sub
```

Before displaying the hint, the subroutine executes the confirm command, displaying a pop-up dialog window that requires the player to reconfirm his decision to see the hint message. If the player clicks on the button labeled Yes, the notice command is used to display the hint in a pop-up dialog window. Otherwise, the hint is not shown and gameplay resumes.

Terminating Gameplay

The last subroutine in the program file is the ClosePlay subroutine. It is called when the player clicks on the button labeled Quit (located on the #play window).

```
'This subroutine is called when the Quit button is clicked and is
'responsible for closing the #play window and ending the game
sub ClosePlay handle$

  close #play
  end

end sub
```

This subroutine consists of two statements. The first statement closes the #play window, and the second statement executes the end command, terminating the application's execution.

The Final Result

Okay, that's it. You have finished the development of your next computer application. Assuming that you did not accidentally make typos or skip steps, you should be ready to test the Ask Genie game and put it through its paces. Remember to check out the operation of all the interface controls and to feed the application both valid and invalid data to make sure it reacts appropriately. Once you have everything working, create a distribution package and ask your friends to try it out and give you their feedback.

Summary

In this chapter you learned how to store and retrieve data using variables and arrays. You also learned a little about constants and how you can use them to store data whose value never changes. You discovered the rules that must be followed when naming variables and arrays in Just BASIC. In addition, you read about different data types and how to convert data from strings to numbers and vice versa. You saw examples of different types of functions that are provided by most programming languages for the purpose of manipulating data in various ways. Finally, you learned about Just BASIC reserved words and the importance of not using them as variable and array names.

Before moving on to Chapter 5, set aside a little extra time to work on the Ask Genie game by tackling the following list of challenges.

Do

1. Although the Ask Genie game does provide the player with a Hint option, it does not provide access to any substantive help. Consider adding a Help window to your application that supplies the player with more detailed instruction.

2. As currently written, the game only provides the player with six questions from which to choose. Consider expanding the number of questions. Also, just for fun, consider replacing the listbox control with a combobox control, thus also allowing the player to type in his or her own silly question.

3. Because the texteditor control is used to display Tabethia's responses, an Edit menu is automatically added to the game's #play window. Consider replacing the editor control with a statictext control, thus eliminating the Edit menu.

5

Making Decisions with Conditional Logic

As you have already seen in numerous examples in this book, to create applications of any degree of complexity, a computer program needs a way of evaluating different values to determine a logical direction in which to proceed. This is done through the use of conditional programming statements that use mathematical, comparison, and logical operators to compare different values and decide upon a course of action. By implementing conditional logic, you can create applications that react differently based on the data they are presented with. This not only provides an interactive user experience but also results in programs that are adaptive enough to handle various situations. In addition to learning the fundamentals of conditional programming logic, you step through the development of your next computer game: the Rock, Paper, Scissors game.

Specifically, you will learn the following:

- How to use the if...then statement to set up different types of logical tests
- How to use if...then statements within one another to create more complex logic
- How to use the select case statement to compare one condition against a range of possible values
- How to compare numeric data using comparison operators
- How to use mathematical operators to perform arithmetic calculations
- How to use logical operators to combine comparison operations

Project Preview: The Rock, Paper, Scissors Game

In this chapter, you will learn how to create a new computer game called Rock, Paper, Scissors. This game is a computerized implementation of a classic children's game. In this game, the player is pitted against the computer. Valid moves are Rock, Paper, and Scissors. The player chooses her move from a selection in a combobox control and then clicks on a button control labeled Go. As soon as the player's turn has been completed, the game generates the computer's move by randomly generating a number between 1 and 3 and then associating that number with a move. The winner of each game is determined according to the following set of rules:

- Rock crushes Scissors to win the game
- Paper covers Rock to win the game
- Scissors cut Paper to win the game
- Matching moves result in a tied game

Figure 5.1 shows how the game appears when it's first started. The game is played on a single window containing two graphicbox controls and a combobox control, as well as five textbox controls and a button control.

The player moves by selecting one of three choices from the game's combobox control, as demonstrated in Figure 5.2. Notice that the Go button is disabled. The game will enable it as soon as the player selects a move.

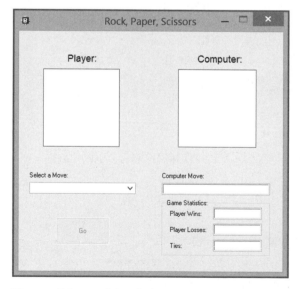

Figure 5.1 Examining the layout of the Rock, Paper, Scissors game's user interface.
© 2016 Cengage Learning®

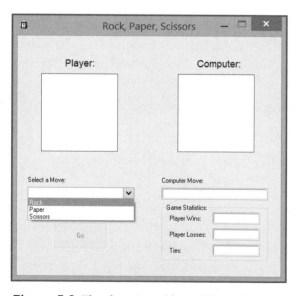

Figure 5.2 The player is unable to click on the Go button until a valid move has been selected.
© 2016 Cengage Learning®

As soon as the player completes her move, the game generates the computer's move and then analyzes and displays the result of the game in a pop-up dialog, as demonstrated in Figure 5.3.

As you can see in Figure 5.4, graphics images are displayed that visually identify both the player's and the computer's move each time a new game is played.

Figure 5.3 A pop-up dialog window informing the player that she has won the game.
© 2016 Cengage Learning®

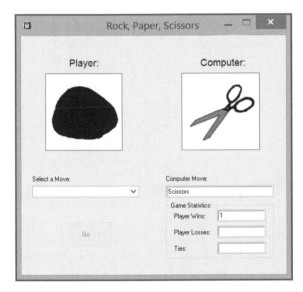

Figure 5.4 The game keeps track of the number of games won, lost, and tied.
© 2016 Cengage Learning®

Building Adaptive Applications with Conditional Logic

In Chapter 3, "Creating Graphical User Interfaces," you developed the Legend of Mighty Molly game. Every programming statement in that game's program file was executed sequentially, starting with the first statement in the program and ending with the last statement. This worked well for that game because there was no complex logic involved. The game simply asked the player a few questions and then plugged whatever input was provided into text strings that were then displayed a screen at a time as the story was told. Although appropriate for simple programs, sequential processing is insufficient for applications that have any level of complexity or that need to interact with the user.

Most applications require some level of conditional execution. For example, a program that displays a graphical user interface (GUI) and accepts user input may need to analyze that input and validate it. If the data is good, the program then executes a given set of programming statements. However, if there is something wrong with the data input, a different set of programming statements might be executed. Another example of how conditional logic might be applied is a program that retrieves data from a file and then processes that data in some way. The program statements that are executed after the file is opened might vary based on whether the file had any data in it as well as the different types of data found inside the file.

Conditional logic is a relatively easy concept to understand because we use it all the time in our everyday lives. For example, any time you visit the grocery store and consider which of two brands of peanut butter to purchase, you are deciding between two distinct courses of action, as depicted in Figure 5.5.

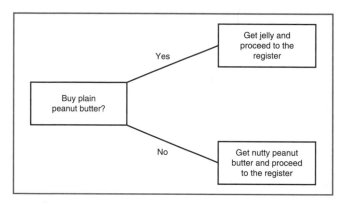

Figure 5.5 Choosing between two courses of action.
© 2016 Cengage Learning®

Based on the value of the condition being tested (whether or not to buy plain peanut butter), either of two possible courses of action is outlined. Fundamentally, you can apply this same type of logic to a computer program, as demonstrated in Figure 5.6.

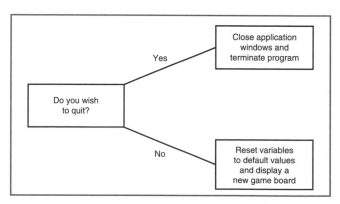

Figure 5.6 An example of the programming logic used to determine when to terminate an application.
© 2016 Cengage Learning®

Hint

Figures 5.5 and 5.6 are examples of simple flowcharts. A *flowchart* is a graphical depiction of all or part of a program's logical flow. Programmers often use flowcharts to outline the overall design of the logic involved in designing a computer program. This gives them a high-level overview of the overall logic involved and provides an opportunity to discover potential logical errors before any mistakes are made in writing program code.

Flowcharts are also useful for large projects that involve more than one programmer because they can be used to identify different parts of an application that can then be more easily divided up, with each programmer having a good understanding of the work that is expected of him.

Here, either of two distinct courses of action is outlined based on the user's decision of whether or not to quit the application. This flowchart view of the logic behind the decision of whether to terminate a computer program can be directly translated into program code, as demonstrated here:

```
confirm "Are you sure you want to quit?"; answer$

   if answer$ = "yes" then   'The player clicked on Yes

      close #play   'Close the #play window
      end   'Terminate the game

   else

      noOfTurns = 0
      call startNewGame

   end if
```

Here, the `confirm` command is used to display a text message in a pop-up dialog window that prompts the player for confirmation before terminating the application. The player indicates her decision to quit playing by clicking on the Yes button, in which case the `close` and `end` commands are then executed. Alternatively, the player can click on the No button, in which case the application continues to execute.

The key to understanding how programming languages apply conditional logic when analyzing data and determining which particular course of action should be taken is that, at its core, conditional logic involves an evaluation as to whether a condition is `true` or not. Based on the result of this analysis, conditional logic results in the execution of either of two possible outcomes (one for `true` and one for `false`).

Just BASIC supplies programmers with access to two different conditional logic statements, listed next, each of which is designed to address specific types of situations:

- **if...then.** This statement tests a condition and then alters the execution flow of an application based on the result of its analysis.
- **select case.** This statement sets up a series of conditional tests, each of which is compared to a single value. The programming statements associated with a test that evaluates as being true are executed, and the programming statements associated with tests that evaluate as being false are not processed.

Working with the if...then Statement

The if...then statement is so fundamental to the development of software programs that it is virtually impossible to write any but the most simple program without using it. In fact, you have already seen assorted variations of the if...then statement at work in the computer games that you have developed in this book. To get a good understanding of the mechanics involved in the application of the if...then statement, consider the following example:

```
if The big game comes on at 8pm then
 I'll stay up and watch it
else
   I'll read for a while
   I'll try to get to sleep by 9pm
end if
```

This pseudo code (English-like outline) shows how you can apply the if...then statement to analyzing a typical everyday situation. Here, the opening statement defines the condition being evaluated. The second statement shows the action to be taken if the condition evaluates as being true. The statements following the else keyword outline the actions to be taken if the condition evaluates as false.

Hint

Pseudo code is a term that refers to an English-like outline of all or part of the programming logic that makes up a computer program. By outlining the high-level programming logic required in pseudo code, programmers develop an outline they can follow when writing actual program code. As such, pseudo code gives programmers the chance to focus on the logic required to solve a problem without having to worry about the specific programming statements required to implement it. When used this way, a pseudo code outline can simplify application development and help to reduce programming logic errors.

Understanding if...then Syntax

The if...then statement has a flexible syntax that allows programmers to implement it in many different formats. The syntax of the if...then statement, as implemented in Just BASIC, is outlined here:

```
if condition then
     statements
else

end if
```

condition represents the expression to be tested. statements represents one or more code statements that will be executed based on the truth or falseness of the test. else is an optional keyword that, when used, allows programmers to specify an alternate set of programming statements to be executed when the condition being tested evaluates as false. The if...then statement can be used in many different variations, including these:

- Single line if...then statements
- Multiple line if...then blocks
- if...then...else blocks

Hint

Some programming languages, like Visual Basic, also support an optional elseif keyword, which allows programmers to specify alternative conditions to be tested if the condition specified by the opening if...then statement evaluates as false.

Creating Single Line if...then Statements

In its most basic form, you can write the if...then statement on a single line, as demonstrated here:

```
x = 10
if x = 10 Then notice "We have a match."
```

Here a numeric variable named x is assigned a value of 10. Next, an if...then statement is set up that checks to see if x equals 10, which of course it does. Therefore, the notice command is executed. If the value of x is changed prior to the if...then statement to something other than a value of 10, the if...then statement evaluates as false and the notice command is not executed.

You have already seen the single-line version of the if...then statement used in this book. For example, back in Chapter 3 when you created the BASIC Crazy 8 Ball game, you used a series of single-line if...then statements to analyze the value of the game's randomly generated number, as shown here:

```
RandomNumber = int(rnd(1)*3) + 1

if RandomNumber = 1 then answer$ = "YES"
if RandomNumber = 2 then answer$ = "MAYBE"
if RandomNumber = 3 then answer$ = "NO"
```

Here, a random value was assigned to a variable name RandomNumber. Three if...then statements were then executed to determine whether the value assigned to RandomNumber was 1, 2, or 3. Only one of these three statements will result in a value of true. The matching test results in the assignment of a value to a variable named answer$.

Trap

Take note that the closing end if keywords are not included at the end of each of these three if...then statements shown above. This is because in the single-line version of the if...then statement, adding the closing end if keywords results in an error.

An advantage of using the single-line if...then statement is that it allows you to set up simple conditional tests that do not require the specification of an action if they evaluate as false. This helps to streamline your program code and make it easier to read.

Creating Multiple-Line if...then Statements

The single-line version of the if...then statement is good for writing streamlined code that only needs to perform a single action when a given conditional evaluates as true. However, the multiline version of the if...then statement allows you to define a code block made up of as many code statements as you want that will be executed if the condition being evaluated proves true, as demonstrated here:

```
x = 10
if x = 10 Then
    x = x + 1
    notice "x equals "; x
end if
```

Here, two programming statements are executed when x evaluates as being equal to 10. The first statement increments the value of x by 1, and the second statement displays x's new value in a pop-up dialog.

Hint

Instead of identifying the code block associated with an if…then statement using the then and end if keywords, some programming languages, such as Perl and C++, use curly braces, as demonstrated here:

```
if (x = 10) {
  Code block statements go here
}
```

You have seen other examples of the multiline if…then statement in action already in this book. For example, in Chapter 4, "Working with Variables and Arrays," when you developed the Ask Genie game, you used a multiline if…then statement to conditionally display a hint. The hint was displayed only after the confirm command was used to prompt the player to click on the Yes button to reconfirm the request to display the game's hint, as shown here:

```
confirm "Hints are for wimps! Are you sure you want one?"; answer$

if answer$ = "yes" then   'The player clicked on Yes

  notice "Ask Tabethia" + chr$(13) + "Tabethia hates repetition. Ask " _
    + "her the same question over again and she'll start giving you " _
    + "the information you want."

end if
```

Checking for Alternative Conditions

The single and multiline version of the if…then statements that were just examined were set up to only execute code statements if the tested conditions evaluate as being true. However, the if…then statement becomes even more useful when you add the optional else keyword, thus specifying an alternative set of code statements to be executed when the tested conditional evaluates as false. An example of this type of if…then statement is provided here:

```
prompt "How old are you?"; age

if age < 18 then
  notice "You must have your parent's permission to play."
  end
else
```

```
notice "Thanks for choosing to play this game!"
'Insert additional programming statements here
end if
```

Here, the prompt command has been used to query the user for her age. If the user responds by entering a number less than 18, she is informed that she needs her parent's permission to play. Once the user closes the pop-up dialog, the end command is executed, terminating the application. If, on the other hand, the player responds by entering a value of 18 or more, a thank-you message is displayed.

Exploring the Power of Nesting if...then Statements

Unfortunately, not every situation can adequately be addressed using the various combinations of the if...then statement that you have just examined. Sometimes you'll need to perform one test and, based on the results of that test, perform another test and so on. Fortunately, programming languages easily accommodate this need by letting you embed or nest if...then statements, as demonstrated here:

```
if x = 10 then
  if y = 20 then
    if z = 30 then
      notice "All the stars are aligned! "
    end if
  end if
end if
```

In this example, a series of three conditional if...then statements have been set up. If the first statement evaluates as false, the nested if...then statements are skipped. If the second if...then statement evaluates as false, the third if...then statement is skipped.

Trap

You might be wondering if there is a limitation to the number of conditional statements that you can nest within one another. The answer is no. However, the deeper you nest statements within one another, the more difficult your application will be to read, understand, and maintain.

Nested if...then statements are really quite common. In fact, you used them in this book back in Chapter 1, "Introduction to Programming," when you developed the Knock Knock Joke game.

As shown next, the Knock Knock Joke game used an embedded if…then…else statement to conditionally execute the display of error messages, based on whether the player provided an expected response:

```
if response$ = "" then

  notice "Knock Knock Joke Game" + chr$(13) + _
    "Error: You must respond by entering 'Who is there?'"

else

  response$ = "Disease who?"

  prompt "Knock Knock Joke Game" + chr$(13) + "Disease!"; response$

  if response$ = "" then

    notice "Knock Knock Joke Game" + chr$(13) + _
      "Error: You must respond by entering 'Disease who?'"

  else

    notice "Knock Knock Joke Game" + chr$(13) + _
      "Disease jokes seem funny to you?"

  end if

end if
```

Working with the select…case Statement

In addition to the if…then statement, Just BASIC supports the use of the select case statement. Although you can accomplish the same thing through the use of multiple if…then statements, the select case statement is better suited to situations in which you want to compare a single value or condition to a whole range of possible matching values. The syntax for the select case statement is shown here:

```
select case expression
  case value
    statements
      .
      .
      .
  case value
    statements
```

```
case else
    statements
end select
```

As you can see, the select...case statement is used to create a code block that includes one or more case statements. The condition to be tested is specified at the end of the opening select case statement, and each case statement specifies a unique value against which the select case statement's expression is compared. If a match occurs in one of the case statements, the statements associated with that case statement are then executed. If none of the case statements matches the expression or value being evaluated, any statements associated with an optional case else statement are executed, if this statement was included.

Hint

Some programming languages, like C and C++, don't support the use of the select case statement, instead providing a switch statement. Other programming languages, including Perl and AppleScript, do not have an equivalent statement and instead rely solely on variations of the if...then statement to implement conditional logic.

To get a feel for the logic behind a typical select...case statement, look at the following pseudo code example:

```
select case game-time
  case If the big game comes on at 8pm, stay up and watch it
  case If the big game comes on at 9pm, stay up and watch the first half
  case If the big game comes on at 10pm, stay up and just watch the pre-game show
  case else Read for a while and get to sleep by 10pm
end select
```

In this pseudo code example, you can see that three case statements have been set up to evaluate different conditions against a single value (game-time). If one of the case statements proves to be true, its associated code block is executed. If none of the case statements results in a match, the case else statement executes.

Typically, you'll need fewer code statements to lay out a select case statement than you will to lay out the equivalent series of tests using if...then statements. As a result, your program code will be easier to understand and maintain.

You will get the opportunity to work with the select case statement again in this chapter when you develop the Rock, Paper, Scissors game. Specifically, you will use three select case statements to analyze the game's results and determine a winner. As a sneak peak, take a look at the following statements, which analyze the results of a game in which the player selects Rock as her move:

```
if playerMove$ = "Rock" then
    select case
    case computerMove$ = "Rock"
        result$ = "Tie!"
        ties = ties + 1
        print #play.textbox4, ties
    case computerMove$ = "Paper"
        result$ = "The computer wins!"
        losses = losses + 1
        print #play.textbox3, losses
    case computerMove$ = "Scissors"
        result$ = "The player wins!"
        wins = wins + 1
        print #play.textbox2, wins
    end select
end if
```

As you can see, the select case statement has been set up inside an if…then statement that executes only when the player's move is a Rock. This select case statement has been set up a little differently this time. Instead of specifying an expression or value at the end of the select case statement, each case statement has been set up to evaluate its own expression. This example demonstrates the versatility of the select case command. If you prefer, you can rewrite the preceding code statements as shown next and achieve the same result:

```
if playerMove$ = "Rock" then
    select case computerMove$
    case "Rock"
        result$ = "Tie!"
        ties = ties + 1
        print #play.textbox4, ties
    case "Paper"
        result$ = "The computer wins!"
        losses = losses + 1
        print #play.textbox3, losses
    case "Scissors"
        result$ = "The player wins!"
        wins = wins + 1
        print #play.textbox2, wins
    end select
end if
```

Here, the variable `computerMove$` has been added to the end of the `select case` statement, and each `case` statement has been rewritten to check for a specific string match.

Performing Different Types of Comparison Operations

So far, I have restricted all the comparison operations that you have seen in this book to equality tests using the = operator. Like all programming languages, Just BASIC offers a number of different comparison operators, allowing programmers to set up comparisons for ranges of data. For example, rather than set up a test to determine if the value of x was equal to the value of y, you might instead want to check whether the value of x was greater than y. This type of comparison is achieved through comparison operators. Just BASIC supports a number of different comparison operators, as outlined in Table 5.1.

TABLE 5.1 JUST BASIC COMPARISON OPERATORS	
Operator	**Description**
=	Equal
<	Less than
>	Greater than
<=	Less than or equal to
>=	Greater than or equal to
<>	Not equal

Hint

Most programming languages, including Just BASIC, use the equals (=) sign to perform an equals comparison. However, some programming languages, including C++ and Perl, use two equals signs (==).

To see a few examples of how you might use the different comparison operators listed in Table 5.1, look at the following examples:

```
x= 10
y = 20
```

```
if x = y then notice "x equals y"                    'false
if x > y then notice "x is greater than y"           'false
if x <= y then notice "x is less than or equal to y"  'true
if x <> y then notice "x and y are not equal"         'true
```

Here, two numeric variables have been defined and assigned values. Next, four if…then statements have been set up that perform a number of different comparisons.

Performing Mathematic Calculations

Like other programming languages, Just BASIC supplies programmers with a collection of mathematic operators that can be used to perform calculations on numeric data. For example, using the + operator, you can add any two numbers together, as demonstrated here:

```
x = 5 + 10    'x now equals 15
```

You can also use Just BASIC's mathematic operators to work with numeric variables just as easily as literal numeric data, as shown here:

```
x = 5
y = 10
z = y − 5    'z now equals 5
```

Anyone who has ever worked with a calculator should easily recognize Just BASIC's mathematical operators, which are outlined in Table 5.2.

TABLE 5.2 JUST BASIC MATHEMATICAL OPERATORS

Operator	Description	Example
+	Addition	x = 5 + 10
-	Subtraction	x = 10 - 5
*	Multiplication	x = 5 * 10
/	Division	x = 10 / 5
^	Exponentiation	x = 5 ^ 2

Hint

Just BASIC only supports binary operators. However, many programming languages such as C++ and Visual Basic also support unary operators. A *unary* operator is an operator that works with a single value. For example, two of the most commonly used unary variables are the ++ and - - operators. These operators are used to decrement and increment the value of a numeric variable by 1. For example, in Just BASIC, you increment the value assigned to a numeric variable using the + binary operator, as demonstrated here:

```
x = x + 1
```

Although you can increment the value assigned to a variable the same way in a Visual Basic application, it's more common to instead use the ++ unary operator, as shown here:

```
x = x++
```

Order of Precedence

Like all programming languages, Just BASIC evaluates numeric expression based on a predefined set of rules, often referred to as *order of precedence*. Table 5.3 outlines the order of precedence that Just BASIC follows.

TABLE 5.3 JUST BASIC ORDER OF PRECEDENCE

Operator	Description
^	Exponentiation occurs first
*, /	Multiplication and division occur second
+, -	Addition and subtraction occur last

Just BASIC calculates operators starting from left to right when cases of equal precedence occur. To help you understand how Just BASIC's operator precedence works, consider the following statement:

```
x = 5 + 10 * 3 / 2 - 4 * 2
```

When executed, Just BASIC processes this statement as shown here:

1. Working from left to right, all multiplication and division operations are completed, so 10 is multiplied by 3 yielding a value of 30. This value is then divided by 2 yielding a value of 15. Next, 4 is multiplied by 2 yielding a value of 8.

2. At this point, based on the calculations already performed by Just BASIC, the statement has been processed and simplified as shown here:

```
x = 5 + 15 - 8
```

3. Next, addition and subtraction occur, so 5 is added to 15 yielding 20, from which 8 is then subtracted. The final result is that x is assigned a value of 12.

Overriding the Rules of Precedence

Sometimes programmers need to be able to control the order in which expressions are evaluated in a manner that is contrary to a programming language's predefined order of precedence. Using parentheses to identify portions of an expression that you want to be calculated first does this. To see how this works, look at the following statement:

```
x = (5 + 10) * 3 / (2 - 4 * 2)
```

As you can see, this statement is almost identical to the previous example, except that two sets of parentheses have been added. As a result, the expression is evaluated differently, resulting in a completely different answer, as explained next.

1. Working from left to right, anything embedded inside parentheses is calculated first. So 5 is added to 10 yielding 15, and then 4 is multiplied by 2 and subtracted from 2 yielding –6.

2. At this point, based on the calculations just performed, the statement has been processed and simplified as shown here:

```
x = 15 * 3 / (-6)
```

3. Once everything within parentheses has been calculated, multiplication and division are performed on a left to right basis. As a result, 15 is multiplied by 3 yielding 45, which is then divided by –6, yielding a final value of –7.5.

Combining and Negating Comparison Operations

In addition to comparison and mathematic operators, most computer languages support a group of operators known as *logical operators*. Just BASIC supports four logical operators, as outlined in Table 5.4.

TABLE 5.4 JUST BASIC LOGICAL OPERATORS

Operator	Type	Example
and	Both comparisons must be true for the evaluation to be true	x > 5 and x < 10
or	One or both comparisons must be true for the comparison to be true	x = 5 or x = 10
xor	To evaluate as being true, only one comparison can evaluate as being true	x = 5 xor x = 10
not	Reverses the value of a comparison	not (x > 5)

© 2016 Shoptalk Systems

The first three operators listed in Table 5.4 give programmers the ability to combine different comparison operations. For example, the following set of comparison operations uses two if...then statements:

```
if x = 1000000 then
  if y = 2000000 then
    notice "We are rich!"
  end if
end if
```

Using the and comparison operator, you can rewrite the preceding example as shown here:

```
if x = 10000000 and y = 2000000 then
  notice "We are rich!"
end if
```

Because of using the logical and operator, two lines of code have been removed, and the overall logic being implemented is easier to read and understand.

Hint

Programming languages may use different characters to represent logical operators. For example, in C and C++, the && characters are equivalent to the and operator in BASIC. Perl, on the other hand, works with both the && and and operators.

The fourth logical operator supported by Just BASIC allows programmers to set up logical comparison operators that reverse the test being performed, as demonstrated here:

```
if not (x = 1000000) then
  notice "I need a job."
end if
```

Here, instead of checking to see if x is equal to 1000000, the if…then statement has been modified to reverse the condition being tested, looking to see if x is not equal to 1000000.

Back to the Rock, Paper, Scissors Game

Okay. Now it is time to turn your attention back to the development of this chapter's game project: the Rock, Paper, Scissors game. In this game, you will develop a player-versus-computer version of the Rock, Paper, Scissors game. In doing so, you will get your first opportunity to put the combobox and groupbox controls to use. You will also make ample use of both the if…then and select case statements.

Designing the Game

The design of the Rock, Paper, Scissors game will follow the same basic pattern we have been using for all preceding games. Namely, we'll build it in a series of steps. This game will use several bitmap images representing different moves that the computer and player can make. Figure 5.7 shows what these three bitmap images look like. You will find copies of them available as part of the source code download file on this book's companion website at www.cengageptr.com/downloads.

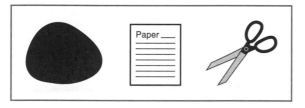

Figure 5.7 Bitmap images used in the generation of the graphics displayed in the Rock, Paper, Scissors game.
© 2016 Cengage Learning®

You will create the development of the Rock, Paper, Scissors game in five steps, as outlined here:

1. Create a new BASIC file and document its purpose.
2. Display the game's user interface.
3. Set up control over when the player may make a move.
4. Add the programming logic needed to manage gameplay.
5. Terminate the game's execution.

Creating a Just BASIC File Script

The first step in creating the Rock, Paper, Scissors game is to create a new Just BASIC file and add the following statements to it. The first 11 lines shown next are comments that document the name of the application, its author's name and creation date, and a brief description of the game. The last statement executes the nomainwin command to suppress the display of the mainwin window, which is not needed by Rock, Paper, Scissors.

```
' ********************************************************************

'
' Script Name: RockPaperScissors.bas (The Rock, Paper, Scissors Game)
' Version:     1.0
' Author:      Jerry Lee Ford, Jr.
' Date:        January 20, 2015
'
' Description: This game is a Just BASIC version of the classic children's
'              Rock, Paper, Scissors game.
'
' ********************************************************************


nomainwin    'Suppress the display of the default text window
```

Designing the Application's User Interface

The next step in the development of the Rock, Paper, Scissors game is the setup of a few global variables followed by the design of the game's user interface. The code to accomplish this is shown next and should be added to the end of the script file:

```
'Declare three global variables used to keep track of game statistics
global wins, losses, ties

WindowWidth = 500  'Set the width of the window to 500 pixels
WindowHeight = 480 'Set the height of the window to 480 pixels

'The following array contains a list of valid game moves that will be
'displayed in the game's combobox control
moves$(0) = "Rock"
moves$(1) = "Paper"
moves$(2) = "Scissors"

'Load rock, paper, and scissors bitmap files into memory
loadbmp "rockImage", "C:\images\rock.bmp"
```

```
loadbmp "paperImage", "C:\images\paper.bmp"
loadbmp "scissorsImage", "C:\images\scissors.bmp"

'Add a graphicbox control in order to graphically represent the player's
'and computer's moves
graphicbox #play.gboxPlayer, 45, 70, 144, 144
graphicbox #play.gboxComputer, 300, 70, 144, 144

'Use variables to store text strings displayed in the window
Instructions1$ = "Player:"
Instructions2$ = "Computer:"
Instructions3$ = "Select a Move:"
Instructions4$ = "Computer Move:"

'Define the format of statictext controls displayed on the window
statictext #play.statictext1, Instructions1$, 90, 40, 90, 20
statictext #play.statictext2, Instructions2$, 335, 40, 90, 20
statictext #play.statictext3, Instructions3$, 20, 260, 80, 20
statictext #play.statictext4, Instructions4$, 270, 260, 80, 20

'Add a combobox control to the window and load the contents of the
'moves$() array into it
combobox #play.combobox, moves$(), doubleClick, 20, 280, 200, 80

'Add a button control to the window
button #play.button1 "Go", PlayHand, UL, 70, 345, 100, 50

'Add a textbox control to the window (to display the computer's move)
textbox #play.textbox, 270, 280, 200, 22

'Add a groupbox control to the window (to group a collection of
'textbox controls)
groupbox #play.groupbox, "Game Statistics:", 270, 310, 200, 105

'Define the format of statictext controls displayed inside the groupbox
'control
statictext #play.statictext5, "Player Wins:", 285, 330, 70, 14
statictext #play.statictext6, "Player Losses:", 285, 360, 70, 14
statictext #play.statictext7, "Ties:", 285, 390, 70, 14
```

```
'Add three textbox controls and place them inside the groupbox control
textbox #play.textbox2, 365, 325, 90, 22
textbox #play.textbox3, 365, 355, 90, 22
textbox #play.textbox4, 365, 385, 90, 22

'Open the window with no frame and a handle of #play
open "Rock, Paper, Scissors" for window_nf as #play

'Set up the trapclose event for the window
print #play, "trapclose ClosePlay"

'Disable the button control to prevent the player from clicking on it
'until the player has selected a valid move
print #play.button1, "!disable"

'Set the font type and size for the specified statictext controls
print #play.statictext1, "!font Arial 11"  'Player label
print #play.statictext2, "!font Arial 11"  'Computer label

'Pause the application to wait for the player's instruction
wait
```

The first statement shown here defines three global variables: wins, losses, and ties. These variables are used throughout the application to keep track of and display game statistics. Next, the special variables WindowWidth and WindowHeight are set to specify the dimension of the game window. An array named moves$(), made up of three items, is then defined. The contents of this array will be used later in the application to populate the contents of the game's combobox control.

Next, three bitmap image files are loaded into memory using the loadbmp command. These image files are stored in the C:\Images folder. You will need to modify this file path if you decide to store them elsewhere. These image files will be displayed in either of two graphicbox controls when the game is run. The statements required to add the graphicbox controls are followed by the specification of four string variables, which are then used by four statictext controls that serve as labels for other interface controls.

The user interface's combobox control is added next. Note that it has been set up to load the contents of the moves$() array and to call on a subroutine named doubleClick whenever the player selects a combobox item. A button control is then added and assigned a label of Go and an event handler of PlayHand. When clicked, this button's event handler will generate the computer's move and then compare it to the player's move to determine who won the game.

Next, a textbox control is added; it will be used to display a text string identifying the computer's moves. After that, a groupbox control is added to the user interface; it will be used to store three statictext controls, which are defined next. These controls will display win, loss, and tie game statistics while the game is running. The open command is then used to display the game's window, displaying a title bar string of Rock, Paper, Scissors. The window has no frame, so the player will not be able to resize it. It is assigned a handle of #play.

The next statement sets up a trapclose event for the window, which will execute whenever the player tries to close the game. A print command is then used to disable the game's button control. This control will remain disabled until the player selects a move from the combobox control to prevent the player from attempting to make a move without first selecting Rock, Paper, or Scissors. The print command is used to set the font type and the size of the statictext controls over the two graphicbox controls (which graphically display images representing the player and computer turns). Lastly, the wait command is executed to pause application execution and give the player the chance to make a move.

Set Up Control Over Player Moves

To make a move, the player must select Rock, Paper, or Scissors from the combobox control drop-down list and then click on the Go button. To prevent the player from clicking on the button control without first making a valid move selection, the button control is disabled when the user interface is first loaded. It remains in this state until the player selects a move from the combobox, at which time the combobox control's doubleClick event handler executes, calling on the doubleClick subroutine to execute. The code statements for this subroutine are shown next and should be added to the end of the program file:

```
'This subroutine enables the button control labeled Go whenever the
'player selects a valid move
sub doubleClick handle$

  'Enable the game's button control
  print #play.button1, "!enable"

end sub
```

When called, this subroutine uses the print command to enable the button control, thus allowing the player to submit a move. Once the player's move is made, the PlayHand subroutine is called (by the button control's event handler). This handler is responsible for again disabling the button control, thus preventing the player from clicking on it until a new move is selected.

Managing Gameplay

The code statements that compose the PlayHand subroutine are shown next and should be added to the end of the program file. This subroutine is responsible for retrieving the player's move, generating a move on behalf of the computer, and then analyzing the result.

Hint

The PlayHand subroutine is a rather large subroutine. To help make it more understandable, I have embedded comments liberally throughout. In Chapter 7, "Improving Program Organization with Functions and Subroutines," you will learn all about subroutines and functions, after which you will learn how to further organize programming logic into more manageable chunks of related programming logic.

```
'This subroutine is called when the player clicks on the Go button
sub PlayHand handle$

  'Retrieve the player's move
  #play.combobox "selection? playerMove$"

  'Use the flush command to prevent graphics images from being overridden
  print #play.gboxPlayer, "flush"
  print #play.gboxComputer, "flush"

  'Display a bitmap image representing the player's move
  if playerMove$ = "Rock" then
    print #play.gboxPlayer, "drawbmp rockImage 1 1"
  end if

  if playerMove$ = "Paper" then
    print #play.gboxPlayer, "drawbmp paperImage 1 1"
  end if

  if playerMove$ = "Scissors" then
    print #play.gboxPlayer, "drawbmp scissorsImage 1 1"
  end if

  'Use the rnd() function to retrieve a random number between 1 and 3 and
  'assign the result to a variable named RandomNumber
  RandomNumber = int(rnd(1)*3) + 1
```

```
'Select the computer's move based on the value assigned to the
'RandomNumber variable and display the appropriate bitmap image
if RandomNumber = 1 then
  computerMove$ = "Rock"
  print #play.gboxComputer, "drawbmp rockImage 1 1"
end if

if RandomNumber = 2 then
  computerMove$ = "Paper"
  print #play.gboxComputer, "drawbmp paperImage 1 1"
end if

if RandomNumber = 3 then
  computerMove$ = "Scissors"
  print #play.gboxComputer, "drawbmp scissorsImage 1 1"
end if

'Use the flush command to prevent graphics images from being overridden
print #play.gboxPlayer, "flush"
print #play.gboxComputer, "flush"

'Display a text string identifying the computer's move in the textbox
'control
print #play.textbox, computerMove$

'See who won if the player picked Rock
if playerMove$ = "Rock" then
  select case
  case computerMove$ = "Rock"
      result$ = "Tie!"
      ties = ties + 1
      print #play.textbox4, ties
  case computerMove$ = "Paper"
      result$ = "The computer wins!"
      losses = losses + 1
      print #play.textbox3, losses
  case computerMove$ = "Scissors"
      result$ = "The player wins!"
      wins = wins + 1
```

```
            print #play.textbox2, wins
      end select
end if


'See who won if the player picked Paper
if playerMove$ = "Paper" then
   select case
   case computerMove$ = "Rock"
         result$ = "The player wins!"
         wins = wins + 1
         print #play.textbox2, wins
   case computerMove$ = "Paper"
         result$ = "Tie!"
         ties = ties + 1
         print #play.textbox4, ties
   case computerMove$ = "Scissors"
         result$ = "The computer wins!"
         losses = losses + 1
         print #play.textbox3, losses
   end select
end if


'See who won if the player picked Scissors
if playerMove$ = "Scissors" then
   select case
   case computerMove$ = "Rock"
         result$ = "The computer wins!"
         losses = losses + 1
         print #play.textbox3, losses
   case computerMove$ = "Paper"
         result$ = "The player wins!"
         wins = wins + 1
         print #play.textbox2, wins
   case computerMove$ = "Scissors"
         result$ = "Tie!"
         ties = ties + 1
         print #play.textbox4, ties
   end select
end if
```

```
'Announce the winner
notice "Rock, Paper, Scissors" + chr$(13) + result$

print #play.button1, "!disable"  'Disable the button labeled Go

print #play.combobox, "selectindex 0"  'Clear out the previous move

end sub
```

The PlayHand subroutine begins by retrieving the player's move. This is done using the following command, which assigns the currently selected combobox item (string) to a variable named playerMove$:

```
#play.combobox "selection? playerMove$"
```

Now that the game knows the player's move, it is time to generate the computer's move and to display graphics representing both moves. These next two statements use the print command to execute the flush command for the game's graphicbox controls; this prevents the image from being overwritten if the player moves another application window over the game's window.

To determine which bitmap image to display to represent the player's move, the game must analyze the player's move. This is accomplished using a series of three if…then statements, each of which checks for a different move. Only one of these if…then statements will execute, displaying the appropriate bitmap image.

A random number between 1 and 3 is then generated and assigned to a variable named RandomNumber. Following that, a series of three if…then statements is executed that examines the value assigned to RandomNumber and assigns a string to a variable named computerMove$, identifying the computer-assigned move. If RandomNumber equals 1, the computer is assigned a move of Rock. If RandomNumber equals 2, the computer is assigned a move of Paper. If RandomNumber equals 3, the computer is assigned a move of Scissors. In addition, the corresponding bitmap image is loaded using the print statement and the drawbmp command. To make sure that the graphics images representing the player's and the computer's move stick, the flush command is executed again for each graphicbox control. Also, the value assigned to the computerMove$ variable is displayed in a textbox control, thus explicitly identifying the computer's assigned move.

At this point, both the player's and the computer's moves have been displayed. It is time to compare the two moves and determine a result. This analysis is accomplished using three if…then statements, each of which contains a select case statement. The first if…then statement is responsible for performing an analysis if the player's move was Rock. The second if…then statement is responsible for performing an analysis if the player's move was Paper, and the third if…then statement is responsible for performing an analysis if the player's move was Scissors. The select case statements located within each if…then statement are responsible for comparing the computer's assigned move against the player's move to determine a winner. The following rules are applied when performing this analysis:

- Rock crushes Scissors to win the game.
- Paper covers Rock to win the game.
- Scissors cut Paper to win the game.
- Matching moves result in a tied game.

Each time a win, loss, or tie occurs, the appropriate global variable is incremented (wins, losses, or ties), and the print statement is used to update the appropriate textbox control. Finally, the notice command is used to display a pop-up dialog that informs the player of the results of the game. The Go button is again disabled, and the combobox control is reset by setting its index to zero, setting the game up for a new round of play.

Terminating Application Execution

The last set of statements to be added to the program file are those associated with the application's trapclose event. These statements compose the ClosePlay subroutine, which is executed whenever the player attempts to close the application window:

```
'This subroutine is called when the player closes the #play window
'and is responsible for ending the game
sub ClosePlay handle$

  'Get confirmation before terminating program execution
  confirm "Are you sure you want to quit?"; answer$

  if answer$ = "yes" then   'The player clicked on Yes

    close #play   'Close the #play window
    end   'Terminate the game

  end if

end sub
```

As you can see, the purpose of the ClosePlay subroutine is to get confirmation from the player before terminating the game. The confirm command is used to display a message requiring confirmation. If the player clicks on the pop-up dialog's Yes button, the close command is used to close the #play window, and the application is terminated using the end command. Otherwise, if the player clicks on the pop-up dialog's No button, gameplay continues.

The Final Result

All right, if you have followed along with all the steps, then your copy of the Rock, Paper, Scissors game should be ready to go. Go ahead and test it. As you play, make sure that the game correctly displays the appropriate graphics for both the player's and the computer's moves. In addition, make sure that the data displayed in the groupbox control is being correctly tabulated. Once you are 100 percent confident that everything is working as it should, build a distribution package for your latest creation and give it to a few friends. Ask them to test it as well and to provide you with feedback as to what you might be able to do to make the game more enjoyable.

Summary

In this chapter, you learned how to work with different variations of the `if` statement and the `select case` statement to implement conditional programming logic. You also saw how to nest conditional statements within one another to develop more complex programming logic. In addition, you discovered how to use mathematic operators to perform numeric calculations. You learned how to use comparison operators to perform conditional tests based on different types of equality. Finally, you discovered how to work with logical operators to set up programming logic that evaluates the combined results of different comparison operations before taking an action.

Before moving on to Chapter 6, "Using Loops to Process Data," take a little extra time to work on the Rock, Paper, Scissors game by tackling the following list of challenges.

Challenges

1. The Rock, Paper, Scissors game assumes that players already know the basic rules for playing the game. Rather than taking this assumption for granted, provide access to another application window where players can go to learn about the rules of the game.

2. As currently designed, the player has to click on the button control labeled Go to make a move. Consider simplifying the user interface by using the combobox control's event handler as the trigger for making moves.

3. Consider enhancing the information provided in the Game Statistics groupbox control by calculating and displaying the percentage of games won, lost, and tied.

4. Consider using the `prompt` command to collect the player's name when the game is started. That way you could address the player by name in any pop-up dialogs. You might also want to display the player's name over the left-hand graphicbox control.

6

Using Loops to Process Data

In this chapter, you will learn how to create and work with loops. Loops are code blocks that repeat a series of programming statements over and over again. As such, they facilitate the development of applications that can process large amounts of data, using a minimum number of programming statements. You can use loops to process the contents of arrays and text files. You can also use loops to control an application's interaction with the user, repeatedly executing the same process until instructed not to. This chapter will teach you how to use a number of different loops and will explain the types of situations to which each type of loop is best applied. This chapter will also show you how to create your next computer game: the Guess My Number game.

Specifically, you will learn the following:

- How to set up do...while, do...until, for...next, and while...wend loops
- How to avoid creating endless loops
- How to prematurely exit out of loops
- How to terminate programs caught up in a loop

Project Preview: The Guess My Number Game

In this chapter, you will learn how to create a new computer game called Guess My Number. This game challenges the player to guess a number between 1 and 100 in as few guesses as possible. The player submits guesses by typing a number into the designated textbox control and then clicking on a button control labeled Guess.

When the game starts, these two controls are disabled, preventing the player from entering a guess until the Start Game button is clicked, as shown in Figure 6.1.

A random number is generated when the player clicks on the Start Game button. In addition, the textbox input control and the Guess button are enabled, allowing the player to start making guesses. The Start Game button is then disabled and stays that way until the player manages to guess the game's secret number, as shown in Figure 6.2.

Figure 6.1 A new game is started when the player clicks on the Start Game button.
© 2016 Cengage Learning®

Figure 6.2 To control player input, the game enables and disables its button controls.
© 2016 Cengage Learning®

Figure 6.3 shows an example of what the game looks like as the player enters a guess.

Each time a guess is made, the game responds by displaying a hint that the player can use to guide her next guess, as demonstrated in Figure 6.4.

Help is available at any time. To access it, all the player has to do is click on the Help button. In response, the game displays the Help window shown in Figure 6.5.

Gameplay continues until the player guesses the secret number, at which time the pop-up dialog shown in Figure 6.6 is displayed.

Figure 6.3 A guess of 66 has been entered, but it will not be processed until the player clicks on the Guess button.
© 2016 Cengage Learning®

Figure 6.4 Hints help the player hone in on the game's secret number.
© 2016 Cengage Learning®

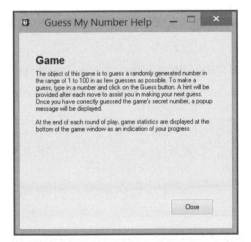

Figure 6.5 The Help window provides the player with instruction on how to play the game.
© 2016 Cengage Learning®

Figure 6.6 A pop-up dialog window notifies the player when the game's secret number has been guessed.
© 2016 Cengage Learning®

After clicking on OK to dismiss the pop-up dialog, the player can start a new game by clicking on the now re-enabled Start Game button again.

Using Loops to Repeat Statement Execution

A *loop* is a set of programming statements that are repeatedly executed within a computer program. Without loops, programmers would have to write enormous programs to be able to process large amounts of data. Likewise, without loops, performing repetitive actions, such as processing a collection of records stored in a file, would become a tedious chore. The power of loops can be easily demonstrated in even small programs. Take, for example, the following Just BASIC program:

```
print 1
print 2
print 3
print 4
print 5
print 6
print 7
print 8
print 9
print 10
```

As you can see in this example, things were done the hard way. To count to 10, ten separate print statements were used. Suppose you wanted to count to 100, 1,000, or 1,000,000. The number of print statements required to count this many times is clearly prohibitive. However, using loops, you can write a program that can count to any number you want using just a handful of statements. For example, consider the following:

```
i = 1

do

   print i
   i = i + 1

loop while i <= 10
```

Here, a do…while loop has been set up to print out ten numbers (see Figure 6.7), displaying the same output as the previous example.

By changing the value of 10 to 1,000,000 in the previous statement, you can modify the loop to count to a million without adding a single line of code.

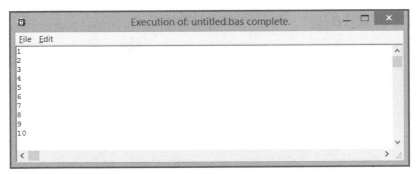

Figure 6.7 Setting up a do…while loop that counts to 10.
© 2016 Cengage Learning®

Obviously, using fewer programming statements to get something done makes for more stream-lined and easier to support applications. Without loops, the programmer's job would be a lot harder. You can use loops to process the contents of arrays or to control an interactive applica-tion that repeatedly prompts the user to provide input. You can also use loops when processing files by extracting records a line at a time. As you have just witnessed, you can also use loops whenever you need to repeat a series of statements over and over again, as when displaying com-puter animation.

Like other programming languages, Just BASIC offers a number of different ways that you can construct loops, including these:

- **Do…While.** Creates a loop that executes at least once and repeats as long as a specified con-dition is `true`.

- **Do…Until.** Creates a loop that executes at least once and repeats until a specified condition is `true`.

- **For…Next.** Creates a loop that repeats a set number of times.

- **While…Wend.** Creates a loop that repeats for as long as a specified condition is `true`.

This chapter will teach you how to formulate and work with each of these types of loops.

Hint

You will find examples of similar types of loops in most programming languages, like C++ and Visual Basic. However, some programming languages, such as AppleScript, go a slightly dif-ferent direction, using the `repeat` statement to create different types of loops. For example, in AppleScript, the `repeat while` and `repeat until` loops are roughly the equivalent of the do…while and do…until loops, and the `repeat with` loop Is pretty similar to Just BASIC's for…next loop.

The do...while Loop

The do...while loop is designed to repeat a code block as long as a specified condition remains true. To set up a do...while loop, you must know in advance what condition must occur for the loop to terminate (for example, what will cause the condition to evaluate as false). You might, for example, set up a do...while loop that allows the user to enter an unlimited amount of input, terminating only when the user enters a command signaling the end of input. The syntax of the do...while loop is outlined here:

```
do
   statements
loop while condition
```

statements is a set of one of more program statements that are to be executed each time the loop repeats. condition is an expression that is evaluated at the end of each iteration of the loop and must resolve to a value of true or false. Because the condition being tested is defined at the end of the loop, do...while loops always execute at least one time, even if the value of condition is false.

Hint

As you can see from the syntax of the do...while loop, the expression being tested is located at the end of the loop, ensuring that the loop executes at least one time. In many other programming languages, such as Visual Basic, the do...while loop supports a second format in which the condition is moved to the opening do statement, as shown here:

```
do while condition
   statements
loop
```

This form of the do...while loop only executes if the value of the tested condition is true. If that is not the case, the loop never executes.

You have already seen an example of a do...while loop that counted to 10 earlier in this chapter. To become more familiar with the do...while loop, take a look at the following example:

```
displayString$ = ""
name$ = ""

do

   name$ = ""
   prompt "Enter a name."; name$
   name$ = upper$(name$)
```

```
  if name$ <> "" and name$ <> "QUIT" then
    displayString$ = displayString$ + name$ + chr$(13)
  end if

loop while upper$(name$) <> "QUIT"

notice "Names" + chr$(13) + displayString$
```

Here, a do…while loop has been set up to allow the user to input a series of names, each of which is appended to a string. As each new name is added, it is appended to the end of the `displayString$` variable followed by a linefeed character. The user may input as many names as desired. The program stops accepting input only when the user enters the `quit` command. Note the use of the `upper$()` function, which converts any input presented by the user to all uppercase characters. This simplifies things by eliminating the requirement that the user enter the `quit` command in a particular format, allowing any use of case when keying in the command.

Figure 6.8 shows an example of the pop-up dialog that is repeatedly displayed, prompting the user to enter another name.

Figure 6.8 Using a loop to collect user input.
© 2016 Cengage Learning®

Figure 6.9 demonstrates how this example's output might look if the user enters five names and then types `quit`.

Figure 6.9 Displaying the output generated by a do…while loop.
© 2016 Cengage Learning®

Hint

Almost all programming languages have an equivalent set of statements that serve the same purpose as Just BASIC's do…while loop. For example, in C++ and Perl, the do…while loop has the following syntax, using curly brackets to enclose the code block portion of the loop:

```
do {
  statements
} while (condition);
```

The do…until Loop

The do…until loop is similar to the do…while loop—the only difference being that the do…until loop executes as long the tested condition is false instead of true. The syntax of the do…until loop is shown here:

```
do
  statements
loop until condition
```

Hint

As you can see from the syntax of the do…until loop, the condition being tested is located at the end of the loop, ensuring that the loop executes at least one time. In many other programming languages, including Visual Basic, the do…until loop supports a second format in which the condition is moved to the opening do statement, as shown here:

```
do until condition
  statements
loop
```

This form of the do…until loop only executes if the value of the tested condition is false. If that is not the case, the loop never executes.

---

statements is a set of one or more program statements that are executed each time the loop repeats. condition is the expression that is evaluated at the end of each iteration of the loop and must resolve to a value of true or false. Because the condition being tested is defined at the end of the loop, do…until loops always execute at least one time, even if the value of the condition is true.

To get a better appreciation of the do...until loop, take a look at the following example:

```
i = 1

do

  print i
  i = i + 1

loop until i > 10
```

As you can see, this example is similar to the do...while loop that was presented earlier. Both loops have been set up to count from 1 to 10. Instead of being set up to count from 1 to 10 while i is less than or equal to 10, this example has been set up to repeat until i is greater than 10. As this example demonstrates, the do...until and do...while loops are pretty much interchangeable.

Hint

Like the do...while loop, other programming languages provide an equivalent set of statements that perform the same basic function as Just BASIC's do...while loop. For example, the following syntax outlines C++ and Perl's do...while statement:

```
do {
  statements
} until (condition);
```

The for...next Loop

The for...next loop is typically when you know in advance the number of times that a loop must repeat. The loop keeps track of the number of times that it has executed using a counter, which is just a numeric variable that is automatically incremented each time the loop repeats. The syntax of the for...next statement is outlined here:

```
for counter = begin to end [step StepValue]
    statements
next counter
```

statements is a set of one of more program statements that will be executed each time the loop repeats. counter is a numeric variable that keeps track of the number of times the loop executes. begin sets the counter variable's initial value, and end sets its ending value, which, when reached, terminates the loop's execution. StepValue is an optional parameter that, when used, sets the incremental value to be used to increase the value of *counter* each time the loop repeats itself. If not specified, a value of 1 is assumed for *StepValue*.

Trick

Note that in Just BASIC, you must add `counter` to the end of the `next` statement. Not all BASIC programming languages have this same requirement.

Hint

The `for...next` loop is common among other programming languages. For example, in C++ and Perl, it has the following syntax:

```
for (initialization; condition; increment) {
    statements
}
```

To get a better feel of how the for...next loop works, take a look at the following example:

```
for i = 1 to 10
    print i
next i
```

Here, a for...next loop has been set up that counts from 1 to 10, just as was previously done with the do...until and do...while loops. As this example demonstrates, you can often use the for...next loop in place of the do...while or do...until loops. The for...next loop is often used in conjunction with arrays, as demonstrated here:

```
dim merchandise$(9)

merchandise$(0) = "Nails"
merchandise$(1) = "Screws"
merchandise$(2) = "Bolts"
merchandise$(3) = "Nuts"
merchandise$(4) = "Wire"
merchandise$(5) = "Hammers"
merchandise$(6) = "Paint"
merchandise$(7) = "Wood"
merchandise$(8) = "Washers"
merchandise$(9) = "Levels"
```

```
for i = 0 To 9
   notice "Inventory" + chr$(13) + merchandise$(i)
next i
```

Here, an array named `merchandise$()` has been created and populated with 10 items. Rather than process each item in the array a statement at a time, a `for...next` loop has been set up that processes the entire loop.

If necessary, you can include the `StepValue` parameter and specify a numeric value other than 1. For example, if you added it to the previous example and assigned it a value of 2, every other item in the `merchandise$()` array would be displayed. You can also assign a negative number as the `StepValue`, which, in the case of the previous example, could be modified to process the contents of the array in reverse order, as demonstrated here:

```
dim merchandise$(9)

merchandise$(0) = "Nails"
merchandise$(1) = "Screws"
merchandise$(2) = "Bolts"
merchandise$(3) = "Nuts"
merchandise$(4) = "Wire"
merchandise$(5) = "Hammers"
merchandise$(6) = "Paint"
merchandise$(7) = "Wood"
merchandise$(8) = "Washers"
merchandise$(9) = "Levels"

for i = 9 To 0 step -1
   notice "Inventory" + chr$(13) + merchandise$(i)
next i
```

The while...wend Loop

Just BASIC also supports the use of `while...wend` loops. A `while...wend` loop is one that repeats as long as a specified condition remains `true`. The syntax of the `while...wend` loop is outlined here:

```
while condition
   statements
wend
```

`condition` is an expression that is evaluated and must resolve to a value of `true` or `false`. `statements` is a set of one or more program statements that is to be executed each time the loop repeats.

Hint

Many other programming languages provide an equivalent functionality to BASIC's while...wend loop. For example, an equivalent loop in C++ and Perl has the following syntax:

```
while (condition) {
    statements
}
```

To see an example of the while...wend loop in action, take a look at the following example:

```
i = 1

while i <= 10
    print i
    i = i + 1
wend
```

When executed, this example counts from 1 to 10.

Hint

In Visual Basic, the while loop is the equivalent of the while...wend loop and has the following syntax:

```
while expression
    statements
end while
```

However, the use of this type of loop is discouraged. Instead, the do...until and do...while loops are preferred because they provide equivalent capabilities and the tested condition to be added to either the beginning of the loop or the end of it, making these statements far more flexible than the while...wend loop.

Looking Out for Endless Loops

One situation that all programmers must constantly be on the lookout for when working with loops is endless loops. An *endless loop* is one that never ends. Endless loops occur because of mistakes made when setting up loops. For example, you might want to create a loop that that counts from 1 to 10 as shown here:

```
i = 1
do
  print i
  i = i + 1
loop while i <= 10
```

However, suppose you accidentally type a minus sign in place of the plus sign, like so:

```
i = 1
do
  print i
  i = i - 1
loop while i <= 10
```

In this example, the loop counts backward starting at 1 and never stops because the value of i never reaches 10.

The point that you need to take from this example is to take extra care when working with loops in your applications. A loop is a powerful programming technique. However, its power can be turned against you when the loop is miscoded. Besides being careful when writing your program code, you need to test your applications thoroughly. Test every line of code—even code for parts of the application you may not often use.

Trick

If, despite your best efforts, you realize when testing the execution of one of your Just BASIC programs within the Just BASIC code editor that your program has gotten stuck in an endless loop, all hope is not lost. In many situations, you can terminate the program's execution. To do so, click on the Run menu and select the Kill BASIC Programs menu item. In response, Just BASIC will display a context menu listing any of the Just BASIC programs currently executing, as demonstrated in Figure 6.10.

Figure 6.10 Killing a Just BASIC program that is stuck in an endless loop.
© 2016 Shoptalk Systems

To force the termination of a particular Just BASIC program, select its name from the list and then click on Yes when prompted to terminate its execution. If this does not work or if you are running a standalone copy of your application outside of the Just BASIC editor, you can still stop your program by using the Task Manager window, which you can access by pressing the Ctrl+Alt+Del keys simultaneously. Once it's opened, you can select your application and then click on the End Task button. Windows will then display a pop-up dialog asking for confirmation before forcing the application's termination.

Busting Out of Loops

Sometimes something happens in a loop that requires the loop to stop executing. For example, you might set up a loop that is designed to collect a series of names from the user. One way that you might handle this situation is to set up a do...while loop that executes until the user enters a command such as quit. When this occurs, you use the exit command to terminate the loop. Once the exit command has been executed, processing resumes with the program statement that follows the loop.

You can use the exit command to break out of do...until, do...while, while...wend, and for...next loops. The following list shows the syntax the exit command uses to break out of each of the aforementioned loops:

- exit do
- exit while
- exit for

Note

You can also use the exit command to break out of subroutines and functions. When you use it to break out of a subroutine, you use the following syntax:

exit sub

When you use the exit command to break out of a function, you use this syntax:

exit function

To get a better understanding of how to work with the exit command, take a look at this example:

```
nomainwin

dim names$(100)
i = 0

do while i <= 100

    prompt "Enter a new name. "; inputName$

  if inputName$ = "quit" then
    exit do
```

```
else
   names$(i) = inputName$
   inputName$ = ""
   i = i + 1
end if
```

```
loop
```

Here, a loop has been set up to collect and populate an array with up to 101 names. Each time the user enters a new name in the pop-up dialog and clicks on the OK button, a new name is added to the names$() array. In this example, the do…while loop has been set up to terminate only under two conditions. The first is when the value of i becomes equal to 100, at which time the array has been filled. The other condition occurs when the user enters quit into the pop-up dialog.

Back to the Guess My Number Game

All right, now that you have learned all about loops and the steps involved in setting them up, let's turn your attention back to the development of this chapter's game project. As you work your way through this project, you will gain hands-on experience in controlling interface controls, including modifying their attributes and controlling their availability. You will also learn how to create and control a Help window and to programmatically terminate the application when one or both application windows are open.

Designing the Game

The design of the Guess My Number game will follow the same pattern already established through the development of earlier programming projects. In total, you will create the development of the Guess My Number game in seven steps, as outlined here:

1. Create a new BASIC file and add initial comment statements.
2. Design the Guess My Number game's user interface.
3. Analyze player guesses and determine whether the game has been won.
4. Start a new game.
5. Create and display a Help window.
6. Close the Help window.
7. Terminate the game's execution.

Creating a Just BASIC File

Let's begin the creation of the Guess My Number game by setting up a new BASIC file and adding the code statements shown here:

```
'  ***************************************************************************
'
'  Script Name: GuessMyNumber.bas (The Guess My Number Game)
'  Version:       1.0
'  Author:        Jerry Lee Ford, Jr.
'  Date:          January 25, 2015
'
'  Description: This game is a Just BASIC number guessing game that
'                    challenges players to guess a number between 1 and 100 in
'                    as few guesses as possible.
'
'  ***************************************************************************

nomainwin     'Suppress the display of the default text window
```

As you can see, there is nothing new here—just a few opening comments followed by the `nomainwin` command, which suppresses the display of the application's default mainwin text window.

Designing the Game's User Interface

The next step in the development of the Guess My Number game is to set up the game's primary window, from which the game is played. This is accomplished by adding the programming statements shown here to the end of the program file:

```
'Declare global variables used to keep track of game statistics
global secretNumber, avgNoGuesses, noOfGamesPlayed, guessCount, helpOpen$

'Assign default values to global variables
secretNumber = 0     'Keeps track of the game's randomly generated number
avgNoGuesses= 0      'Stores the calculated average number of moves per game
noOfGamesPlayed = 0 'Keeps track of the total number of games played
guessCount = 0       'Keeps track of the total number of guesses made
helpOpen$ = "False" 'Keeps track of when the #help window is open

WindowWidth = 510    'Set the width of the window to 510 pixels
WindowHeight = 500   'Set the height of the window to 500 pixels

ForegroundColor$ = "Darkblue"   'Set the window font color to dark blue
```

```
'Define the format of statictext controls displayed on the window
statictext #play.statictext1, "G U E S S    M Y    N U M B E R", _
  30, 50, 460, 40
statictext #play.statictext2, "Copyright 2015", 395, 90, 100, 20
statictext #play.statictext3, "Games Played:", 40, 400, 80, 20
statictext #play.statictext4, "Avg. No. Guesses:", 265, 400, 90, 20
statictext #play.statictext5, "Enter Your Guess:", 200, 140, 120, 20
statictext #play.statictext6, "Hint:", 42, 300, 30, 20

'Add button controls to the window
button #play.button1 "Guess", AnalyzeGuess, UL, 210, 225, 80, 30
button #play.button2 "Help", DisplayHelp, UL, 400, 318, 70, 25
button #play.button3 "Start Game", StartGame, UL, 400, 288, 70, 25

'Add four textbox controls and place them inside the groupbox control
textbox #play.textbox1, 200, 160, 110, 50
textbox #play.textbox2, 130, 395, 90, 22
textbox #play.textbox3, 370, 395, 90, 22
textbox #play.textbox4, 40, 320, 340, 22

'Open the window with no frame and a handle of #play
open "Guess My Number" for window_nf as #play

'Set up the trapclose event for the window
print #play, "trapclose ClosePlay"

'Display the appropriate variable values in the following textbox controls
print #play.textbox3, avgNoGuesses
print #play.textbox2, noOfGamesPlayed

'Set the font type, size, and properties for each of the static controls
print #play.statictext1, "!font Arial 20 bold"
print #play.statictext2, "!font Arial 8"
print #play.statictext5, "!font Arial 8 bold"
print #play.statictext6, "!font Arial 8 bold"
print #play.textbox1, "!font Arial 24";

print #play.button3, "!setfocus"    'Set focus to the Start Game button
print #play.button1, "!disable"     'Disable the Guess button
```

```
print #play.textbox1, "!disable"    'Disable the input textbox

'Pause the application to wait for the player's instruction
wait
```

As you can see, the first thing that happens is the definition of five global variables that will be used to keep track of data used throughout the application. Each of these five variables is then assigned an initial value. Note that the purpose of each variable is documented in comments embedded within the program code. The last variable, helpOpen$, merits additional discussion. It will be used to keep track of the status of the game's Help window. Because the Help window is not opened by default, an initial status of "False" is assigned to helpOpen$. Later, should the player open the Help window, its value will be changed to "True". If the player decides to stop playing the Guess My Number game, the value assigned to helpOpen$ will be checked to determine if the application needs to close the Help window before terminating its execution.

The next several statements set the height and width of the window and its foreground color to dark blue. Six statictext controls are then added to the window. These controls will be used to display the game's name and copyright information and to provide labels for other controls.

Next, three button controls are added to the window and assigned labels of Guess, Help, and Start Game. When the player clicks on the Guess button, the AnalyzeGuess subroutine is called. This subroutine compares the player's guess to the game's randomly generated number to see if the player has won. If this is not the case, a hint is provided. Clicking on the Help button calls on the DisplayHelp subroutine, which displays the game's Help window. Clicking on the Start Game button executes the StartGame subroutine, which allows the player to start up a new round of play.

Four textbox controls are then added to the window. The first textbox control will be used to allow the player to type in and submit guesses. The other three textbox controls will be used to display a hint that helps to guide the player's next guess as well as display game statistics, showing the number of games played and the average number of guesses made per game.

The next statement displays the window using the open command, assigning it a handle of #play. The window's trapclose event handler is then set up, calling on the ClosePlay subroutine whenever the player attempts to close the #play window (requiring confirmation before closing any open windows and executing the end command).

The next seven statements use the print command to display the values assigned to the avgNoGuesses and noOfGamesPlayed variables (both are initially assigned a value of 0) and to set the font size, type, and attributes of various statictext and textbox controls. The last three print statements set focus to the Start Game button and disable access to the Guess button and its associated input textbox control. Finally, the wait command is executed, pausing application execution to await user interaction.

Analyzing the Player's Guesses

The AnalyzeGuess subroutine is responsible for analyzing player guesses. It provides hints based on player input and determines when the game has been won. The code statements that make up the AnalyzeGuess subroutine are shown next and should be added to the end of the program file:

```
'This subroutine analyzes player guesses and determines when the game
'has been won
sub AnalyzeGuess handle$

  'Retrieve the player's guess and assign it to a variable
  print #play.textbox1, "!contents? playerGuess"

  'Validate that an acceptable value has been entered
  if playerGuess < 1 or playerGuess > 100 then

    'Inform the user that an invalid guess has been made
    print #play.textbox4, "Your guess must be between 1 and 100. Try again."
    print #play.textbox1, ""  'Clear out the input textbox
    print #play.textbox1, "!setfocus"  'Set focus to the input textbox
    exit sub  'Exit the subroutine without processing any remaining
              'subroutine statements

  end if

  'Determine if the player's guess is too low
  if playerGuess < secretNumber then

    'Increment the variable that tracks the total number of guesses made
    guessCount = guessCount + 1

    'Inform the user that the guess was too low
    print #play.textbox4, "Your guess was too low. Try again."
    print #play.textbox1, ""  'Clear out the input textbox
    print #play.textbox1, "!setfocus"  'Set focus to the input textbox
    exit sub  'Exit the subroutine without processing any remaining
              'subroutine statements

  end if
```

```
'Determine if the player's guess is too high
if playerGuess > secretNumber then

    'Increment the variable that tracks the total number of guesses made
    guessCount = guessCount + 1

    'Inform the user that the guess was too high
    print #play.textbox4, "Your guess was too high. Try again."
    print #play.textbox1, ""   'Clear out the input textbox
    print #play.textbox1, "!setfocus"  'Set focus to the input textbox
    exit sub   'Exit the subroutine without processing any remaining
               'subroutine statements

end if

'Determine if the player's guess was correct
if playerGuess = secretNumber then

    'Let the player know he has won the game
    notice "Guess My Number" + chr$(13) + "Game over! You win!"

    'Increment the variable that tracks the total number of guesses made
    guessCount = guessCount + 1

   'Increment the variable that tracks the total number of games played
   noOfGamesPlayed = noOfGamesPlayed + 1

    'Calculate the average number of guesses per game
    avgNoGuesses = guessCount / noOfGamesPlayed

    'Display the appropriate variable values in the following textbox
    'controls
    print #play.textbox3, avgNoGuesses
    print #play.textbox2, noOfGamesPlayed

    print #play.textbox1, ""             'Clear out the input textbox
    print #play.button3, "!enable"       'Enable the Start Game button
    print #play.button3, "!setfocus"     'Set focus to the Start Game button
    print #play.textbox1, "!disable"     'Disable the input textbox
```

```
      print #play.button1, "!disable"     'Disable the Guess button
      print #play.textbox4, ""            'Clear out the Hint textbox control

      exit sub   'Exit the subroutine without processing any remaining
                 'subroutine statements

  end if

end sub
```

This subroutine begins by storing the player's guess in a variable named `playerGuess`. It then uses an `if…then` statement to determine if the player's guess is valid (that is, it is not less than 1 or greater than 100). Note the use of the `or` operator, which allows the `if` statement to perform two separate comparison operations. If the player's guess is invalid, an error message is displayed and the input textbox control is cleared and assigned focus, preparing it for the player's next guess.

If the player's guess is valid (that is, it is greater than or equal to 1 and less than or equal to 100), three separate `if…then` statements are executed. The first `if…then` statement executes when the player's guess is too low. The second `if…then` statement executes when the player's guess is too high, and the last `if…then` statement executes when the player's guess matches the game's secret number. The first two `if…then` statements increment the value of `guessCount` by 1 and display an appropriate hint message. The last `if…then` statement also increments the value of `guessCount` as well as the value of `noOfGamesPlayed` by 1. It then divides the value of `guessCount` by `noOfGamesPlayed` to calculate the value assigned to `avgNoGuesses`. Next, a series of `print` statements is executed to enable the Start Game button and assign it focus as well as to disable the Guess button and the input textbox control.

Starting a New Game

The `StartGame` subroutine, shown next, is called when the player clicks on the Start Game button. It is responsible for generating the game's random number (in the range of 1 to 100) and for enabling the Guess button and input textbox controls:

```
'This subroutine is called when the player clicks on the Start Game button
sub StartGame handle$

  'Generate a new random number for the game
  secretNumber = int(rnd(1)*100) + 1

  print #play.button1, "!enable"     'Enable the Guess button
  print #play.textbox1, "!enable"    'Enable the input textbox
```

```
print #play.button3, "!disable"      'Disable the Start Game button
print #play.textbox1, "!setfocus"    'Set focus to the input textbox

end sub
```

Creating a Help Window

The code statements responsible for generating and displaying the game's Help window are shown next and should be added to the end of the program file. This subroutine is called when the player clicks on the Help button:

```
sub DisplayHelp handle$

  helpOpen$ = "True"   'Identify the #help window as being open

  WindowWidth = 400    'Set the width of the window to 400 pixels
  WindowHeight = 400   'Set the height of the window to 400 pixels

  'Use variables to store text strings displayed in the window
  HelpHeader$ = "Game Instructions"
  helpText1$ = "The object of this game is to guess a randomly generated" _
    + " number in the range of 1 to 100 in as few guesses as possible. " _
    + "To make a guess, type in a number and click on the Guess button. " _
    + "A hint will be provided after each move to assist you in making " _
    + "your next guess. Once you have correctly guessed the game's secret" _
    + " number, a popup message will be displayed."
  helpText2$ = "At the end of each round of play game statistics are " _
    + "displayed at the bottom of the game window as an indication of " _
    + "your progress."

  'Define the format of statictext controls displayed on the window
  statictext #help.helptext1, HelpHeader$, 30, 40, 140, 20
  statictext #help.helptext2, helpText1$, 30, 70, 330, 80
  statictext #help.helptext3, helpText2$, 30, 160, 330, 50

  'Add button controls to the window
  button #help.button "Close", CloseHelpWindow, UL, 280, 310, 80, 30

  'Open the window with no frame and a handle of #play
  open "Guess My Number Help" for window_nf as #help
```

```
'Set the font type, size, and properties for specified statictext control
print #help.helptext1, "!font Arial 12 bold"
```

```
end sub
```

As you can see, the code statements in this subroutine are pretty straightforward. However, there is one statement that you should pay particular attention to. It is the first statement in the subroutine. This statement assigns a value of "True" to the helpOpen$ string variable. This identifies the Help window as being open. Later, when the player tries to terminate the Guess My Number game, the game's trapclose event handler will examine the value assigned to helpOpen$ to determine whether the Help window needs to be closed before executing the end command and terminating application execution.

Closing the Help Window

The CloseHelpWindow subroutine, shown next, is executed whenever the player closes the game's Help window. As you can see, it executes two statements. The first statement sets the value of helpOpen$ to "False", and the second statement closes the window:

```
'This subroutine is called when the player closes the #help window
sub CloseHelpWindow handle$
```

```
helpOpen$ = "False"   'Identify the #help window as being closed
```

```
   close #help   'Close the #help window
```

```
end sub
```

Terminating Application Execution

The application's last subroutine is ClosePlay. Its job is to get confirmation from the player before terminating the game. If confirmation is provided, the subroutine closes the #play window and, if open, it also closes the game's Help window (#help) and then executes the end command, neatly terminating application execution:

```
'This subroutine is called when the player closes the #play window
'and is responsible for ending the game
sub ClosePlay handle$
```

```
   'Get confirmation before terminating program execution
   confirm "Are you sure you want to quit?"; answer$
```

```
  if answer$ = "yes" then   'The player clicked on Yes

    close #play   'Close the #play window

    'See if the #help window is open and close it if it is
    if  helpOpen$ = "True" then

      call CloseHelpWindow "X"   'Close the #help window

    end if

    end   'Terminate the game

  end if

end sub
```

The Final Result

That's it. Assuming that you have followed along carefully without missing any steps, your copy of the Guess My Number game should be ready to test. As you put the game through its paces, try entering both valid and invalid data to ensure that the application handles it correctly. Keep an eye on the game statistics provided at the bottom of the game window, and validate that they are being properly tabulated. Lastly, make sure that the Guess and Start Game button controls are appropriately enabled and disabled as the game progresses and that the hints that are provided are consistent with the number that the game generates.

Summary

In this chapter you learned how to work with different types of loops, including the do…while, do…until, for…next, and while…wend loops. This chapter also guided you in terms of which loops are best applied for various situations. In addition, you discovered how to use the exit command to break out of loops and terminate programs that have become hung up in loops. By learning how to work with loops, you have laid the foundation required to develop applications that can process huge amounts of data or repeat any set of program statements over and over again as required to perform a particular task.

Before moving on to Chapter 7, "Improving Program Organization with Functions and Subroutines," take a little extra time to work on the Guess My Number game by tackling the following list of challenges.

Challenges

1. The Help window belonging to the Guess My Number game provides only a minimal amount of useful information. Consider spending a little time beefing up the content this window offers.

2. Currently, the game has only two hints, stating whether the player's guess is too high or too low. Consider adding programming logic that supplies additional hints. For example, you might want to display a different hint message when the player's guesses begin to get close to the game's secret number.

3. Consider enforcing a limit on the number of guesses that the player can make and then end gameplay when that limit is reached. You might also want to track and display the number of games lost as an additional game statistic.

Improving Program Organization with Functions and Subroutines

The larger your applications become, the more complicated your program code becomes and the more difficult things are to maintain. One effective way of making your programs easier to create and maintain is to break them up into small parts, which you can then use as building blocks to create a larger program. One way of accomplishing this is through procedures. You've used procedures in the development of most of the game applications you've already created in this book. In this chapter, you will discover how to work with two types of procedures: subroutines and functions. You will learn how to pass data to your subroutines and functions for processing. You will also learn how to return data back from functions. You will also get the opportunity to put your newfound understanding of subroutines and functions to use in this chapter's game project: the BASIC BlackJack game.

Specifically, you will learn the following:

- How to improve the overall organization and manageability of your applications through subroutines and functions
- How to streamline program code by placing reusable code within subroutines and functions
- How to pass data to subroutines and functions for processing
- How to return data from functions back to calling statements

Project Preview: The BASIC BlackJack Game

This chapter's game project is the BASIC BlackJack game. This game is a lite version of the popular BlackJack casino game that pits the player against the dealer (computer) in a virtual card game whose object is to come as close as possible to 21 without going over. This game, like many applications, begins by displaying a splash screen, as shown in Figure 7.1.

After a four-second delay, the splash screen closes and the game's main window is displayed. An initial hand is automatically dealt for both the player and the dealer, as shown in Figure 7.2.

Figure 7.1 The splash screen is displayed for four seconds and then automatically disappears.

© 2016 Cengage Learning®

Figure 7.2 In this game, the player must complete his hand before the dealer plays out its hand.

© 2016 Cengage Learning®

The object of the game is to get the highest possible hand without going over 21, which would cause the player to bust and automatically make the dealer a winner. The player is required to always play out her hand first. To get additional cards, the player must click on the Hit Me button. The value of the player's hand is automatically updated each time the Hit Me button is clicked, as demonstrated in Figure 7.3.

The player may ask for as many cards as she wants, provided the value of her hand does not exceed 21. If the player's hand goes over 21, she automatically busts and loses that hand. The player may stop adding cards to her hand at any time and allow the dealer to play out its hand by clicking on the Stay button. The dealer's method of play is simple: it will continue to ask for a card as long as its hand is less than 17 or until it busts. Once its hand exceeds 17, assuming it has not busted, it stops adding new cards to its hand and holds.

If neither the player nor the dealer has busted, the game compares both hands to determine the results of the game. Figure 7.4 shows an example of a hand in which the player and the dealer have tied.

Figure 7.3 The player's turn ends when she clicks on the Stay button or when she goes bust.
© 2016 Cengage Learning®

Figure 7.4 The results of each hand are displayed at the bottom of the window.
© 2016 Cengage Learning®

The player can start a new hand at the end of each round of play by clicking on the Play Again button. Again, play continues until the player or dealer busts or stays. Figure 7.5 shows an example of a hand in which the dealer has gone bust.

Figure 7.5 Any hand over 21 results in an automatic loss.
© 2016 Cengage Learning®

Working with Subroutines and Functions

As your applications become larger, they become more complicated and difficult to maintain. One way of making your programs easier to create and maintain is to organize them into small parts, which can then be used as building blocks in the creation of a larger program. This is where procedures come into play.

A *procedure* is a collection of programming statements that can be called upon to execute from different locations within an application. Most programming languages support two types of procedures: subroutines and functions. A *subroutine* is a collection of one or more code statements that can be called upon to execute. A *function* is similar to a subroutine except that a function also can return a value to the statement that called upon it. Subroutines and functions help to make application development easier by allowing you to break down an application into manageable sections, which you can develop one at a time.

Hint

In Chapter 3, "Creating Graphical User Interfaces," you were introduced to the use of labels as a means of identifying locations within program code. By specifying a label as the event handler for a user interface control or by using the goto or gosub commands, you learned how to group and execute collections of code statements. However, as was stated in that chapter, this method of programming is frowned upon. Instead, professional programmers rely on subroutines and functions to group and execute related code statements.

Procedures give programmers several advantages. For starters, they make program development easier by letting programmers build programs in small chunks, each of which is designed to accomplish a specific task. Secondly, procedures allow programmers to reduce the amount of code required to develop applications by providing the ability to group commonly executed statements into a named collection, which can then be called upon to run over and over again as necessary. Organizing programming logic into separate procedures also helps to streamline programming logic and create modular code. This can reduce errors, too.

Suppose, for example, that you created a program for a retail store that performs a number of different tasks, including the calculation of sales tax for each sale made in the store. You now need to modify the program because the sales tax rate had changed. If you did not use procedures when initially developing the program, your job will be more difficult, especially if you are working on a large program. By organizing the program into procedures, you simplify its maintenance by grouping related code statements. To change the part of the program that calculates the sales tax, all that you have to do is locate the procedure where the sales tax calculation is performed and make the appropriate modification. Thus, by placing related code statements into subroutines and functions, programmers can isolate different logical processes and reduce the chances that a change made in one part of a program might affect another part.

Defining Subroutines

Subroutines begin with a declaration statement (sub) and end with an end sub statement. When called, subroutines execute, and, when complete, they return control to the statement that called upon them. To define a subroutine within a Just BASIC application, you must use the following syntax:

```
sub SubroutineName Parameter1,... ParameterN
  statements
end sub
```

SubroutineName represents the name of the subroutine being defined. Subroutines can accept and process any number of arguments passed to them when called, as represented by *Parameter1* ... *ParameterN* (that is, *Parameter1* "through" *ParameterN*). statements represents the statements that will be executed each time the subroutine is called.

Trap

Procedure names for both subroutines and functions must be unique throughout an application. You cannot assign the same name to more than one subroutine or function. Nor can you assign a subroutine or function name to a variable.

In many programming languages, including C++ and Just BASIC, programmers are required to declare the data type of any parameters defined in a procedure. Because Just BASIC supports only two data types—numeric and string—data type is identified by the absence or presence of the $ character at the end of the parameter name.

The following statements define a small subroutine that accepts two arguments and uses them in the formulation of a string, which is then displayed in a pop-up window:

```
sub HappyBirthday name$, age

  notice "Happy birthday, " + name$ + "! Today you are " + str$(age) _
    + " years old."

end sub
```

As you can see, the name assigned to the subroutine is HappyBirthday. The first parameter defined by the subroutine is a string variable named name$. The second parameter is a numerical variable named age.

Within Just BASIC, subroutines can be called in either of two ways. The first way of calling a sub-routine is as an event handler. The second is to explicitly call the subroutine using the call command. Both of these options are explained in the sections that follow.

Using a Subroutine as an Event Handler

You have used procedures in most of the game projects that you have worked on so far. For exam-ple, in most of the chapter game projects, you have set up subroutines as event handlers that exe-cute whenever the player clicks on user interface controls.

When defining a subroutine that will be used as the event handler for an interface control, you must always define at least one parameter. That's because, when called in this manner, the sub-routine is passed an argument containing a string representing the name of the control that called the subroutine. If you forget to add a parameter representing this argument, you'll get an error. For example, in the Guess My Number game that you created in Chapter 6, "Using Loops to Process Data," you created a subroutine called ClosePlay, as shown next. As you can see, this subroutine includes a parameter definition named handle$. handle$ is really just a string vari-able that receives the name of the user interface control whose event triggered the execution of the subroutine:

```
sub ClosePlay handle$

  'Get confirmation before terminating program execution
  confirm "Are you sure you want to quit?"; answer$

  if answer$ = "yes" then   'The player clicked on Yes

    close #play   'Close the #play window

    'See if the #help window is open and close it if it is
    if  helpOpen$ = "True" then

      call CloseHelpWindow "X"   'Close the #help window

    end if

    end   'Terminate the game

  end if

end sub
```

If you did not include the required parameter as part of this subroutine's definition, your program would crash and generate an error similar to the one shown in Figure 7.6.

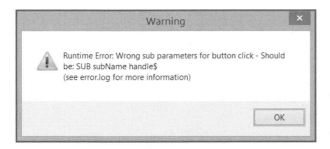

Figure 7.6 Just BASIC has generated an error because a subroutine was called and passed an argument for which it did not have a corresponding parameter defined.
© 2016 Cengage Learning®

Programmatically Calling a Subroutine

In addition to setting up procedures as event handlers for window and user interface controls, you can execute them using the `call` command. The syntax for the `call` command is outlined here:

```
call ProcedureName Parameter1, ... ParameterN
```

ProcedureName represents the procedure to be executed, and *Parameter1,... ParameterN* represents one or more optional arguments that may be passed to the procedure. For example, you could use the following statement to call on a procedure named `HappyBirthday` and pass it two arguments (a string and a number), as demonstrated here:

```
call HappyBirthday "William", 9
```

> **Hint**
>
> An *argument* is a value, literal or variable, that is passed to a subroutine or function for processing. A *parameter* is a variable defined within a subroutine or function that maps up to an argument that the subroutine or function is passed.

When executed, the `HappyBirthday` subroutine maps each argument that is passed to it to one of its parameters. The data type of each argument that is passed must match the data type of each parameter defined by the subroutine or function; otherwise, an error will occur:

```
sub HappyBirthday name$, age

  notice "Happy birthday " + name$ + "! Today you are " + str$(age) _
    + " years old."

end sub
```

Hint

In many programming languages, including Visual Basic, you can call on a procedure by simply keying in its name, as demonstrated here:

```
HappyAnniversary()
```

Here, a function named HappyAnniversary() has been called upon to execute. In Visual Basic, the call command is regarded as a legacy statement that is seldom used anymore. However, Just BASIC still requires it.

Prematurely Terminating a Subroutine

If necessary, you can terminate the execution of a subroutine at any time using the following statement:

```
exit sub
```

For example, the following subroutine, taken from the Guess My Number game, used the exit sub command in a number of different places to terminate the execution of the AnalyzeGuess subroutine when validating and processing the player's guess:

```
sub AnalyzeGuess handle$

  print #play.textbox1, "!contents? playerGuess"

  if playerGuess < 1 or playerGuess > 100 then
    print #play.textbox4, "Your guess must be between 1 and 100. Try again."
    print #play.textbox1, ""
    print #play.textbox1, "!setfocus"
    exit sub
  end if

  if playerGuess < secretNumber then
    guessCount = guessCount + 1
    print #play.textbox4, "Your guess was too low. Try again."
    print #play.textbox1, ""
    print #play.textbox1, "!setfocus"
    exit sub
  end if
```

```
  if playerGuess > secretNumber then

    guessCount = guessCount + 1
    print #play.textbox4, "Your guess was too high. Try again."
    print #play.textbox1, ""
    print #play.textbox1, "!setfocus"
    exit sub
  end if

  if playerGuess = secretNumber then
    notice "Guess My Number" + chr$(13) + "Game over! You win!"
    guessCount = guessCount + 1
    noOfGamesPlayed = noOfGamesPlayed + 1
    avgNoGuesses = guessCount / noOfGamesPlayed
    print #play.textbox3, avgNoGuesses
    print #play.textbox2, noOfGamesPlayed
    print #play.textbox1, ""
    print #play.button3, "!enable"
    print #play.button3, "!setfocus"
    print #play.textbox1, "!disable"
    print #play.button1, "!disable"
    print #play.textbox4, ""
    exit sub
  end if

end sub
```

As you can see, the exit sub command was used four times in four separate if…then statements to terminate the subroutine's execution as soon as any of the tested conditions evaluated as being true.

Defining Functions

As has already been stated, a function is almost the same thing as a subroutine except that functions also allow programmers to return a value to the statement that called upon them to execute. To define a function within a Just BASIC application, you must use the following syntax:

```
function FunctionName(Parameter1,... ParameterN)
  statements
end sub
```

FunctionName represents the name of the function being defined. A function can accept and process any number of arguments passed to it, as represented by *Parameter1* through *ParameterN*. *statements* represents the statements that will be executed each time the function is executed.

You can pass as many arguments to your subroutines and functions as you want, provided that you have the same number of corresponding parameters defined inside the subroutine or function.

The following statements are an example of a function that generates a random number in the range of 1 to 10 and then returns the number that is generated to the statement that called upon the function to execute:

```
function GetRandomNumber()

  RandomNumber = int(rnd(1)*10) + 1

  GetRandomNumber = RandomNumber

end function
```

As the previous example demonstrates, to return a value from a function, you must create a variable within the function that has the same name as the function and assign it the value that you want returned.

Hint

Different programming languages have different ways of returning values from functions. For example, in Visual Basic, you can return a value from a function using the same approach as Just BASIC (for example, creating a variable with the same name as the function and assigning the value to be returned to it). C++, on the other hand, uses the `return` command to explicitly specify the value that is to be returned. Languages like Perl and Ruby will automatically return the last expression that was evaluated if the `return` statement is not specified.

Executing Functions

Using the following statement, you can call upon the GetRandomNumber function shown in the previous example from anywhere inside the application that contains it:

```
gameNumber = GetRandomNumber()
```

Of course, instead of returning values to and from functions, you can use global variables, accessing them whenever necessary from within your subroutines and functions. However, it is a much better programming practice to limit the scope of your variables as much as possible, pass arguments to your functions, and return any required result to calling statements. Limiting variable scope in this manner helps to prevent the unintentional modification of variable values and helps make your program code easier to maintain.

Prematurely Terminating a Function

As with subroutines, you can terminate the execution of a function at any time using the following statement:

```
exit function
```

As an example of how to use the `exit function` statement, consider the following example:

```
prompt "Give me a number and I'll double it!"; x


notice DoubleNumber(x)


function DoubleNumber(x)

  DoubleNumber = x + x

  if DoubleNumber > 100 then
    notice "Sorry, I don't like large numbers! How about 2 + 2 instead?"
    DoubleNumber = 4
    exit function
  end if


end function
```

Here, in this somewhat silly example, a function named DoubleNumber has been defined. It accepts a single argument in the form of a numeric value, which is mapped to a parameter named x. Next, the function adds the value of x to itself, thus creating a new numeric value that is twice the value of the argument that was passed to the function. By assigning this new value to a variable with the same name as the function, this value is passed back to the statement that called upon the function so long as the if…then statement that follows proves false. The if…then statement executes only if the value being returned is greater than 100. If this is the case, the notice command is used to inform the user that it does not appreciate being asked to calculate a large number, and the value of DoubleNumber is instead reassigned an arbitrary value of 4, which is then returned to the statement that called upon the function.

Different Ways to Pass Arguments to Procedures

Variables defined within a subroutine or function are local in scope, meaning they cannot be accessed outside of the subroutine or function where they are defined. However, you can share access to data throughout your Just BASIC applications by declaring your variables as global. Alternatively, you can pass variables as arguments to subroutines and functions where they can then be acted upon. You can also pass arguments by reference, in which case your subroutine or function can modify the value assigned to any argument that is passed to it.

Passing Arguments by Value

By default, any argument passed to a subroutine or function is passed by value, meaning that the subroutine or function may do whatever it wants to the value of the argument within itself, but any modification of the value is not visible outside the procedure. To get a better feeling for how this works, consider the following example:

```
age = 10

call ChangeValue age
notice "You are " + str$(age) + " years old."

sub ChangeValue x
   x = x + 5
end sub
```

Here, a numeric variable named age is defined and assigned a value of 10. Next, the call command is used to execute a subroutine named ChangeValue, to which age is passed as an argument. Within the subroutine, the value of age is mapped to a variable named x. The value of x is then increased by 5. However, because the argument passed to the subroutine was passed by value, the modification of x's value had no effect on the value of age, as proven when the subroutine ends and the notice statement is executed, showing that the value assigned to age is still 5.

Passing Arguments by Reference

Arguments passed by reference affect the value of the argument passed, both within the procedure and outside of it. To see how this works, take a look at the following example:

```
age = 10

call ChangeValue age
notice "You are " + str$(age) + " years old."

sub ChangeValue byref x
   x = x + 5
end sub
```

As you can see, in this example the subroutine definition includes the byref keyword. As a result, any change made to the value of x inside the subroutine is also reflected outside the subroutine in the value of age, which is proved when the notice statement executes and age is shown to have a value of 15 and not 10.

Taking Advantage of Built-In Function Libraries

Although you can certainly create your own custom functions to perform all kinds of operations, you will find that most programming languages include their own collection of predefined functions that you can call upon to execute commonly performed calculations or tasks. By taking advantage of these built-in functions, you reduce the size and complexity of your programs. You also reduce the time required to create your applications.

You have already seen a number of Just BASIC's functions in action. For example, you have used the rnd() function to generate random numbers, the int() function to convert a floating-point number to an integer, and the str$() function to convert a numeric value to a string value. Table 7.1 shows a list of functions that Just BASIC provides. You'll see a number of these functions in use throughout this book. For any function that is not covered, you can learn more about it by referencing Just BASIC's Help.

TABLE 7.1 JUST BASIC'S BUILT-IN FUNCTIONS

Function Name	Function Name	Function Name
abs()	left()	sin()
acs()	len()	space()
asn()	loc()	sqr()
atn()	lof()	str$()
chr$()	log()	tab()
cos()	lower$()	tan()
date$()	mid$()	time$()
eof()	midipos()	trim$()
exp()	mkdir()	upper$()
input$()	right$()	using()
instr()	rmdir()	val()
int()	rnd()	

Back to the BASIC BlackJack Game

All right, that is enough about subroutines and functions for now. Let's turn your attention back to the development of this chapter's game project: the BASIC BlackJack game. This game will consist of two windows—one will serve as a splash screen, and the other will serve as the main window. To create the splash screen, you need to download copies of the two bitmap image files shown in Figure 7.7 from this book's companion website.

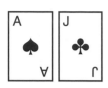

Figure 7.7 Reviewing copies of the two bitmap images displayed on the game's opening splash screen window.
© 2016 Cengage Learning®

Hint

You can download copies of these two bitmap images along with the source code for this application from this book's companion website, at www.cengageptr.com/downloads.

Designing the Game

The design of the BASIC BlackJack game relies heavily on the use of subroutines and functions. You will follow the same pattern already established through the development of previous game projects. In total, you will create the BASIC BlackJack game in 12 steps, as outlined here:

1. Create a new BASIC file.
2. Initiate the game by defining global variables and executing the `DisplaySplash` subroutine.
3. Create the `DisplaySplash` subroutine.
4. Create the `CloseSplashWindow` subroutine.
5. Create the `ManageGamePlay` subroutine.
6. Create the `DealCard` subroutine.
7. Create the `DealerTurn` subroutine.
8. Create the `RestartGame` subroutine.
9. Create the `DealOpeningHand` subroutine.
10. Create the `GetRandomNumber` function.
11. Create the `ResetGame` subroutine.
12. Create the `ClosePlay` subroutine.

Creating a Just BASIC File Script

Following the same pattern that has been established with the creation of all Just BASIC game applications that you have worked on in this book, let's begin by adding a few comment statements to the beginning of the program file:

```
' *************************************************************************
'
' Script Name: BlackJack.bas (The BASIC BlackJack Game)
' Version:     1.0
' Author:      Jerry Lee Ford, Jr.
' Date:        January 25, 2015
'
' Description: This game is a Just BASIC implementation of the BlackJack
'              casino card game which pits the player against the
'              computer (dealer).
'
' *************************************************************************
```

Next, because the application will not make use of its default text window, add the following statement to the end of the program file telling Just BASIC to suppress its display at runtime:

```
nomainwin    'Suppress the display of the default text window
```

Initializing the Game

The next step in the development of the BASIC BlackJack game is to define a pair of global variables. The `dealerCard` variable will be used to keep track of the numeric value of the dealer's hand during gameplay. Likewise, the `playerCard` variable is used to keep track of the value of the player's hand. Next, the `call` command is used to execute the `DisplaySplash` subroutine. This subroutine is responsible for displaying the game's splash screen and then initializing gameplay:

```
global dealerCard, playerCard 'Assign default values to global variables

call DisplaySplash   'Call on the subroutine that displays the game's
                     'splash screen

wait   'Pause the application and wait for the player's instruction
```

Creating the DisplaySplash Subroutine

The code statements that make up the `DisplaySplash` subroutine are shown next and should be added to the end of the program file:

```
'This subroutine displays a splash screen at game start-up
sub DisplaySplash

  loadbmp "AceImage", "C:\images\Ace.bmp"    'Load the specified bitmap
                                             'file into memory
  loadbmp "JackImage", "C:\images\Jack.bmp" 'Load the specified bitmap
                                             'file into memory

  'Define the format of statictext controls displayed on the window
  statictext #splash.statictext1, "B A S I C   B L A C K J A C K", _
    5, 30, 440, 30
  statictext #splash.statictext2, "Copyright 2015", 230, 60, 80, 20

  'Add two graphicbox controls to the #splash window
  graphicbox #splash.gboxAce, 65, 120, 77, 116
  graphicbox #splash.gboxJack, 175, 120, 77, 116

  'Open the window with no frame and a handle of #splash
  open "BASIC BlackJack" for window_nf as #splash

  'Set the font type, size, and attributes
  print #splash.statictext1, "!font Arial 14 bold"

  'Use the flush command to prevent the contents of the graphicbox control
  'from being overwritten when the window is first generated
  print #splash.gboxAce, "flush"
  print #splash.gboxJack, "flush"

  'Display the preloaded bitmap images in the graphicbox control
  print #splash.gboxAce, "drawbmp AceImage 1 1"
  print #splash.gboxJack, "drawbmp JackImage 1 1"

  'Use the flush command to prevent the contents of the graphicbox controls
  'from being overwritten if the user opens or moves another window on top
  'of the #splash window
  print #splash.gboxAce, "flush"
  print #splash.gboxJack, "flush"
```

```
'Wait 4 thousand milliseconds (4 seconds) and then call upon the
'subroutine that closes the game's splash screen
timer 4000, CloseSplashWindow
```

```
end sub
```

The `DisplaySplash` subroutine begins by using the `loadbmp` command to preload graphics bitmap files into memory. Statictext and graphicbox controls are then added to the window. After that, the window is displayed using the `open` command and assigned a handle of `#splash`. The rest of the subroutine consists of statements that perform the following set of actions:

- Set the window's font type, size, and attributes.
- Use the `flush` command to prevent bitmap files from being overwritten.
- Use the `drawbmp` command to display the bitmap images.
- Use the `timer` command to pause the subroutine's execution for four seconds before calling on the `CloseSplashWindow` subroutine.

Hint

The `timer` command uses the computer's internal hardware timer to allow programmers to implement programming logic that relies on the passage of time. For example, you might use the `timer` command to drive the execution of programming statements that control the display of animation in a computer game.

The syntax of the `timer` command is shown here:

```
timer delay, EventHandler
```

delay is a placeholder that represents the amount of time, in milliseconds, that the `timer` command will wait before executing the specified *EventHandler* (for example, call to a subroutine, function, or label). One second is equivalent to 1,000 milliseconds. So, to tell the time to wait 5 seconds, you would specify a value of 5,000 for *delay*.

Creating the CloseSplashWindow Subroutine

The `CloseSplashWindow` subroutine, shown next, is responsible for closing the game's splash screen window:

```
'This subroutine closes the game's splash screen window
sub CloseSplashWindow

  timer 0          'Turn the timer off
```

```
close #splash  'Close the #splash window

call ManageGamePlay  'Call on the subroutine that manages gameplay

end sub
```

The first statement in the subroutine disables the execution of the timer command by passing a value of zero. Next, the close command is used to close the #splash window. Finally, the call command is used to execute the ManageGamePlay subroutine, which is responsible for initializing gameplay.

Creating the ManageGamePlay Subroutine

The code statements that make up the ManageGamePlay subroutine are shown next and should be added to the end of the program file. This subroutine will display the game's main window and facilitate gameplay:

```
'This subroutine displays the game board and controls interaction with the
'player
sub ManageGamePlay

  WindowWidth = 400    'Set the width of the window to 400 pixels
  WindowHeight = 400   'Set the height of the window to 400 pixels

  'Define the format of statictext controls displayed on the window
  statictext #play.statictext1, "B A S I C   B L A C K J A C K", _
     12, 20, 440, 30
  statictext #play.statictext2, "Copyright 2015", 310, 60, 80, 20
  statictext #play.statictext3, "Player's Hand", 50, 110, 70, 20
  statictext #play.statictext4, "Dealer's Hand", 270, 110, 70, 20

  'Define textbox control that will be used to display data
  textbox #play.textbox1, 50, 140, 70, 50
  textbox #play.textbox2, 270, 140, 70, 50
  textbox #play.textbox3, 50, 280, 290, 50

  'Add button controls to the window
  button #play.button1 "Hit Me!", DealCard, UL, 30, 210, 50, 30
  button #play.button2 "Stay!", DealerTurn, UL, 90, 210, 50, 30
  button #play.button3 "Play Again", RestartGame, UL, 270, 210, 70, 30
```

```
'Open the window with no frame and a handle of #play
open "BASIC BlackJack" for window_nf as #play

'Set up the trapclose event for the window
print #play, "trapclose ClosePlay"

Call DealOpeningHand  'Call the subroutine that deals the player's and
                        'dealer's initial hands

'Set the font type, size, and attributes
print #play.statictext1, "!font Arial 16 bold"
print #play.textbox1, "!font Arial 24 bold"
print #play.textbox2, "!font Arial 24 bold"
print #play.textbox3, "!font Arial 18 bold"

print #play.button1, "!setfocus";  'Set focus to the Hit Me button
print #play.button3, "!disable"    'Disable the Play Again button

'Pause the application and wait for the player's instruction
wait

end sub
```

The first two statements specify the window's dimensions. Then a series of statictext, textbox, and button controls are added to the window. Each of the button controls calls on a different subroutine as its event handler. The Hit Me button calls on the DealCard subroutine, which adds another card to the player's hand when executed. The Stay button calls on the DealerTurn subroutine, which is responsible for managing the dealer's hand. The Play Again button calls on the RestartGame subroutine, which resets the game board and resets the game's variables, readying the game to play a new hand.

The open command is used next to display the window, which is assigned a handle of #play. Next, the window's trapclose event handler is set up to call on the ClosePlay subroutine whenever the player attempts to close the #play window. The DealOpeningHand subroutine is then called. This subroutine sets font type, size, and attributes for various interface controls. Lastly, the Hit Me button is assigned focus, and the Play Again button is disabled and will stay that way until the end of the current hand.

Creating the DealCard Subroutine

The code statements that make up the DealCard subroutine are provided next and should be added to the end of the program file. This subroutine is responsible for adding a new card to the player's hand when called. This is accomplished by calling on the GetRandomNumber function and adding the number that is returned to the current value assigned to the playerCard variable:

```
'This subroutine is called when the player clicks on the Hit Me button
sub DealCard handle$

  'Add another card to the player's hand
  playerCard = playerCard + GetRandomNumber()

  'The player busts if his hand exceeds 21
  if playerCard > 21 then
     print #play.textbox1, playerCard          'Display the player's card
     print #play.textbox3, "You have busted!"  'Display a summary of the
                                               'results

     print #play.button1, "!disable"    'Disable the Hit Me button
     print #play.button2, "!disable"    'Disable the Stay button
     print #play.button3, "!enable"     'Enable the Play Again button

  else
     print #play.textbox1, playerCard   'Display the player's card
  end if

end sub
```

Next, an if…then…else statement is set up to analyze the value of the player's hand. If it is over 21, the player has gone bust, losing the game. If this is the case, the value of the player's hand is updated, a message is displayed explaining what has happened, and the Hit Me and Stay buttons are disabled while the Play Again button is enabled. This prevents the player from doing anything else at this point other than starting a new game. If, however, the player's hand is less than 21, all that happens is that the display of the player's score is updated.

Creating the DealerTurn Subroutine

The code statements that make up the DealerTurn subroutine are shown next and should be added to the end of the program file:

```
'This subroutine manages the dealer's turn
sub DealerTurn handle$
```

```
print #play.button1, "!disable"     'Disable the Hit Me button
print #play.button2, "!disable"     'Disable the Stay button
print #play.button3, "!enable"      'Enable the Play Again button

do

   'Add another card to the dealer's hand
   dealerCard = dealerCard + GetRandomNumber()

   print #play.textbox2, dealerCard 'Display the player's card

   'The dealer busts if its hand exceeds 21
   if dealerCard > 21 then

       print #play.textbox3, "The dealer busts!" 'Display a summary of the
                                                 'results

       exit sub  'Exit out of the subroutine

   end if

loop while dealerCard < 17  'Keep looping as long as the dealer's hand
                            'is less than 17

'Analyze the results of the game once both the player and dealer have
'rested
if playerCard = dealerCard then  'Check for a tie
  print #play.textbox3, "Tie!"
end if

if playerCard < dealerCard then  'See if the dealer has won
  print #play.textbox3, "You lose!"
end if

if playerCard > dealerCard then  'See if the player has won
  print #play.textbox3, "You win!"
end if

end sub
```

This subroutine begins by disabling the Hit Me and Stay buttons and enabling the Play Again button. Next, a do...while loop is set up. This loop is responsible for adding new cards to the dealer's hand, stopping only when the value of the dealer's hand (the value assigned to the dealerCard variable) exceeds 17. New cards are added to the dealer's hand by calling on the GetRandomNumber() function and adding the value that is returned to dealerCard. The display of the dealer's hand is then updated. Each time the loop repeats, the value of dealerCard is checked to see if it exceeds 21, in which case the dealer has busted. Note that if the dealer has busted, the exit sub command is executed, immediately terminating the execution of the DealerTurn subroutine. If the do...while loop ends without the dealer going bust, three if...then statements are executed. These statements compare the player's and the dealer's hands to determine the result of the game.

Creating the RestartGame Subroutine

The RestartGame subroutine is shown next. When called, this subroutine calls on the ResetGame subroutine and enables the Hit Me and Stay buttons, allowing the player to begin adding new cards to her hand or to elect to hold onto her current hand. The last statement in this subroutine calls on the DealOpeningHand subroutine, which deals an initial card for the player and the dealer.

```
'This subroutine gets the game ready to play a new hand
sub RestartGame handle$

  call ResetGame   'call on the subroutine that resets the game

  print #play.button1, "!enable"     'Enable the Hit Me button
  print #play.button2, "!enable"     'Enable the Stay button
  print #play.button3, "!disable"    'Disable the Play Again button

  call DealOpeningHand   'Call on the subroutine that deals the player's
                         'and dealer's opening hands

end sub
```

Creating the DealOpeningHand Subroutine

The code statements that make up the DealOpeningHand subroutine are shown next and should be added to the end of the program file:

```
'This subroutine deals the player's and dealer's opening hands
sub DealOpeningHand

  playerCard = GetRandomNumber()   'Retrieve  the player's first card
  dealerCard = GetRandomNumber()   'Retrieve the dealer's first card
```

```
   print #play.textbox1, playerCard   'Display the player's card
   print #play.textbox2, dealerCard   'Display the dealer's card

end sub
```

The first statement adds a card to the player's and computer's hands by assigning the value returned by the GetRandomNumber() function. Two print statements then update the display of the player's and the computer's hands.

Creating the GetRandomNumber Function

The GetRandomNumber() function, shown next, is responsible for generating a numeric value and returning it to the statement that called upon the function:

```
'This function generates and returns cards
function GetRandomNumber()

  RandomNumber = int(rnd(1)*13) + 1   'Retrieve a number between 1 and 13

  if RandomNumber = 1 then RandomNumber = 11   'A 1 is converted to 11 (ace)
  if RandomNumber > 10 then RandomNumber = 10  '11, 12, and 13 are equivalent
                                               'to jacks, queens, and kings,
                                               'which have a value of 10

  GetRandomNumber = RandomNumber     'Return the selected card

end function
```

As you can see, random numbers are generated in the range of 1 to 13. If a value of 1 is generated, it is considered to be an ace, and a value of 11 is returned in its place. Any number greater than 10 represents a face card (jack, queen, or king), and a value of 10 is returned. Any other value (2–10) is returned without modification or replacement.

Creating the ResetGame Subroutine

The code statements that make up the ResetGame subroutine are shown next and should be added to the end of the program file. When called, this subroutine resets the value of dealerCard and playerCard back to zero and clears out any numbers or text displayed in the game's textbox controls, readying the game to play a new hand:

```
'This subroutine resets the player's and dealer's hands and clears out
'the game board
sub ResetGame
```

```
dealerCard = 0   'Reset the dealer's hand to zero
playerCard = 0   'Reset the player's hand to zero

'Clear out the textbox controls on the game board
print #play.textbox1, ""
print #play.textbox2, ""
print #play.textbox3, ""

end sub
```

Creating the ClosePlay Subroutine

The last procedure to be added to the BASIC BlackJack game is the ClosePlay subroutine, whose code statements are shown next. This subroutine is called when the #play window's trapclose event handler is executed:

```
'This subroutine is called when the player closes the #play window
'and is responsible for ending the game
sub ClosePlay handle$

  'Get confirmation before terminating program execution
  confirm "Are you sure you want to quit?"; answer$

  if answer$ = "yes" then  'The player clicked on Yes

    close #play  'Close the #play window

    end   'Terminate the game

  end if

end sub
```

When called, this subroutine uses the confirm command to display a pop-up window that requires the player to reconfirm her intention to terminate the game. If the player responds by clicking on the Yes button, the close command is executed, followed by the end command.

The Final Result

Okay, you have seen all the steps involved in the creation of the BASIC BlackJack game. Assuming that you didn't make any typos or miss keying in any statement, the game should be ready to run. So put it through its paces and see how well you fare when playing against the computer.

Summary

In this chapter, you learned how to work with subroutines and functions. This included defining them and setting them up to process arguments. You discovered how to create functions that could return a result. In addition, you read about variable scope within subroutines and functions. Using this information, you will be able to develop applications whose source code is better organized and more manageable.

Before moving on to Chapter 8, "Working with Text Files," take a little extra time to work on the BASIC BlackJack game by addressing the following list of challenges.

Challenges

1. The BASIC BlackJack game's splash screen currently displays the game's name and a copyright statement. It also displays two graphics images of playing cards. However, to truly leverage the usefulness of the splash screen, you should consider displaying additional information on it. For example, you might want to display the URL of your website.

2. Consider tracking the number of games won, lost, and tied. Also, think about making this information available to the player by displaying it either on the main window as the game is played or in a separate window that the user can open at her discretion.

3. Consider making the game a little more exciting by giving the player an arbitrary amount of money when the game is started, say $10, and adding or subtracting a dollar from this amount for each game won or lost. You would want to terminate the game if the player goes broke.

8

Working with Text Files

Like most other programming languages, Just BASIC allows programmers to interact with the computer's file system, creating and deleting files and folders. It can also be used to build applications that can create and work with external files. As such, it gives you the ability to create reports, documents, and log files. In addition to teaching you the basics of working with files and folders, this chapter will show you how to create your next application project: the Tic Tac Toe game.

Specifically, you will learn the following:

- How to indicate absolute and relative path and filenames
- How to open and close files
- How to read from and write to text files
- How to perform file administration tasks

Project Preview: The Tic Tac Toe Game

In this chapter, you will learn how to create a new computerized Tic Tac Toe game. Individual game board squares will be represented by bmpbutton controls because they are well suited to this task. Using each bmpbutton control's click event, the game will be able to respond to player clicks and then display bitmap images (of Xs and Os) representing each player's move.

In total, nine bmpbutton controls will be used and will be lined up in three consecutive rows. Figure 8.1 shows how these controls will appear when the game is started.

Initially a blank (all white) bitmap image is loaded onto each bmpbutton control to represent an unselected game board square. As Figure 8.2 demonstrates, as gameplay continues, bitmap images representing Xs and Os are displayed on bmpbutton controls as Player X and Player O select them.

Figure 8.1 Player X starts each game by clicking on one of the available game board squares.
© 2016 Cengage Learning®

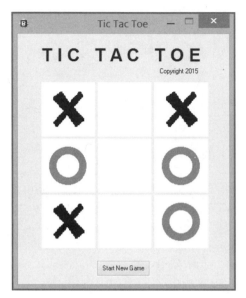

Figure 8.2 Player X and Player O alternate turns when selecting squares.
© 2016 Cengage Learning®

Players are only allowed to choose from unselected squares. If a player attempts to select a square that has already been chosen, the pop-up dialog shown in Figure 8.3 is displayed, informing the player of her mistake.

Gameplay continues until one of the players wins or until all nine game board squares have been selected without either player having won. At the end of each game, a pop-up dialog is displayed that informs the players of the result. For example, Figure 8.4 shows the pop-up dialog that is displayed when Player X wins.

After dismissing the pop-up dialog showing the results of the game, the game board continues to display the results of the previous game, as demonstrated in Figure 8.5. At this point, the players can click on the Start New Game button to play another round, or they can click on the close button (X) located in the upper-right corner of the window to terminate the game.

Figure 8.3 Any attempt to click on a square that has already been selected results in an error.
© 2016 Cengage Learning®

Figure 8.4 At the conclusion of each round of play, a pop-up dialog is displayed announcing the result.
© 2016 Cengage Learning®

Figure 8.5 Player X has won by lining up three squares diagonally.
© 2016 Cengage Learning®

Working with Files and Folders

Some programming languages such as JavaScript have limited execution environments. In the case of JavaScript, this means that it can only be used to create scripts that run within web browsers. As a result, these programming languages cannot interface with the Windows file system and thus cannot be used to create text files or reports. However, desktop programming languages like Visual Basic, C++, and Just BASIC do not have this restriction.

> ### Hint
>
> Today, many programming languages have been expanded to the point at which they are capable of developing applications that can be run on many different platforms. One of the best examples of this is Visual Basic, which can be used to create desktop applications as well as web-based applications. Visual Basic also supports application development on a range of portable devices, including PDAs and cell phones.

In this chapter, you will learn how to create Just BASIC applications that are capable of interacting with the Windows file system. The programming techniques presented here, although specific to Just BASIC, can be generally applied to other programming languages and will give you a solid understanding of the basic steps involved in developing applications that interact with the Windows file system.

Retrieving Drive Information

To work with files and folders, you must understand how to interact with the Windows file system, which consists of one or more disk drives represented by a letter followed by a colon. For example, C: is the standard designation for a computer's primary disk drive. Many computers today have more than one drive. With Just BASIC, you can retrieve a string representing all the drives available on a computer using the Drives$ special variable. For example, the following statement uses the print command to display the value of Drives$:

```
print Drives$
```

When it's executed, output similar to the following is displayed:

```
c: d: e: f:
```

As you can see, the computer on which this example was executed contains four drives. Using the Drives$ special variable you could, as the following example demonstrates, populate a combobox (or a listbox) control with a list of all the drives available on a computer and then allow the user to select one:

```
nomainwin

global selection$
dim mydrives$(10)

call GenerateDriveList
call DisplayWindow

wait
```

```
sub GenerateDriveList

  i = 0
  do
    mydrives$(i) = word$(Drives$, i + 1)
    i = i + 1
  loop until word$(Drives$, i + 1) = ""

end sub

sub DisplayWindow

  combobox #main.combobox, mydrives$(), DisplaySelection, 100, 100, 100, 100
  open "Select Drive" for window_nf as #main
  wait

end sub

sub DisplaySelection handle$

  print #main.combobox, "contents? selection$"
  notice "You picked " + selection$
  close #main
  end

end sub
```

In this example, an array named mydrives$ is defined that is capable of storing up to 11 elements. Next, a subroutine called GenerateDriveList is called. This subroutine uses a do...until loop to iterate through the list of drives stored in the Drives$ special variable to populate the mydrives$() array.

Hint

Note the use of the word$() function in the GenerateDriveList subroutine. This function returns a specified word from a string based on the word's position in the string and has the following syntax:

word$(*string*, *i* [,*delimiter*])

string represents the string that is parsed. The variable *i* is used to keep track of each word in the string. *delimiter* is optional; when used, it specifies the character in the string that is used to delimit words. If *delimiter* is omitted, blank spaces are used as delimiters.

Once the `GenerateDriveList` subroutine is done, the `DisplayWindow` subroutine is called. This subroutine displays a window that contains a combobox control. The combobox control has been set up to display the contents of the `mydrives$()` array. In addition, the combobox control has been set up to execute the program's remaining subroutine, `DisplaySelection`. When called, this subroutine retrieves the drive letter that the user has selected from the combobox control and displays it.

Retrieving Information About the Current Working Directory

In Just BASIC, if you specify a filename without also providing path information, Just BASIC looks to the special variable `DefaultDir$` to determine which folder to look in to find the file. By default, `DefaultDir$` contains a text string identifying the absolute path and name of the folder where the Just BASIC application being executed resides. For example, suppose you created a new Just BASIC program named `text1.bas` that contains the following statement:

```
print DefaultDir$
```

If you save this program in `C:\Basic\Just BASIC v1.01` and then execute it, the following output is displayed:

```
c:\Basic\Just BASIC v1.01
```

Collecting Data About Files and Folders

Programmers can use the `files` command to retrieve information about files and folders. To use this statement, you must first create a two-dimensional array, which you will use to store the data returned by the `files` command, as demonstrated here:

```
dim folderInfo$(3, 3)
files "C:\temp", folderInfo$()
```

Here, a two-dimensional array named `folderInfo$()` has been defined that can store up to four pairs of entries. Next, the `files` command is executed and passed two arguments. The first argument is the path of the folder for which information is to be retrieved. The second argument is the name of the array that will be used to store this information. Once the command is executed, you can retrieve information about the specified folder by examining the information that has been stored in the array, as demonstrated here:

```
print "Files: " + folderInfo$(0, 0) 'Retrieves the number of files
print "Folders: " + folderInfo$(0, 1) 'Retrieves the number of folders
print "Drive: " + folderInfo$(0, 2) 'Retrieves the drive
print "Path: " + folderInfo$(0, 3) 'Retrieves the path
```

Hint

As was discussed back in Chapter 4, "Working with Variables and Arrays," a one-dimensional array is an indexed list of values. A two-dimensional array is like a table or a spreadsheet, made up of rows and columns. When using the `files` command to retrieve information about a folder, you retrieve the information from the first column of the array, which has an index value of 0. Because data is retrieved from a two-dimensional array by specifying a pair of numbers, when retrieving folder data, you always use 0 as the first number when specifying array coordinates. Thus, the value representing the number of files found in a folder is located at (0,0), whereas the number of subfolders found in the folder is found at (0,1). File information, on the other hand, is stored in the second column of the array and thus is retrieved by specifying a value of 1 as the first coordinate. For example, the name of the file is stored at coordinates (1,0), and the size of the file is found at (1,1).

When executed, these statements generate output similar to the following:

```
Files: 2
Folders: 2
Drive: c:\
Path: temp\
```

You can just as easily use the `files` command to collect information about individual files, as demonstrated here:

```
dim fileInfo$(2, 2)
files "C:\temp\", "Application.log", fileInfo$()

print "File name: " + fileInfo$(1, 0) 'Retrieves the file's name
print "File size: " + fileInfo$(1, 1) 'Retrieves the file's size
print "Date/time: " + fileInfo$(1, 2) 'Retrieves the file's date and time
```

Here, the `files` command has been used to retrieve information about a file named `Application.log` stored in `C:\temp`. The data retrieved from the command is stored in the `fileInfo$()` array and then displayed using a series of `print` commands.

Trick

You can also use wildcard characters when specifying filenames for the `files` command. For example, you can use the `?` wildcard character to substitute any single character, whereas you can use the `*` wildcard character to substitute any number of characters. To better understand what all this means, take a look at the following example:

```
dim fileInfo$(2, 2)
files "C:\temp\", "*.log", fileInfo$()

for i = 1 to val(fileInfo$(0, 0))
    print "File name: " +fileInfo$(i, 0)
next i
```

Here, the `*` wildcard character has been used to tell the `files` command to add information about every file found in the `C:\temp` folder that has a `.log` file extension. A string showing the number of files found will be stored in `fileInfo$(0, 0)`. You can convert this to a numeric value using the `val()` function. As such, you can use it to control the execution of a for...next loop that iterates through all the output stored in the `fileInfo$()` array, displaying output similar to that shown here:

```
File name: Application.log
File name: Error.log
File name: System.log
```

As you can see, three files with a `.log` file extension were found in `C:\temp`.

Ensuring That Files Exist

If you write a program that needs to work with a specific file and that file is not present when the program attempts to access it, an error occurs. To avoid this problem, you can use the `files` command to determine whether the file exists. If it does, your program can go ahead and open it. If the file does not exist, your program could create and then open it. To see how you might do this, take a look at the following example:

```
dim fileInfo$(0, 0)
files "C:\temp\", "Application.log", fileInfo$()

if val(fileInfo$(0, 0)) = 0 then
  print "File not found!"
end if
```

Here, an array named `fileInfo$()` has been defined to hold a single pair of items. The `files` command is then executed. Next, an `if…then` statement has been set up to examine `fileInfo$(0, 0)`. If a value of 0 is found, the file does not exist. At this point, you can insert additional programming statements to handle the situation as appropriate.

Specifying Absolute File and Path Names

Like most programming languages, Just BASIC allows you to specify the location of files and folders using either absolute or relative paths. An *absolute path* is one that specifies the complete path to a file or folder, including the drive specification and any folders included in the path between the drive specification and the target file or folder. For example, the following statement specifies the absolute path of the `temp` folder (`C:\temp`):

```
dim fileInfo$(0, 0)
files "C:\temp\", "Application.log", fileInfo$()
```

Use of absolute path when specifying file and folder names is convenient when you can count on the location of the files and folders being where you expect them to be, which is the case on your own desktop computer. This might also be the case in a tightly controlled corporate environment where desktop computers are controlled and monitored by a central desktop support team. However, often you cannot count on knowing the exact location of a file of folder. For example, if you create a distribution package for one of your Just BASIC games and share it with your friends, there is no guaranteeing that they will install the game in the location you expect when they set it up on their computer. In these types of situations, using relative path names is usually the better way to go.

Specifying Relative Path Names

With relative paths, you identify the location of a file or folder relative to the location of the current working directory (folder). For example, if you have created an application that works with a text file that is located within the same location as the application itself, you can specify its name and location as demonstrated here:

```
open "CustomerData.txt" for input as #1
```

Because your Just BASIC program and the text file reside in the same folder, it is not necessary to specify the absolute path of the text. Instead, by simply specifying the name of the text file, Just BASIC knows to look in the current working directory.

Now let's suppose that when your application is installed, your installation package automatically adds a number of files and folders to the computer. Using relative paths, you can navigate backward and forward within this file structure. For example, consider the following statement:

```
open "inventory\PartsList.txt" for input as #1
```

Here, the open command has been instructed to look in a subfolder of the current working directory named inventory and to open a file named PartsList.txt. Using relative paths, you can also navigate your way backward, as demonstrated here:

```
open "..\SystemCodes.txt" for input as #1
```

Here, using the .. characters, the open command has been instructed to look in the parent folder of the current working directory for a file named SystemCodes.txt. If necessary, you can go backward an additional level, as demonstrated here:

```
open "..\..\Accounting.txt" for input as #1
```

Here, the open command has been instructed to go back to the parent folder of the parent folder of the current working directory and open a file named Accounting.txt. You can get as creative as necessary using relative paths to specify the location of a file:

```
open "..\..\..\books\ISBNS.txt" for input as #1
```

Here, the open command has been told to back up three levels from the current working directory and then to go forward one level into a folder named books to find and open a file named ISBNS.txt.

Using the filedialog Window to Allow the User to Select a File

You can use the filedialog command to display a dialog window that allows the user to select a file using a standard Windows Explorer dialog window. The dialog window will return a string representing the absolute path and filename of the file the user selects. For example, take a look at the following statement:

```
filedialog "Open a File", "C:\temp\*.txt", selectedFile$
```

Here, a filedialog window is opened and configured to display a list of all text files located in the C:\temp folder, as demonstrated in Figure 8.6.

In this example, a string representing the absolute file and path name of the file selected by the user is then captured and stored in a variable name selectedFile$.

> **Note**
>
> You can find more information on how to work with the filedialog command in Chapter 3, "Creating Graphical User Interfaces."

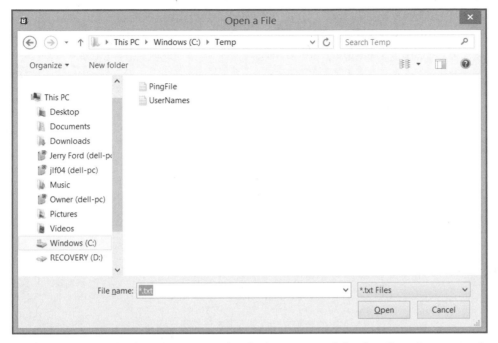

Figure 8.6 Using the filedialog command to display a pop-up dialog that allows the user to select a file.
© 2016 Shoptalk Systems

Working with Files

Just BASIC allows programmers to store data in and read it back from different types of files, including sequential, binary, and random access files. In this chapter, you will learn the basic steps involved in storing and retrieving data in sequential files.

Hint

A *sequential file* is one that contains plain text. Sequential files are processed sequentially, from beginning to end. A *binary file* is one that contains more than plain text. Binary files are capable of storing graphics files, sound files, and more. A *random access file* is one that can be read from or written to at any location within the file. To learn more about how to work with binary and random access files, consult Just BASIC's help system.

Opening Files

To work with a sequential file, you must first open it. In Just BASIC, files are opened using the open command, which has the following syntax:

```
open resource for purpose as #handle [len = n]
```

The open command is an extremely powerful and flexible command that can perform a number of different actions, including opening files, windows, and serial communications. With respect to opening files, *resource* identifies the file to be opened, and the *purpose* is input. The last parameter, *[len = n]*, is used only when working with random access files.

As an example of how to use the open command, take a look at the following example:

```
open "C:\temp\Sample.txt" for input as #targetFile
```

Here, the open command has been set up to open a file named Sample.txt located in C:\temp. Once it's opened, the file can be referenced within the program as #targetFile.

Hint

Remember, it is always a good idea to first check whether a file exists before trying to open it.

Closing Files

Any file that is opened should be closed when the program is finished working with it. You accomplish this using the close command, which has the following syntax:

```
close #reference
```

#reference is the handle assigned to the file when it was opened using the open command. To avoid errors, it is critical that you always remember to close a file previously opened by your application, as demonstrated in the following example:

```
open "C:\temp\Sample.txt" for input as #targetFile
'Add statements here that process the contents of the file
close #targetFile
```

If you forget to close a previously opened file, an error is generated when you try to terminate the execution of your program, as demonstrated in Figure 8.7.

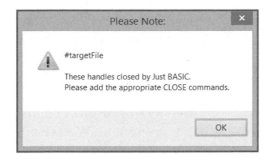

Figure 8.7 Errors result when a program is stopped while files remain open.
© 2016 Shoptalk Systems

Reading from Files

Once you have opened a text file, you can read from it and write to it. Just BASIC processes text files sequentially, starting at the beginning of the file and moving to its end. You cannot open a text file and begin reading it anywhere other than at the beginning. To read from a text file, you can use the input and line input commands.

The input command reads from the text file, stopping at the first comma or carriage return that it finds. A subsequent input command resumes reading where the previous command stopped, terminating at the first comma or carriage return that it runs into. When used to read from a text file, the input command has the following syntax:

```
input #handle, variableName
```

#handle is the reference previously set up for the file by the open command, and variableName is the name of a variable into which the contents of the text file are to be copied. For example, the following statements open a file named Sample.txt and read the first line from it (assuming that the first line does not have a comma in it):

```
open "C:\temp\Sample.txt" for input as #targetFile
input #targetFile, variableName$
print variableName$
close #targetFile
```

Once the input command has been used to read the first line and store its contents, the print command is used to display what was read in the default mainwin window.

Using the line input command, you can read from a file a line at a time, ignoring any commas that may be found along the way. The syntax of the line input command is shown here:

```
line input #handle, variablename
```

To get a better feel for how this command works, suppose you have a text file named Story.txt that contains the text shown in Figure 8.8.

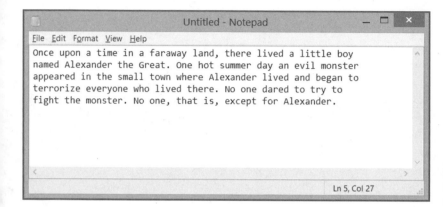

Figure 8.8 An example of a small text file.

© 2016 Cengage Learning®

Using the line input command within a loop, you can create a program that reads through and processes every line in the text file, as demonstrated here:

```
nomainwin

WindowWidth = 360
WindowHeight = 300

texteditor #main.texteditor1, 10, 10, 335, 230

open "Story" for window_nf as #main

call DisplayStory

wait

sub DisplayStory

    open "C:\temp\Story.txt" for input as #targetFile
```

```
while eof(#targetFile) = 0
    line input #targetFile, variableName$
    print #main.texteditor1, variableName$
wend

close #targetFile
```

```
end sub
```

As you can see, this example starts by displaying a small application window that contains a text-editor control. The texteditor control has been sized so that it fills up most of the window. A call is then made to a subroutine named DisplayStory, which uses a while...wend loop and the line input command to copy the contents of the text file into the texteditor control. When it's executed, the contents of the text file are visible to the user, as demonstrated in Figure 8.9.

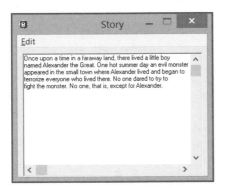

Figure 8.9 Using a text file to populate the contents of a texteditor control.
© 2016 Cengage Learning®

Trick

To read a file a line at a time from beginning to end as demonstrated earlier, you need to use the eof() function. You use this function to determine when the end of the file that is being read has been reached. If the end of the file is not reached, the function returns a value of –1. When the end of the file has been reached, the function returns a value of 0.

Writing to Files

Writing to a text file is just about as easy as reading from one. Just BASIC gives you two options for doing so, as outlined here:

- **output.** Opens a new file and writes to the beginning of it.
- **append.** Opens an existing file and writes to the end of it.

Creating and Writing to New Files

To create a new file and write to it, you need to open the file for output, as demonstrated here:

```
open "C:\temp\Story.txt" for output as #targetFile
```

When you open a file in this manner, any text written to the file starts at the beginning of the file. Once you have opened the file in for output mode, text is written to the file using print commands. If a file of the same name already exists, it is replaced by a new empty file to which text is then written. It is a good idea to first check whether the file that you want to write to already exists. If this is the case and you want to preserve any text that may have already been written to the file, you will want to instead open the file for append, as discussed in the next section.

To get a good feel for how to write output to a file, take a look at the following example:

```
open "C:\temp\Story.txt" for output as #x

print #x, "Once upon a time in a faraway land, there lived a little boy"
print #x, "named Alexander the Great. One hot summer day an evil monster"
print #x, "appeared in the small town where Alexander lived and began to"
print #x, "terrorize everyone who lived there. No one dared to try to"
print #x, "fight the monster. No one, that is, except for Alexander."

close #x
```

As with the reading of files, any file opened for writing must be closed to prevent an error from occurring. As each line of output is written to the file, Just BASIC automatically adds a carriage return to the end of the line. When executed, this example creates the Story.txt file that you worked with earlier in the chapter when learning how to read from text files.

Appending Text to the End of an Existing File

As was alluded to in the previous section, you can open a file in for append mode to preserve its current contents. Once opened in this manner, any print statements that write output to the file are added to the end of the file instead of to the beginning of it, as demonstrated in the following example:

```
open "C:\temp\Story.txt" for append as #x
print #x, ""
print #x, "The End"
close #x
```

When executed, this example opens the Story.txt file that you created previously and adds a blank line followed by a second line that reads The End to the end of the text file.

File and Folder Administration

You have already learned how to create and write to new files. Just BASIC also gives you a number of commands that you can use to interact with and control the Windows file system. Using these commands, you can rename and delete files. You can also create and delete folders.

Renaming Files

To rename a file, use the name command, which has the following syntax:

```
name CurrentName as NewName
```

CurrentName is the name of the file that you want to rename. *NewName* is the new filename. For example, you could use the following statement to rename a file named mini-parts.txt located in the current working directory to small-parts.txt:

```
name "mini-parts.txt" as "small-parts.txt"
```

Trap

Be careful not to assign the file a name the same as another file. Otherwise, you'll get an error.

Deleting Files

Provided that you have the appropriate security permissions, you can use the kill command to delete a file from the computer. The kill command has the following syntax:

```
kill FileName
```

FileName is the name of the file to be removed. For example, you can use the following statement to delete a file named small-parts.txt from the current working directory:

```
kill small-parts.txt
```

Trap

Be careful when working with the kill command. Once you've executed that command, you cannot reverse its effects. The file is permanently deleted from the computer; you will not find a copy of it in the Recycle Bin.

Creating New Folders

In addition to creating new files, Just BASIC lets you programmatically create new folders. This is achieved through the mkdir() function, which has the following syntax:

```
mkdir("FolderName")
```

FolderName is a text string that specifies the name and path of the folder to be created. For example, the following statement creates a new folder named WorkPapers in the C:\Temp folder:

```
result = mkdir("C:\Temp\WorkPapers")

if result <> 0 then
  notice "Something went wrong. C:\temp\WorkPapers was not created."
end if
```

When executed, the mkdir() function returns a numeric value indicating the success or failure of its operation. A value of zero indicates that the folder was successfully created. A nonzero value indicates that an error occurred and the folder was not created, which would be the case if a folder of the same name already existed at the specified location.

Deleting Folders

Just BASIC also lets you delete empty folders using the rmdir() function. If the delete operation is successful, the function returns a value of zero. The rmdir() function has the following syntax:

```
rmdir("FolderName")
```

Using this command, you can programmatically delete any folder from the computer for which you have the appropriate set of security permissions, as demonstrated here:

```
result = rmdir("C:\temp\WorkPapers")

if result <> 0 then
  notice "Something went wrong. C:\temp\WorkPapers was not deleted."
end if
```

In this example, the WorkPapers folder is deleted from the C:\temp folder if it is found and if it is empty. It the folder is not found or if the folder is not empty, an error occurs.

Trap

Be careful when working with the rmdir() function. Once you've executed it, you cannot reverse its effects. The folder is permanently deleted from the computer; you will not find a copy of it in the Recycle Bin.

Back to the Tic Tac Toe Game

Okay, it is time to turn your attention back to the development of this chapter's game project. In developing this application, you will gain experience working with the bmpbutton control. You will use it to display different bitmap images. Specifically, this application will display various combinations of the three graphics bitmap images shown in Figure 8.10 as the players play the game. You can download copies of all three of these files from this book's companion website at www.cengageptr.com/downloads.

Figure 8.10 Copies of the three bitmap images used to represent available game board squares as well as squares selected by Player X and Player Y.
© 2016 Cengage Learning®

Designing the Game

The design of the Tic Tac Toe game will rely on the use of subroutines. In total, you will create the Tic Tac Toe game in eight steps, as outlined here:

1. Create a new BASIC file and add initial comment statements.
2. Define global variables and start the gameplay.
3. Create the `ManageGamePlay` subroutine.
4. Create the `ProcessMove` subroutine.
5. Create the `SwitchPlayerTurn` subroutine.
6. Create the `LookForEndOfGame` subroutine.
7. Create the `ResetGameBoard` subroutine.
8. Create the `ClosePlay` subroutine.

Creating a Just BASIC File Script

The first step is to create a new BASIC file. After creating the program file, add the following statements to it:

```
'  ************************************************************************

'

'  Script Name: TicTacToe.bas (The Tic Tac Toe Game)
'  Version:      1.0
'  Author:       Jerry Lee Ford, Jr.
'  Date:         January 31, 2015
'
```

```
' Description: This game is a Just BASIC implementation of the classic
'              children's Tic Tac Toe game. This game pits two players
'              against one another to see who can line up three
'              consecutive characters in a row.
'
' *********************************************************************

nomainwin    'Suppress the display of the default text window
```

The first 13 lines are introductory comment statements that help to document the program and its purpose. The last statement executes the nomainwin command to prevent the mainwin window from being displayed when the application is started.

Defining Global Variables and Initiating Gameplay

The next step in the development of the Tic Tac Toe game is to define the game's global variables and to call upon the subroutine that displays the game board window. This is accomplished by adding the following statements to the end of the program file:

```
'Assign default values to global variables
global currentPlayer$, noMoves
global a1$, a2$, a3$, b1$, b2$, b3$, c1$, c2$, c3$

currentPlayer$ = "X"   'Player X always starts off each game

call ManageGamePlay 'Call the subroutine responsible for managing gameplay

wait   'Pause the application and wait for the player's instruction
```

In this version of Tic Tac Toe, Player X starts each new game by going first. Players take turns making moves. The game keeps track of whose turn it is based on the value assigned to currentPlayer$, which is set to "X" at the beginning of each new game.

The game board will consist of nine bmpbutton controls named A1, A2, A3, B1, B2, B3, C1, C2, and C3. As players take turns selecting game board squares, a graphic is displayed on each bmpbutton identifying when it has been selected and which player has selected it. The game keeps track of the status of each game board square (bmpbutton) by assigning a value of "X" or "O" to variables named a1$, a2$, a3$, b1$, b2$, b3$, c1$, c2$, and c3$. Part of knowing when a game has ended is knowing how many moves the players have made, which is tracked using the noMoves variable. Finally, gameplay is started by calling the ManageGamePlay subroutine.

Displaying the Game Board

The Tic Tac Toe game consists of a single window, which displays the game board. The ManageGamePlay subroutine, shown next, is responsible for creating and displaying the game's main window (#play). You should add these statements to the end of the program file:

```
'This subroutine displays the game board and controls interaction with the
'player
sub ManageGamePlay

  WindowWidth = 400    'Set the width of the window to 400 pixels
  WindowHeight = 500   'Set the height of the window to 500 pixels

  loadbmp "_", "C:\images\_.bmp"    'Load the specified bitmap
                                    'file into memory
  loadbmp "O", "C:\images\o.bmp"    'Load the specified bitmap
                                    'file into memory
  loadbmp "X", "C:\images\x.bmp"    'Load the specified bitmap
                                    'file into memory

  'Define the format of statictext controls displayed on the window
  statictext #play.statictext1, "T I C   T A C   T O E", 45, 20, 440, 35
  statictext #play.statictext2, "Copyright 2015", 265, 62, 80, 20

  'Add nine bmpbutton controls representing the game board to the window

  'First row
  bmpbutton #play.a1, "C:\images\_.bmp", ProcessMove, UL, 45, 90
  bmpbutton #play.a2, "C:\images\_.bmp", ProcessMove, UL, 150, 90
  bmpbutton #play.a3, "C:\images\_.bmp", ProcessMove, UL, 255, 90

  'Second row
  bmpbutton #play.b1, "C:\images\_.bmp", ProcessMove, UL, 45, 194
  bmpbutton #play.b2, "C:\images\_.bmp", ProcessMove, UL, 150, 194
  bmpbutton #play.b3, "C:\images\_.bmp", ProcessMove, UL, 255, 194

  'Third row
  bmpbutton #play.c1, "C:\images\_.bmp", ProcessMove, UL, 45, 298
  bmpbutton #play.c2, "C:\images\_.bmp", ProcessMove, UL, 150, 298
  bmpbutton #play.c3, "C:\images\_.bmp", ProcessMove, UL, 255, 298
```

```
'Add the game's button control to the window
button #play.button1 "Start New Game", ResetGameBoard, UL, _
    147, 420, 100, 30

'Open the window with no frame and a handle of #play
open "Tic Tac Toe" for window_nf as #play

'Set up the trapclose event for the window
print #play, "trapclose ClosePlay"

'Set the font type, size, and attributes
print #play.statictext1, "!font Arial 20 bold"

print #play.button1, "!setfocus";   'Set focus to the button control

'Pause the application and wait for the player's instruction
wait

end sub
```

The ManageGamePlay subroutine begins by defining the height and width of the game's window and preloading three images, representing Player X, Player Y, and an unselected (blank) game board square. Next, the game defines the controls that make up its user interface. These controls include two statictext controls used to display the game's name and copyright information as well as nine bmpbutton controls, representing each of the game's nine game board squares. The last control to be added to the window is a button control, which allows the players to clear the game board and start a new game at any time during gameplay.

Next, the open statement is used to display the window, and the window's trapclose event handler is defined. The last few statements set the font type, size, and attributes of the statictext control that displays the name of the game and sets focus to the Start New Game button. The wait command is then executed, pausing the game to allow Player X to make the first move.

Processing Player Moves

Players make their moves by clicking on one of the bmpbutton controls. Each bmpbutton control has the ProcessMove subroutine set up as its event handler. The code statements that make up this subroutine are shown next and should be added to the end of the program file:

```
'This subroutine processes player moves, deciding when moves are
'valid and invalid and assigning game board squares accordingly
sub ProcessMove handle$
```

```
'Set up a select case code block to process player moves
select case handle$

    case "#play.a1"  'The player selects the 1st square on the 1st row
       if a1$ = "" then  'Let the player have the square if it's available
          a1$ = currentPlayer$  'Assign the square to the current player
          print #play.a1, "bitmap " + currentPlayer$  'Display bitmap image
       else
          notice "Sorry, but this square is already assigned. Try again!"
          exit sub  'There is no need to keep going, so exit the subroutine
       end if

    case "#play.a2"  'The player selects the 2nd square on the 1st row
       if a2$ = "" then  'Let the player have the square if it's available
          a2$ = currentPlayer$  'Assign the square to the current player
          print #play.a2, "bitmap " + currentPlayer$  'Display bitmap image
       else
          notice "Sorry, but this square is already assigned. Try again!"
          exit sub  'There is no need to keep going, so exit the subroutine
       end if

    case "#play.a3"  'The player selects the 3rd square on the 1st row
       if a3$ = "" then  'Let the player have the square if it's available
          a3$ = currentPlayer$  'Assign the square to the current player
          print #play.a3, "bitmap " + currentPlayer$  'Display bitmap image
       else
          notice "Sorry, but this square is already assigned. Try again!"
          exit sub  'There is no need to keep going, so exit the subroutine
       end if

    case "#play.b1"  'The player selects the 1st square on the 2nd row
       if b1$ = "" then  'Let the player have the square if it's available
          b1$ = currentPlayer$  'Assign the square to the current player
          print #play.b1, "bitmap " + currentPlayer$  'Display bitmap image
       else
          notice "Sorry, but this square is already assigned. Try again!"
          exit sub  'There is no need to keep going, so exit the subroutine
       end if
```

```
case "#play.b2"   'The player selects the 2nd square on the 2nd row
   if b2$ = "" then   'Let the player have the square if it's available
      b2$ = currentPlayer$   'Assign the square to the current player
      print #play.b2, "bitmap " + currentPlayer$   'Display bitmap image
   else
      notice "Sorry, but this square is already assigned. Try again!"
      exit sub   'There is no need to keep going, so exit the subroutine
   end if

case "#play.b3"   'The player selects the 3rd square on the 2nd row
   if b3$ = "" then   'Let the player have the square if it's available
      b3$ = currentPlayer$   'Assign the square to the current player
      print #play.b3, "bitmap " + currentPlayer$   'Display bitmap image
   else
      notice "Sorry, but this square is already assigned. Try again!"
      exit sub   'There is no need to keep going, so exit the subroutine
   end if

case "#play.c1"   'The player selects the 1st square on the 3rd row
   if c1$ = "" then   'Let the player have the square if it's available
      c1$ = currentPlayer$   'Assign the square to the current player
      print #play.c1, "bitmap " + currentPlayer$   'Display bitmap image
   else
      notice "Sorry, but this square is already assigned. Try again!"
      exit sub   'There is no need to keep going, so exit the subroutine
   end if

case "#play.c2"   'The player selects the 2nd square on the 3rd row
   if c2$ = "" then   'Let the player have the square if it's available
      c2$ = currentPlayer$   'Assign the square to the current player
      print #play.c2, "bitmap " + currentPlayer$   'Display bitmap image
   else
      notice "Sorry, but this square is already assigned. Try again!"
      exit sub   'There is no need to keep going, so exit the subroutine
   end if

case "#play.c3"   'The player selects the 3rd square on the 3rd row
   if c3$ = "" then   'Let the player have the square if it's available
      c3$ = currentPlayer$   'Assign the square to the current player
```

```
      print #play.c3, "bitmap " + currentPlayer$   'Display bitmap image
   else
      notice "Sorry, but this square is already assigned. Try again!"
      exit sub   'There is no need to keep going, so exit the subroutine
   end if

end select

noMoves = noMoves + 1   'Increment the variable representing the number of
                        'moves made so far in this game

'Call the subroutine responsible for determining when the game is over
call LookForEndOfGame

'Call the subroutine responsible for controlling whose turn it is
call SwitchPlayerTurn

end sub
```

As you can see, this subroutine mainly consists of a Select Case statement that contains nine case statements, each of which sets up a code block that's designed to process a specific game board square (bmpbutton). The first case statement is set up to execute when one of the players clicks on the bmpbutton control named #play.a1 (when the value of handle$ is equal to "play.a1").

Hint

Remember, a subroutine set up as an event handler is automatically passed an argument, which is a text string that identifies the name of the window or control whose event has triggered the subroutine's execution

---

The first thing that each case statement's code block does when executed is examine the value of its associated global variable, which in the case of #play.a1 is a1$. If a1$ is equal to an empty string(""), then it has not been chosen yet, and the next statement assigns the value of currentPlayer$ (either Player "X" or Player "O") to a1$. Next, the bitmap image associated with the current player is displayed on the bmpbutton control.

Hint

The game's three bitmap images were preloaded into memory earlier in the program file. To display them on a bitmap control, you must use the `print` command to pass a string to the control for processing. This string consists of two parts. The first part is the keyword `bitmap`. The second part of the string is a reference to the file that was established earlier by the `loadbmp` commands to preload each bitmap file (_ represents a blank bitmap file. 0 represents a bitmap file that displays the letter O, and X represents a bitmap file that displays the letter X).

If the value of `a1$` is not equal to an empty string, the game board square has already been assigned to one of the players, and it cannot be reassigned again. The player is then notified of the selection error via a pop-up dialog, and the `exit sub` statement is executed (because no further action needs to be taken when an invalid move is made).

The next eight `case` statement code blocks operate identically to the first `case` statement code block except that each is set up to process the move associated with different game board squares. At the end of the subroutine are a few additional code statements, which are executed only if the player selected an available game board square when making a turn. The first of these statements increments the value of `noMoves` by 1, allowing the games to keep track of the number of valid moves made so far. Next, the `LookForEndOfGame` subroutine is executed. The subroutine scans the game board and determines when either player has won the game by managing to line up three squares in a row. The `SwitchPlayerTurn` subroutine is called next. This subroutine is responsible for controlling when each player gets to take a turn.

Controlling Player Turns

The code statements that make up the `SwitchPlayerTurn` subroutine are shown next and should be added to the end of the program file:

```
'This subroutine is responsible for switching between Player X and
'Player O's turns
sub SwitchPlayerTurn

  'If Player X just went, then it is Player O's turn
  if currentPlayer$ = "X" then
    currentPlayer$ = "O"   'Make Player O the current player
    exit sub   'There is no need to keep going, so exit the subroutine
  end if

  'If Player O just went, then it is Player X's turn
  if currentPlayer$ = "O" then
    currentPlayer$ = "X"   'Make Player X the current player
```

```
      exit sub  'There is no need to keep going, so exit the subroutine
   end if

end sub
```

As you can see, this subroutine consists of two if…then code blocks. The first code block executes if Player X has just completed a turn, assigning a value of "O" to currentPlayer$ and then exiting the subroutine. If, however, Player O just moved, the first code block is skipped and the second if…then code block is executed, assigning "X" to currentPlayer$. Thus, by assigning a string value of "X" or "O" to currentPlayer$, the game is able to keep track of player turns.

Looking for the End of the Game

The code statements for the LookForEndOfGame subroutine are shown next. This subroutine is called at the end of each player's turn to determine if the current player has won the game:

```
'This subroutine is called at the end of each player's turn and is
'responsible for determining if the game is over
sub LookForEndOfGame

   'Look horizontally for a winner

   'Check the first row
   if (a1$ = currentPlayer$) and (a2$ = currentPlayer$) and _
     (a3$ = currentPlayer$) then
     notice "Player " + currentPlayer$ + " has won!"
     exit sub  'There is no need to keep going, so exit the subroutine
   end if

   'Check the second row
   if (b1$ = currentPlayer$) and (b2$ = currentPlayer$) and _
     (b3$ = currentPlayer$) then
     notice "Player " + currentPlayer$ + " has won!"
     exit sub  'There is no need to keep going, so exit the subroutine
   end if

   'Check the third row
   if (c1$ = currentPlayer$) and (c2$ = currentPlayer$) and _
     (c3$ = currentPlayer$) then
     notice "Player " + currentPlayer$ + " has won!"
     exit sub  'There is no need to keep going, so exit the subroutine
   end if
```

```
'Look vertically for a winner

'Check the first column
if (a1$ = currentPlayer$) and (b1$ = currentPlayer$) and _
  (c1$ = currentPlayer$) then
  notice "Player " + currentPlayer$ + " has won!"
  exit sub  'There is no need to keep going, so exit the subroutine
end if

'Check the second column
if (a2$ = currentPlayer$) and (b2$ = currentPlayer$) and _
  (c2$ = currentPlayer$) then
  notice "Player " + currentPlayer$ + " has won!"
  exit sub  'There is no need to keep going, so exit the subroutine
end if

'Check the third column
if (a3$ = currentPlayer$) and (b3$ = currentPlayer$) and _
  (c3$ = currentPlayer$) then
  notice "Player " + currentPlayer$ + " has won!"
  exit sub  'There is no need to keep going, so exit the subroutine
end if

'Look diagonally for a winner

'Check from the top-left corner down to the lower-right corner
if (a1$ = currentPlayer$) and (b2$ = currentPlayer$) and _
  (c3$ = currentPlayer$) then
  notice "Player " + currentPlayer$ + " has won!"
  exit sub  'There is no need to keep going, so exit the subroutine
end if

'Check from the top-right corner down to the lower-left corner
if (a3$ = currentPlayer$) and (b2$ = currentPlayer$) and _
  (c1$ = currentPlayer$) then
  notice "Player " + currentPlayer$ + " has won!"
  exit sub  'There is no need to keep going, so exit the subroutine
end if

'If neither player has won and all squares have been chosen the game
'ends in a tie
```

```
if noMoves = 9 then
   notice "Tie. There was no winner this time!"
end if

end sub
```

As you can see, this subroutine consists of a series of if...then statements that determine if the game is over. The first if...then statement checks to see if the current player has won by selecting all three squares in the first row (a1, a2, a3). It does this by checking to see if a1$, a2$, and a3$ are all assigned to the current player. Note the use of the and operator, which simplifies the logic involved in making these comparisons by allowing one if...then statement to be created instead of three if...then statements. If the player has won, a message is displayed in a pop-up dialog notifying the players of the results of the game, after which the exit sub statement executes, terminating the execution of this subroutine.

The next two if...then statements check the second and third rows. The three if...then statements that follow check each column of the game board. The next two if...then statements check diagonally in both directions for a winner. If no winner is found, the last if...then statement executes, checking the value assigned to noMoves to see if it is equal to 9. If it is, the game has ended in a tie with neither player having lined up three consecutive squares and all squares having been chosen. If, on the other hand, the value of noMoves is less than 9, the subroutine ends without taking action, allowing the game to continue.

Preparing for a New Game

The ResetGameBoard subroutine, whose code statements are shown next, is responsible for readying the game for a new round of play. This is achieved by displaying the blank bitmap image file (_.bmp) on each bmpbutton control and then clearing out any assignments made to the game board squares by assigning an empty string to a1$, a2$, a3$, b1$, b2$, b3$, c1$, c2$, and c3$. The subroutine concludes by resetting the value of noMoves to 0 and making Player X the current player in the new game:

```
'This subroutine resets the game board and global variables to
'ready the game for a new round of play
sub ResetGameBoard handle$

   'Display a blank bitmap image in each game board square
   print #play.a1, "bitmap _"
   print #play.a2, "bitmap _"
   print #play.a3, "bitmap _"
   print #play.b1, "bitmap _"
   print #play.b2, "bitmap _"
```

```
print #play.b3, "bitmap _"
print #play.c1, "bitmap _"
print #play.c2, "bitmap _"
print #play.c3, "bitmap _"

'Clear out any game board square assignments
a1$ = ""
a2$ = ""
a3$ = ""
b1$ = ""
b2$ = ""
b3$ = ""
c1$ = ""
c2$ = ""
c3$ = ""

noMoves = 0  'Reset the variable used to keep track of the total number
             'of moves made per game to zero

currentPlayer$ = "X"   'Set Player X as the current player

end sub
```

Terminating Gameplay

The last subroutine in the Tic Tac Toe game is CLosePlay, which should look pretty familiar to you by now. This subroutine should be added to the end of the program file and is responsible for getting player confirmation before terminating the execution of the game:

```
'This subroutine is called when the player closes the #play window
'and is responsible for ending the game
sub ClosePlay handle$

  'Get confirmation before terminating program execution
  confirm "Are you sure you want to quit?"; answer$

  if answer$ = "yes" then  'The player clicked on Yes

    close #play  'Close the #play window
```

```
    end   'Terminate the game

  end if

end sub
```

The Final Result

All right, that is all there is to the development of the Tic Tac Toe game. Assuming that you have not made typing mistakes, everything should be ready for you to test. As you put your new program through its paces, keep an eye on the overall flow of the game, ensuring that the game manages the switching of player moves and the assignment of game board squares correctly.

Summary

In this chapter, you learned how to programmatically interact with the Windows file system. This included accessing information about files and folders and specifying the location of files using absolute and relative path and filenames. You also discovered how to open, close, read from, and write to text files sequentially. Finally, you learned how to create and delete files and folders to perform basic file and folder administration tasks.

Before moving on to Chapter 9, "Working with Sound and Graphics," take a little extra time to work on the Tic Tac Toe game by tackling the following list of challenges.

Challenges

1. As currently written, the game counts on both players remembering whose turn it is. Although this is certainly not an unreasonable expectation, you might want to consider displaying a text message somewhere on the game board that reminds the players whose turn it is.

2. Consider making the Tic Tac Toe game a little more full featured by giving it a splash screen and setting up a Help window that explains the rules for playing the game.

3. Consider making the game a little more user friendly by not only informing players who has won the game but also telling them how the game was won (horizontally, vertically, or diagonally).

4. As currently written, the Tic Tac Toe game does not terminate gameplay when there is a winner. Modify the program to prevent this behavior, forcing players to start a new game before allowing either player to move again.

Working with Sound and Graphics

Many programming languages, like C++ and Visual Basic, support the development of *graphical user interfaces (GUIs)* that give users a stimulating interactive experience. In addition, these programming languages allow programmers to take things a step further by integrating sound and graphics into desktop applications. Just BASIC offers this same basic set of capabilities. In this chapter, you will learn how to incorporate wave and MIDI sounds into your Windows applications. You will also learn how to draw custom graphics.

Specifically, you will learn the following:

- How to work with the pen to draw lines and shapes
- How to configure pen color and size
- How to add text to your drawings
- How to play wave and MIDI files

Project Preview: The Slot Machine Game

In this chapter, you will learn how to create a new game that imitates the operation of a Las Vegas slot machine. The player is assigned a bank account with a $20 balance, and you play the virtual slot machine by clicking on a button labeled Spin. Figure 9.1 shows how the BASIC Slot Machine game looks when it's started.

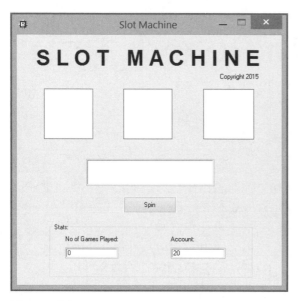

Figure 9.1 You initiate gameplay by clicking on the Spin button.
© 2016 Cengage Learning®

Figure 9.2 The player receives a payout when a match occurs.
© 2016 Cengage Learning®

As you can see, the player's account balance is displayed in a textbox control located at the bottom-right corner of the window. Each time the player clicks on the Spin button, the slot machine runs a brief animation sequence simulating the mechanical spinning of dials in the game's three graphicbox controls. At the end of each spin, a random selection of three fruit is displayed, as demonstrated in Figure 9.2.

The result of the spin is then analyzed and the player's account adjusted accordingly. A jackpot wins the player $3. Two of a kind wins $1. A spin with no matches costs the player $5.

Figure 9.3 shows an example of how the game looks when the player gets a jackpot.

Figure 9.4 provides an example of a losing spin.

Gameplay can potentially last forever as long as the player continues to grow the balance in her account. However, play is immediately halted if the player goes broke.

Figure 9.3 Three matching fruit result in a jackpot.
© 2016 Cengage Learning®

Figure 9.4 Five dollars is deducted from the player's account if a spin ends with no matching fruit.
© 2016 Cengage Learning®

Integrating Graphics and Sound into Applications

In programming languages like Visual Basic and C++, access to graphics commands is provided through the instantiation of a graphics object. (These are object-oriented programming languages.) Using methods (functions) and properties (attributes) associated with the graphics object and other related objects, programmers can incorporate custom graphics and animation into their applications. In the same manner, these programming languages allow programmers to instantiate objects whose methods and properties have sound capabilities.

Just BASIC manages the display of graphics using a coordinate system that employs pixels to set the location and size of drawn images. This system of coordinates begins at 0,0, which is located in the upper-left corner of the graphics window or graphicbox control, as depicted in Figure 9.5.

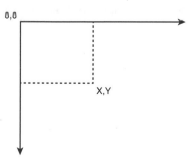

Figure 9.5 A depiction of Just BASIC's graphics coordinate system.
© 2016 Cengage Learning®

Hint

The term *pixel*, which stands for *picture element*, is the smallest addressable area on a control or window.

Just BASIC implements graphics support in the form of graphics commands that can be used in conjunction with the graphics window and the graphicbox control. In addition, Just BASIC has a number of commands specifically tailored to playing and controlling the execution of wave and MIDI files.

Displaying Graphics Images

You have already seen numerous examples of how to use the graphicbox control to display graphic bitmap files on Windows applications. This is accomplished by preloading images that are to be displayed into the computer's memory using the loadbmp command, as demonstrated here:

```
loadbmp "Star", "C:\images\Star.bmp"
```

Here a bitmap file named Star.bmp is loaded into memory and assigned a reference of Star.

Once loaded into memory, bitmap files can be displayed using graphicbox controls, as shown here:

```
graphicbox #play.Star, 100, 80, 93, 93
```

Here, the previously loaded bitmap file is displayed in a graphicbox control by referencing the file's handle and specifying the starting coordinates (100, 80) and then its size in pixels (93, 93).

You have also learned that, to make a graphics image stick after it has been displayed, you must execute the flush command:

```
print #play.Star, "flush"
```

Understanding How Just BASIC Manages Drawings

In Just BASIC, drawing occurs in segments. A *segment* is a collection of drawing operations that have been executed since the last flush command. Once flushed, a segment can be redrawn if a graphics window or graphicbox control needs to be repainted, as is the case when a window is minimized and later restored or when a window or control is temporarily overlaid by another window. Segments accumulate over time. Each time the flush command is executed, a new segment is generated. The first segment generated is assigned a segment ID of 1, and the segment ID assigned to each subsequent segment is incremented by 1.

You can retrieve the segment ID of the current segment using the segment command, as shown here:

```
print #handle "segment"; segmentID
```

Here, the segment ID of the current segment is retrieved and stored in a variable named segmentID. Once this command has been executed, you can delete the previously drawn segments using the delsegment command, as demonstrated here:

```
print #handle "delsegment"; segmentID - 1
```

By periodically removing unnecessary segments from computer memory, you can prevent needless loss of resources and help keep the computer running efficiently.

Just BASIC's Graphics Capabilities

Just BASIC supports several types of drawing options, including these:

- **Turtle Graphics.** This type of graphic involves the creation of custom images drawn using Just BASIC graphics commands. These commands move a virtualized pen around a graphics window or graphicbox control.
- **Shapes.** This type of graphic involves the drawing of shapes by calling on Just BASIC's graphic commands and passing them command coordinates representing the shape's location and dimensions.
- **Text.** This type of graphic involves the drawing of text on a graphics window or graphicbox control.

Turtle graphics, shapes, and text are drawn using a pen. A *pen* has two states: up and down. When the pen is down, any drawing operations result in the generation of a graphic. When the pen is up, you may still execute drawing commands, but no drawing will occur. The pen has two attributes that can be programmatically set: size and color. In addition to specifying pen size and color, Just BASIC allows you to specify the background color displayed on the graphics window and graphicbox control.

Drawing Graphics

To draw in a Just BASIC application, you need a surface upon which to draw. In Just BASIC, either the graphics window or the graphicbox control provides this surface. You also need to be familiar with the many graphics commands that Just BASIC provides.

A Quick Review of Graphics Commands

Just BASIC's collection of graphics commands is extensive. Table 9.1 is a list of commonly used graphics commands and their purpose. Note that although most commands are applicable to both the graphics window and the graphicbox control, some commands work only with one of these resources.

TABLE 9.1 JUST BASIC DRAWING COMMANDS

Command	Description
"autoresize"	Sets a control to resize if its window is resized
"backcolor COLOR"	Sets the background color of the window or graphicbox control
"box x y"	Draws a box from the pen's current position to position x, y
"boxfilled x y"	Draws a filled-in box from the pen's current position to position x, y
"circle r"	Draws a circle using the specified radius
"circlefilled r"	Draws a filled-in circle using the specified radius
"cls"	Clears the graphicbox or window
"color COLOR"	Sets the pen's color
"delsegment n"	Deletes the specified segment number
"delsegment segmentName"	Deletes the specified segment name
"direction"	Sets the current direction (north = 270, south = 90, east = 0, west = 180)
"disable"	Disables the control (graphicbox only)
"discard"	Discards anything drawn in the last flush
"down"	Places the pen in drawing mode
"drawbmp bmpname x y"	Draws the specified bitmap file
"ellipse w h"	Draws an ellipse using the specified width and height
"ellipsefilled w h"	Draws a filled-in ellipse using the specified width and height
"enable"	Enables the control (graphicbox only)
"fill COLOR"	Fills the window or graphicbox control with the specified color
"flush"	Ensures a drawing is redrawn if a window is resized or temporarily overlaid
"flush segmentName"	Flushes the window or control and assigns a segment name
"font facename pointSize"	Specifies the pen's type and size
"getbmp bmpName x y w h"	Creates a bitmap copy of a portion of a graphics windows using the specified coordinates

TABLE 9.1 JUST BASIC DRAWING COMMANDS (CONTINUED)

Command	Description
"go *d*"	Advances the pen the specified distance
"goto *x y*"	Moves the pen to the specified coordinates
"home"	Centers the pen in the graphicbox control or graphics window
"horizscrollbar on/off [min max]"	Enables or disables the horizontal scrollbar
"line *x1 y1 x2 y2*"	Draws a line between two points
"locate *x y w h*"	Repositions the graphicbox control in its window (graphicbox only)
"northpie *w h angle 1 angle2*"	Draws a pie slice
"place *x y*"	Positions the pen at the specific location
"posxy *x y*"	Sets the pen's position to x, y
"print"	Prints the graphics window
"redraw"	Redraws a previously flushed segment
"segment *segmentName*"	Assigns a variable representing the current segment ID
"set *x y*"	Draws a point at x, y
"setfocus"	Sets focus to the control (graphicbox only)
"size *s*"	Sets the pen size
"\text"	Draws text at the current pen position
"trapclose *label*" (window only)	Sets up the trapclose event (graphics window only)
"turn *angle*"	Turns the pen to the specified angle
"up"	Turns off the pen's drawing mode
"vertscrollbar on/off [min max]"	Enables or disables the vertical scrollbar
"when event *EventHandler*"	Instructs the window to respond to the specified event handler

Hint

Note that the double quotation marks are a required part of each command listed in Table 9.1 because graphics commands are formatted as strings.

As you can see from the list of commands in Table 9.1, Just BASIC has commands allowing you to draw points, lines, circles, boxes (squares and rectangles), pie shapes, and so on. In addition, it has commands that allow you to draw filled-in shapes. Other commands are used to control the movement and availability of the pen and to set up event handlers.

Working with the Graphics Window

To draw in a graphics window, you must first open the window using the open command, as demonstrated here:

```
open "Drawing Demo" for graphics as #canvas
```

Once the window is open, you can use the print statement to submit drawing commands to the window, as shown here:

```
nomainwin

open "Drawing Demo" for graphics as #canvas

print #canvas, "backcolor red"
print #canvas, "place 110, 110"
print #canvas, "down"
print #canvas, "boxfilled 200, 200"
print #canvas, "flush"

wait
```

Here, five graphic commands are applied to the graphics window. The first command uses the backcolor command to specify a color of red. The second command moves the pen to a location of 110 pixels down and 110 pixels to the right of the upper-left corner of the graphicbox control. Next, the down command is executed, which places the pen in a down position, readying it for drawing. The boxfilled command is executed next, drawing a filled-in box shape that starts at the current pen location and ends at coordinates 200, 200. The last command flushes the drawing, ensuring that it sticks. Figure 9.6 shows the resulting graphic that is generated when this example is executed.

Working with the Graphicbox Control

Working with the graphicbox control is just as easy as working with the graphics window. To do so, you must add an instance of the control to a window and then open the window using the open command. Once you've accomplished this, you can send graphics commands to the graphicbox control using the print command, as demonstrated in the next code:

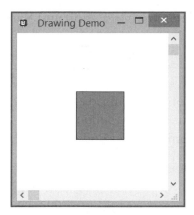

Figure 9.6 Drawing a filled-in red square using graphics commands and the pen.
© 2016 Cengage Learning®

```
nomainwin

graphicbox #main.canvas, 10, 10, 300, 300

open "Drawing Demo" for window as #main

print #main.canvas, "home"
print #main.canvas, "down"
print #main.canvas, "\Hello there!"
print #main.canvas, "flush"

wait
```

Here, you use the home command to move the pen to the center of the graphicbox control. Next, the pen is put into a down position, and a text string is drawn using the \text command. With the \text command, any text that is entered after the \ character is drawn starting at the current pen position. Figure 9.7 shows the resulting graphic that is generated when this example is executed.

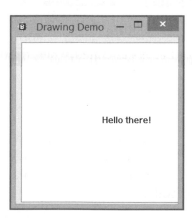

Figure 9.7 Text can be drawn just as easily as a graphic.
© 2016 Cengage Learning®

Trap

Graphics commands only work with the graphics window or the graphicbox control. In addition, not all graphics commands work with both the graphics window and the graphicbox control.

Using Different Colors

As you saw in a previous example where a red square was drawn, you can specify different colors to be used in drawing operations. By default, Just BASIC sets the pen's color to black and the surface area of the graphics window and the graphicbox control to white. However, you can specify any of the colors listed here when setting background and pen color attributes:

Black	Darkblue	Darkpink	Pink
Blue	Darkcyan	Darkred	Red
Brown	Darkgray	Green	White
Cyan	Darkgreen	Lightgray	Yellow

Clearing Out a Drawing

You can clear out any drawing in a graphics window or graphicbox control using the cls command, which has the following syntax:

```
print #handle, "cls"
```

Clearing out a graphics window or graphicbox control removes the drawing from the computer's memory and prepares the drawing area to be reused.

Setting Up Event Mouse and Keyboard Event Handlers

By setting up event handlers that respond to mouse and keyboard input, you can create applications that allow the user to provide input that can be used in drawing operations. Just BASIC supports a large number of mouse and keyboard events for which event handlers can be set up, as shown in Figure 9.2.

By taking advantage of Just BASIC's ability to intercept and react to different mouse and keyboard events, you can, for example, create an interactive drawing application, as demonstrated in the next section.

TABLE 9.2   JUST BASIC EVENTS

Event	Description
characterInput	Executes when a key is pressed while the graphics window or graphicbox control has focus
leftButtonDouble	Executes when the left mouse button is double-clicked
leftButtonDown	Executes when the left mouse button is pressed
leftButtonMove	Executes when the mouse is moved while the left button is pressed
leftButtonUp	Executes when the left mouse button is released
middleButtonDouble	Executes when the middle mouse button is double-clicked
middleButtonDown	Executes when the middle mouse button is pressed
middleButtonMove	Executes when the mouse is moved while the middle button is pressed
middleButtonUp	Executes when the middle mouse button is released
mouseMove	Executes when the mouse is moved
rightButtonDouble	Executes when the right mouse button is double-clicked
rightButtonDown	Executes when the right mouse button is pressed
rightButtonMove	Executes when the mouse is moved while the right button is pressed
rightButtonUp	Executes when the right mouse button is released

Creating a Drawing Application

As an example of how to work with various drawing commands as well as how to set up an event handler to process mouse input, let's take a look at how to create a small drawing application called BASIC Doodle. The code for this application is shown here:

```
nomainwin

WindowWidth = 500
WindowHeight = 500

dim colors$(15)
colors$(0) = "Red"
colors$(1) = "Blue"
colors$(2) = "Yellow"
```

```
colors$(3) = "Brown"
colors$(4) = "Pink"
colors$(5) = "Green"
colors$(6) = "Cyan"
colors$(7) = "White"
colors$(8) = "Black"
colors$(9) = "Darkred"
colors$(10) = "Darkblue"
colors$(11) = "Darkpink"
colors$(12) = "Darkgreen"
colors$(13) = "Darkcyan"
colors$(14) = "Darkgray"
colors$(15) = "Lightgray"

dim pensize$(5)
pensize$(0) = "1"
pensize$(1) = "3"
pensize$(2) = "5"
pensize$(3) = "7"
pensize$(4) = "9"

statictext #main.statictext1, "Pick a color:", 10, 10, 60, 12
statictext #main.statictext1, "Pick a pen size:", 10, 270, 60, 12

combobox #main.combobox1, colors$(), SetColor, 10, 30, 75, 70
combobox #main.combobox2, pensize$(), SetPenSize, 10, 290, 75, 50

graphicbox #main.graphicbox1, 95, 10, 390, 450

button #main.button1, "Clear", ClearArea, UL, 10, 400, 75, 30

open "BASIC Doodle" for window_nf as #main

print #main.combobox1, "select Blue"
print #main.combobox2, "select 7"

print #main.graphicbox1, "color Blue"
print #main.graphicbox1, "size 7"
print #main.graphicbox1, "down"
print #main.graphicbox1, "when leftButtonMove draw"

wait
```

```
sub draw handle$, x, y
    #handle$, "set "; x; " "; y
end sub

sub SetColor handler$
  print #main.combobox1, "selection? selected$"
  print #main.graphicbox1, "color " + selected$
end sub

sub SetPenSize handler$
  print #main.combobox2, "selection? selected$"
  print #main.graphicbox1, "size " + selected$
end sub

sub ClearArea handle$
  #main.graphicbox1, "cls"
end sub
```

Here, a window has been set up that is 500 pixels wide by 500 pixels tall. The window contains two statictext controls, which provide labels for the window's two combobox controls. The first combobox control is loaded with a list of colors stored in the colors$() array, and the second combobox control is loaded with a list of values (saved as strings) from the pensize$() array. Each of the pen size values corresponds to a different pen size. By clicking on entries stored in these two comboboxes, the user can specify the color and pen size used in drawing operations.

The next control added to the window is a graphicbox control, which will provide the virtualized canvas upon which the user will draw. The last control added to the window is a button control labeled Clear that calls upon a subroutine named ClearArea when it's clicked.

Default selections are made for both combobox controls. These color and pen specifications are also assigned to the graphicbox control. This is accomplished using the print command to execute the color blue and size 7 graphics commands. Next, the pen is set up to draw by executing the down graphic command, and an event handler is set up to call upon a subroutine named Draw whenever the user moves and holds down the left mouse button.

Take note of the construction of the draw subroutine. It consists of a single statement that executes the set graphic command. The set command takes two arguments that are automatically passed to it by the leftButtonMove event. These arguments are used to draw a point at the specified coordinates. (For example, x and y specify the location of the pointer when the left mouse button is depressed.) If the user continues to hold down the left mouse button and move the mouse around the graphicbox control, the draw subroutine is repeatedly executed and will draw whatever freehand design the user wants.

Hint

The set command works with strings. It can be passed a pair of literal values, as demonstrated here:

#handle "set 50 100"

However, when the set command is passed variable data, you just reformat the command as shown here:

```
x = 50
y = 100
#handle "set "; x" " "; y
```

This format of the set command ensures that a string is processed as required by the command.

The SetColor subroutine, which follows the draw subroutine, is called whenever the user clicks on a value in the first combobox control and uses the color graphic command to assign a color to the pen. Likewise, the SetPenSize subroutine is called whenever the user clicks on an item in the second combobox control. This subroutine uses the size graphics command to set the pen's size.

The last procedure in the application is the ClearArea subroutine. It is called whenever the user clicks on the Clear button and executes the cls graphic command. This clears out the graphicbox control, allowing the user to begin a new drawing.

Figure 9.8 demonstrates how this application looks when running.

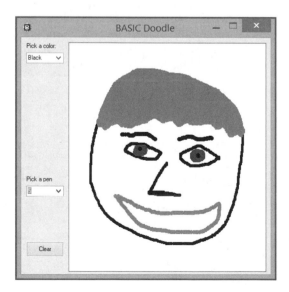

Figure 9.8 Using the BASIC Doodle program to draw a funny face.
© 2016 Cengage Learning®

Getting Your Applications to Make Some Noise

Applications often use sound when communicating with users. For example, some applications use sound to indicate when a long-running process has finished running or to signal when an error has occurred. Like other programming languages, Just BASIC allows programmers to make noise in several different ways, including these:

- Making a beep sound
- Playing wave files
- Playing MIDI files

To facilitate the playing of each of these types of sounds and sound files, Just BASIC supplies you with access to the following commands and functions:

- **beep.** A command used to play the operating system's default wave file, which usually makes a "ding" sound.
- **playwave.** A command used to play, stop, and loop while playing wave audio files.
- **playmidi.** A command used to play MIDI music files.
- **stopmidi.** A command used to stop the playback of MIDI music files.
- **midipos().** A function used to determine the current location of a MIDI file that is being played.

Making Noise

The simplest way to add sound to a Just BASIC application is with the beep command, which has the following syntax:

```
beep
```

When executed, the beep command plays the operating system's default wave file, which, unless you have changed it, makes a "ding" sound.

Playing Wave Files

A *wave* file is a digital audio file that stores uncompressed raw audio data. To play a wave file, you need to work with the playwave command, which has the following syntax:

```
playwave "file" [, mode]
```

file is a placeholder representing the name and path of the wave file to be played, and *mode* is one of the following options:

- **async.** Continues execution without waiting for the wave file to finish playing.
- **sync.** Waits for the wave file to finish playing.
- **loop.** Repeats the playback of a wave file.

The following statements demonstrate how to use different forms of the `playwave` command:

```
playwave "ding.wav", async    'Continues program execution
playwave "ding.wav", synch    'Waits for the wave file to finish
playwave "ding.wav", loop     'Repeatedly plays the wave file
playwave ""                   'Stops wave file playback
```

Take note of the last statement shown in the preceding code, which passes an empty string to the `playwave` command. This stops the playback of any wave file that might be playing currently. To get a better idea of how to work with the `playwave` command, take a look at the following application:

```
nomainwin

global selectedFile$

WindowWidth = 400
WindowHeight = 200

statictext #play.statictext1, "W A V E    P L A Y E R", 50, 20, 440, 30
statictext #play.statictext2, "Copyright 2015", 250, 70, 80, 20

button #play.button1 "Open", GetWaveFile, UL, 40, 100, 60, 30
button #play.button1 "Play", PlayWaveFile, UL, 125, 100, 60, 30
button #play.button1 "Loop", LoopWaveFile, UL, 210, 100, 60, 30
button #play.button1 "Stop", StopWaveFile, UL, 295, 100, 60, 30

open "WAVE Player" for window_nf as #play

print #play.statictext1, "!font Arial 18 bold"

wait
```

```
sub GetWaveFile handle$
  filedialog "Open a File", "c:\Windows\media\*.wav", selectedFile$
end sub

sub PlayWaveFile handle$
  playwave selectedFile$, async
end sub

sub LoopWaveFile handle$
  playwave selectedFile$, loop
end sub

sub StopWaveFile handle$
  playwave ""
end sub
```

When executed, this application displays a window with four button controls labeled Open, Play, Loop, and Stop. Each of these button controls has been set up to execute a subroutine. The GetWaveFile subroutine uses the filedialog command to display a list of wave files from which the user can select. The PlayWaveFile subroutine plays the wave file the user selects. The LoopWaveFile subroutine repeatedly plays the selected wave file, and the StopWaveFile subroutine stops the playing of the currently playing wave file. If no wave file is being played, clicking on the Stop button has no effect. Figure 9.9 shows how this application looks when it's executed.

Figure 9.9 Using the playwave command to play wave files.
© 2016 Cengage Learning®

Trick

A number of wave files are supplied as part of Windows. For example, you will find a large collection of wave files on a computer running Windows 7 or Windows 8.1 in C:\Windows\Media. You can also find any number of wave files on the Internet. Beyond all this, you can create your own wave files using the Sound Recorder utility that Microsoft Windows supplies.

Playing MIDI Files

In addition to playing wave files, Just BASIC allows programmers to play MIDI files. *MIDI (musical instrument digital interface)* is a communications protocol that enables electronic musical instruments and computers to communicate. MIDI files are music files that store MIDI music. Just BASIC gives programmers the following commands for playing MIDI files:

- **playmidi.** Plays the specified MIDI file.
- **stopmidi.** Stops the currently playing MIDI file.
- **midipos().** Returns the current position of the MIDI file being played.

To see how to work with each of these commands and functions, take a look at the following example. Here, a small program has been written that plays a specified MIDI file and then ends once the file has finished playing:

```
nomainwin

playmidi "c:\Sounds\OneMoreTime.mid", duration

timer 1000, CheckForDone

wait

sub CheckForDone

  if duration = midipos() then
    stopmidi
    timer 0
    end
  end if

end sub
```

This example begins by using the playmidi command to play a specific MIDI file. The timer command is then used to run a subroutine every second. This subroutine uses the midipos() function to retrieve a value representing the current playback location in the MIDI file. This value is then compared against the value stored in duration. These two values will become equal once the end of the MIDI file has been reached, in which case the stopmidi command is executed and the timer command is turned off.

Hint

To use the `playmidi` command, you need to supply it with two pieces of information: the name and path of the MIDI file to be played and a variable that the command will use to store the length of the MIDI file. In the case of the previous example, this variable was named `duration`.

Back to the Slot Machine Game

Okay, now it is time to turn your attention back to the development of the BASIC Slot Machine game. This game simulates a Las Vegas slot machine in which the player initiates a virtual pull of the slot machine's lever by clicking on the game's Spin button. During each spin, an animated simulation is executed that imitates the spinning of mechanical dials in the slot machine. The end of the animation sequence is followed by the selection and display of three values, representing the slot machine's final result. Based on this result, the amount of money in the player's account is increased or decreased.

Designing the Game

The Slot Machine game relies on three global variables and a subroutine that is responsible for generating the game's GUI. Interaction with the player occurs when the player clicks on the Spin button, at which time a series of additional subroutine calls are made that analyze the results of the spin and adjust the player's account balance accordingly.

The Slot Machine game uses a cherry, an apple, and a pear image, as depicted in Figure 9.10. Copies of the bitmap image files are available for download on this book's companion website located at www.cengageptr.com/downloads.

Figure 9.10 Slot machine values are represented by images of different types of fruit.
© 2016 Cengage Learning®

In total, you will create the Slot Machine game in eight steps, as outlined here:

1. Create a new BASIC file and document it.
2. Define global variables and initiate gameplay.
3. Create the `ManageGamePlay` subroutine.
4. Create the `AnimateDisplay` subroutine.
5. Create the `DisplayImages` subroutine.
6. Create the `UpdateDisplay` subroutine.

7. Create the RandomSelection subroutine.

8. Create the ClosePlay subroutine.

Creating a Just BASIC File Script

The first step in the creation of the Slot Machine game is to create a new basic file named SlotMachine.bas and add the following statements to it:

```
'  ***********************************************************************
'
'  Script Name: SlotMachine.bas (The Slot Machine Game)
'  Version:      1.0
'  Author:       Jerry Lee Ford, Jr.
'  Date:         February 1, 2015
'
'  Description: This game is a simulation of a Las Vegas-style slot
'               machine. The objective of the game is for the player to
'               win as much money as possible and not go broke.
'
'  ***********************************************************************

nomainwin     'Suppress the display of the default text window
```

In addition to documenting the overall purpose of the application using comment statements, the nomainwin command is executed, suppressing the display of the window.

Initializing Gameplay

The next step in the development of the Slot Machine game is to define and assign starting values for a few global variables and to make a call to the subroutine responsible for displaying the game's user interface. This is accomplished by adding the following statements to the end of the program file:

```
'Assign default values to global variables
global iteration, account, gamesPlayed

iteration = 0     'Used to control the display of animation
account = 20      'Represents the amount of money in the player's account
gamesPlayed = 0   'Keeps track of the total number of games played

call ManageGamePlay 'Call the subroutine responsible for managing gameplay

wait  'Pause the application and wait for the player's instruction
```

The Slot Machine game utilizes three global variables to manage the game's animation sequence and to track the amount of money in the player's account and the number of games played. Gameplay is controlled by the ManageGamePlay subroutine, which is called next. This subroutine is responsible for displaying the window representing the game's slot machine and for calling on other subroutines.

Designing the Game's User Interface

The code statements that make up the ManageGamePlay subroutine are shown next and should be added to the end of the program file:

```
'This subroutine displays the game board and controls interaction with the
'player
sub ManageGamePlay

  WindowWidth = 500    'Set the width of the window to 500 pixels
  WindowHeight = 500   'Set the height of the window to 500 pixels

  loadbmp "Cherry", "C:\images\Cherry.bmp"  'Load the specified bitmap
                                            'file into memory
  loadbmp "Apple", "C:\images\Apple.bmp"    'Load the specified bitmap
                                            'file into memory
  loadbmp "Pear", "C:\images\Pear.bmp"      'Load the specified bitmap
                                            'file into memory

  'Define the format of statictext controls displayed on the window
  statictext #play.statictext1, "S L O T   M A C H I N E", 35, 20, 440, 50
  statictext #play.statictext2, "Copyright 2015", 380, 70, 80, 20

  'Add the controls used to graphically display slot machine values
  graphicbox #play.pic1, 50, 100, 93, 93
  graphicbox #play.pic2, 200, 100, 93, 93
  graphicbox #play.pic3, 350, 100, 93, 93

  'Add a control that will be used to announce the results of each play
  textbox #play.textbox1 130, 230, 240, 50

  'Add a button control to operate the slot machine
  button #play.button1 "Spin", AnimateDisplay, UL, 200, 300, 100, 30

  'Add a groupbox control at the bottom of the window
  groupbox #play.groupbox1 "Stats:", 60, 350, 380, 100
```

```
'Use statictext controls to display two labels inside the groupbox control
statictext #play.statictext3, "No of Games Played:", 90, 372, 105, 20
statictext #play.statictext4, "Account:", 290, 372, 50, 20

'Add two textbox controls inside the groupbox control for displaying
'game statistics
textbox #play.textbox2 90, 395, 100, 20
textbox #play.textbox3 290, 395, 100, 20

'Open the window with no frame and a handle of #play
open "Slot Machine" for window_nf as #play

'Set up the trapclose event for the window
print #play, "trapclose ClosePlay"

'Set the font type, size, and attributes
print #play.statictext1, "!font Arial 24 bold"
print #play.textbox1, "!font Arial 18 bold"

'Display the initial values representing the number of games played and
'the value of the player's account
print #play.textbox3, str$(account)
print #play.textbox2, str$(gamesPlayed)

print #play.button1, "!setfocus";   'Set focus to the button control

'Pause the application and wait for the player's instruction
wait

end sub
```

This subroutine begins by specifying the dimensions of the game window. Next, three bitmap image files, containing images representing a cherry, an apple, and a pear, are preloaded into memory using the loadbmp command. Two statictext controls are then added that display the game's name and copyright statement. Three graphicbox controls are added next and will be used to represent the dials displayed on the slot machine. A textbox control is then added and will be used to display status information at the end of each spin. Spins are initiated when the player clicks on the button control labeled Spin, which is defined next. When clicked, this control will call upon a subroutine named AnimateDisplay. As the name implies, the AnimateDisplay subroutine simulates the spinning of mechanical dials that display slot machine values. Finally, a groupbox control is added to the bottom of the window, into which two statictext and two textbox controls are added. The textbox controls will be used to display information regarding the number of games played and the current amount of money in the player's account.

With all its graphic controls now specified, the #play window is opened as a regular window with the string "Slot Machine" displayed in its title bar. A series of print statements are executed next. These statements set font type, size, and attributes for various statictext and textbox controls and display the starting values in the two textbox controls located at the bottom of the window. The last print statement assigns focus to the Spin button, and then the wait command is executed, pausing the application to give the player the chance to begin playing the game.

Controlling Game Automation

The AnimateDisplay subroutine, shown here, is called whenever the player clicks on the game's Play button. Its purpose is to call on the DisplayImages subroutine every third of a second. When called, the DisplayImages subroutine displays a different set of bitmap image files, thus simulating the spinning of slot machine dials:

```
'This subroutine is responsible for controlling the timing involved in
'displaying the slot machine's animation
sub AnimateDisplay handle$

   timer 333, DisplayImages 'Call the DisplayImages subroutine every
                            '.333 seconds
end sub
```

Animating the Slot Machine's Spin

The code statements that make up the DisplayImages subroutine are shown next and should be added to the end of the program file:

```
'This subroutine displays a different set of bitmap image files in the
'game's three bmpbutton controls each time it is called.
sub DisplayImages

   iteration = iteration + 1   'Keep track of how many times this subroutine
                               'has been called

   'Display a different set of bitmap images upon each call
   if iteration = 1 then call UpdateDisplay "Apple", "Cherry", "Pear"
   if iteration = 2 then call UpdateDisplay "Cherry", "Pear", "Cherry"
   if iteration = 3 then call UpdateDisplay "Pear", "Apple", "Pear"
   if iteration = 4 then call UpdateDisplay "Apple", "Pear", "Cherry"
   if iteration = 5 then call UpdateDisplay "Pear", "Cherry", "Apple"
```

```
'Turn the timer control off on the sixth iteration
if iteration = 6 then
    timer 0                     'Turn the timer off
    iteration = 0               'Reset this value to zero
    call RandomSelection        'Call the subroutine that generates the slot
                                'machine's sixth spin
end if

end sub
```

Each time this subroutine is called upon to execute, it increments the value of a variable named iteration by one. iteration is a global variable, thus allowing its value to be maintained across different executions of the subroutine. As you can see, depending on the value assigned to iteration, the UpdateDisplay subroutine is called and passed different sets of arguments, representing different slot machine values. Because this subroutine is called every third of a second, the net effect of its execution is to simulate the spinning of values in the slot machine's three dials.

Upon the sixth execution of the subroutine, the timer is turned off, and the value of iteration is reset to zero. Finally, the RandomSelection subroutine is called. The RandomSelection subroutine is responsible for generating and displaying a random set of three slot machine values, thus ending the spin animation sequence.

Displaying Slot Machine Graphics

The code statements for the UpdateDisplay subroutine, shown next, take three arguments and use them along with the drawbmp command to display bitmap images representing different slot machine values. After being drawn, the flush command is used to make the images stick, and then the Windows ding.wav file is played using the playwave command:

```
'This subroutine loads the specified bitmap files into the game's three
'bmpbutton controls
sub UpdateDisplay x$, y$, z$

    print #play.pic1, "drawbmp " + x$ + " 1 1" 'Load first image
    print #play.pic2, "drawbmp " + y$ + " 1 1" 'Load second image
    print #play.pic3, "drawbmp " + z$ + " 1 1" 'Load third image

    'Use the flush command to make sure the images stick
    print #play.pic1, "flush"
    print #play.pic2, "flush"
    print #play.pic3, "flush"
```

```
'Let's make a little noise at the end of each spin
playwave "ding.wav", asynch

end sub
```

Hint

The `ding.wav` wave file is provided by default as part of Windows XP's installation and can be found along with a collection of other wave files in `C:\Windows\Media`.

Selecting the Slot Machine's Ultimate Result

The `RandomSelection` subroutine, shown here, is responsible for generating the sixth and final iteration of the slot machine's spin animation sequence:

```
'This subroutine is responsible for determining which bitmap images should
'be displayed for the slot machine's sixth and final spin
sub RandomSelection

  RandomNumber = int(rnd(1)*3) + 1  'Retrieve a number between 1 and 3

  'Select the image to be displayed on the first bmpbutton control
  SELECT CASE RandomNumber
    CASE 1
      print #play.pic1, "drawbmp Cherry 1 1" 'Display the Cherry bitmap
      firstPic = 1  'Set a numeric value representing the selection
    CASE 2
      print #play.pic1, "drawbmp Apple 1 1"  'Display the Apple bitmap
      firstPic = 2  'Set a numeric value representing the selection
    CASE 3
      print #play.pic1, "drawbmp Pear 1 1"   'Display the Pear bitmap
      firstPic = 3  'Set a numeric value representing the selection
  END SELECT

  RandomNumber = int(rnd(1)*3) + 1  'Retrieve a number between 1 and 3

  'Select the image to be displayed on the second bmpbutton control
  SELECT CASE RandomNumber
    CASE 1
```

```
      print #play.pic2, "drawbmp Cherry 1 1" 'Display the Cherry bitmap
      secondPic = 1  'Set a numeric value representing the selection
    CASE 2
      print #play.pic2, "drawbmp Apple 1 1"  'Display the Apple bitmap
      secondPic = 2  'Set a numeric value representing the selection
    CASE 3
      print #play.pic2, "drawbmp Pear 1 1"   'Display the Pear bitmap
      secondPic = 3  'Set a numeric value representing the selection
END SELECT

RandomNumber = int(rnd(1)*3) + 1  'Retrieve a number between 1 and 3

'Select the image to be displayed on the third bmpbutton control
SELECT CASE RandomNumber
    CASE 1
      print #play.pic3, "drawbmp Cherry 1 1" 'Display the Cherry bitmap
      thirdPic = 1  'Set a numeric value representing the selection
    CASE 2
      print #play.pic3, "drawbmp Apple 1 1"  'Display the Apple bitmap
      thirdPic = 2  'Set a numeric value representing the selection
    CASE 3
      print #play.pic3, "drawbmp Pear 1 1"   'Display the Pear bitmap
      thirdPic = 3  'Set a numeric value representing the selection
END SELECT

'Let's make a little noise and display the results of the game
playwave "ding.wav", asynch

'Tabulate the value representing the results of the sixth spin
result = firstPic + secondPic + thirdPic

'Look to see if three cherries or three pears were displayed
if (result = 3) or (result = 9) then
  print #play.textbox1, "Jackpot!"
  account = account + 3  'Add 3 dollars to the player's account
end if
```

```
'A value of 6 means either three apples were displayed or three separate
'values were displayed
if result = 6 then
  if firstPic = secondPic then    'Look for three apples
    print #play.textbox1, "Jackpot!"
    account = account + 3   'Add 3 dollars to the player's account
  else
    'A cherry, apple, and pear were displayed
    print #play.textbox1, "You lose!"
    account = account - 5   'Subtract 5 dollars from the player's account
  end if
end if

'A value other than 3, 6, or 9 means that two of a kind was displayed
if (result <> 3) and (result <> 6) and (result <> 9) then
  print #play.textbox1, "Two of a kind!"
  account = account + 1   'Add 1 dollar to the player's account
end if

if account < 0 then   'End the game if the player goes broke
  notice "You have gone broke. Game Over!"   'Tell the player first
  close #play   'Close the window
  end   'Terminate the game
end if

'Keep track of the total number of games played
gamesPlayed = gamesPlayed + 1

'Update the display of game statistics
print #play.textbox2, str$(gamesPlayed)
print #play.textbox3, str$(account)

end sub
```

As you can see, the subroutine starts off by generating a random number between 1 and 3. Next, the select…case statement is used to set up a code block that determines the value assigned to the slot machine's first dial. A random value of 1 equates to a cherry. A value of 2 equates to an apple, and a value of 3 equates to a pear. Note that a numeric value is added to the firstPic variable representing the value assigned to the first dial. A new random number is then generated and processed by another select…case statement to generate and assign a value to the slot machine's second dial.

Note that a numeric value is added to the secondPic variable representing the value assigned to the second dial. The preceding process is repeated a third time to generate a value for the slot machine's third dial. This time a numeric value is added to a thirdPic variable representing the value assigned to the third dial.

Once values have been assigned to all the dials, the playwave command is used to play the ding.wav file, thus notifying the user that her spin has been completed. The rest of the subroutine tabulates the results of the spin to determine how much to add or deduct from the player's account. This is accomplished by adding the value of firstPic, secondPic, and thirdPic together to establish the total value for the spin and then using a series of conditional tests to analyze the result.

Table 9.3 lists every possible outcome that the lottery machine can generate. If you look closely at the Total column, you will see that the only time a value of 3 or 9 is generated is when three of a kind has been selected. In addition, the only time a value of 6 is generated is when either three of a kind has been generated or when no matches have occurred. To determine which situation applies when a total value of 6 is generated, all you have to do is compare the value of any two dials and determine if they match. If they do, then a jackpot occurred. Otherwise, a set with no matches has to have been generated.

In addition to analyzing the results of each spin, the conditional code blocks are responsible for adding or deducting money as appropriate from the player's account and for displaying a text message informing the player of the result of each spin. In addition, one last if…then statement is used to check on the amount of money left in the player's account. If the player has run out of money, the player is informed that she has gone broke and the game is immediately terminated.

The last few statements in the subroutine increment the value of gamesPlayed by 1 and then update the display of the statistics being tracked by the game (for example, the total number of games played and the value of the player's account).

Terminating Gameplay

The final subroutine in the Slot Machine game is ClosePlay, which is responsible for getting player confirmation before terminating the execution of the game:

```
'This subroutine is called when the player closes the #play window
'and is responsible for ending the game
sub ClosePlay handle$

  'Get confirmation before terminating program execution
  confirm "Are you sure you want to quit?"; answer$

  if answer$ = "yes" then  'The player clicked on Yes
```

```
    close #play   'Close the #play window

    end   'Terminate the game

  end if

end sub
```

TABLE 9.3 SLOT MACHINE VALUES AND RESULTS

First Value	Second Value	Third Value	Total	Results	Transaction
1	1	1	3	Jackpot	+ 3 dollars
2	2	2	6	Jackpot	+ 3 dollars
3	3	3	9	Jackpot	+ 3 dollars
1	1	2	4	Two of a kind	+ 1 dollar
1	1	3	5	Two of a kind	+ 1 dollar
2	2	1	5	Two of a kind	+ 1 dollar
2	2	3	7	Two of a kind	+ 1 dollar
3	3	1	7	Two of a kind	+ 1 dollar
3	3	2	8	Two of a kind	+ 1 dollar
1	2	1	4	Two of a kind	+ 1 dollar
1	3	1	5	Two of a kind	+ 1 dollar
2	1	2	5	Two of a kind	+ 1 dollar
2	3	2	7	Two of a kind	+ 1 dollar
3	1	3	7	Two of a kind	+ 1 dollar
3	2	3	8	Two of a kind	+ 1 dollar
1	2	3	6	No match	– 5 dollars
1	3	2	6	No match	– 5 dollars
2	3	1	6	No match	– 5 dollars
2	1	3	6	No match	– 5 dollars
3	1	2	6	No match	– 5 dollars
3	2	1	6	No match	– 5 dollars

The Final Result

That's everything! Assuming that you followed along carefully and did not leave anything out or make typos along the way, your version of the BASIC Slot Machine game should be ready to go. As with previous games, you'll be well served to spend a little time playing the game yourself before sharing it with others. As you play, keep an eye on the game's statistics, and make sure that they are being correctly tabulated. In addition, make sure that the game is consistently analyzing the results of each spin.

Summary

In this chapter, you discovered how to spruce up your Windows applications by incorporating sound and graphics. This included learning how to play wave and MIDI files and learning how to work with Just BASIC's pen so you could draw lines and shapes. Using the information provided, you saw how to create a wave file player and a small drawing application. In developing the drawing program, you demonstrated your ability to configure pen size and color and to control pen availability by moving it up and down. You also learned how to add drawn text to your graphics.

Before moving on to Chapter 10, "Arcade-Style Computer Game Development," consider setting aside a little extra time to improve the BASIC Slot Machine game by tackling the following list of challenges.

Challenges

1. To liven things up a bit, consider playing a MIDI file in the background while the application is running to help set the right mood for the game. If you do not have a MIDI file that seems to fit, you should be able to find something on the web to play with.

2. You might want to further spice things up by giving the game a splash screen. Given that not everyone may be familiar with the operation of slot machines, it might also be a good idea to add a Help window to the game.

3. Consider expanding on the amount of information presented to the player at the end of each spin. For example, you might include a brief explanation of the amount of money that was just added or deducted from the player's account.

4. You might also want to add programming logic to the game that differentiates types of jackpots, paying out different sums for three cherries versus three apples or three pears.

10

Arcade-Style Computer Game Development

So far you have learned how to work with the Just BASIC development environment and been introduced to the fundamentals of application development. In this chapter, the focus changes to the development of good old fashioned arcade-style games. As a result, you will learn a number of new development techniques. Everything you will learn will then be tied together through the development of this chapter's game project: the Bricks game.

Specifically, you will learn the following:

- Key features found in most computer games
- How to manage sprites in computer games
- How to manage game state and control gameplay with loops
- How to manage event synchronization and game pace
- The fundamentals of capturing and processing player input

Project Preview: The Bricks Game

In the second half of this chapter, you will learn how to create the Bricks game. This game is a close cousin of the classic Atari Breakout game developed back in the 1970s. In this arcade game, the player is challenged to use a paddle and a bouncing ball to clear the screen of bricks while preventing the ball from dropping off the bottom of the play area. Figure 10.1 provides a first look at the Bricks game.

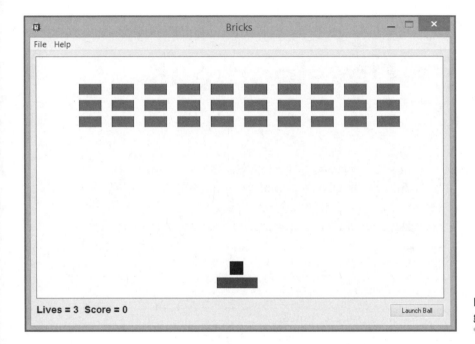

Figure 10.1 The Bricks game when it's started.
© 2016 Cengage Learning®

As you can see, in addition to the ball and paddle, the Bricks game consists of thirty colored bricks (three rows of ten). In addition to keeping the ball in play by bouncing it around the screen, the player is challenged to score as many points as possible by knocking out the bricks. In addition to the primary gaming window, the Bricks game consists of a number of dialog windows, as demonstrated in Figure 10.2, which are used to display game information and collect player input.

Figure 10.2 An example of one of the Bricks game's dialog windows.
© 2016 Cengage Learning®

Figure 10.3 provides another look at the Bricks game as it is being played. As you can see, the player has cleared out close to half the bricks from the screen. Once all thirty bricks have been removed, a new set of bricks is redrawn on the screen, allowing the player to continue to rack up more points. Gameplay ends when the player loses all three of his assigned lives.

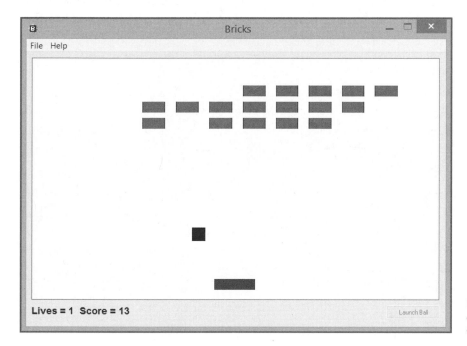

Figure 10.3 An example of the Bricks game in action.
© 2016 Cengage Learning®

Key Features Found in Computer Arcade Games

Arcade-style games are fast-paced action-oriented computer games that challenge players to compete against each other or a computer opponent. These games typically require good eye-hand coordination. They incorporate and combine many different facets of computer programming, including complex programming logic and the integration of graphics and sounds.

At this point, you should have a good understanding of how to display text, draw and position sprites, and integrate sound effects into your Just BASIC applications. These are essential elements of computer game development. However, before you're ready to begin creating your own computer games, you need to learn a few more things, including these:

- Working with sprites using new commands
- Managing game state
- Controlling gameplay with loops
- Controlling the movement of sprites

- Detecting collisions between sprites
- Managing event synchronization
- Capturing user input

Each of these topics is explored in this chapter. In addition, many of them are demonstrated in the development of the Bricks game.

Creating and Managing Sprites

As you learned in Chapter 3, "Creating Graphical User Interfaces," Just BASIC includes a built-in sprite engine that facilitates the management of sprites in Windows applications. Sprites are two-dimensional graphics objects that can be displayed and managed individually. Just BASIC has two graphics environments that work with its sprite engine to support the use of sprites: the graphics window and the graphicbox control.

Sprites are used to represent things like spaceships, tanks, and missiles in computer games. Gameplay involves interaction with and control over game sprites. For example, in a tank versus tank shoot-'em-up game, each tank would graphically be represented by a sprite. Bullets that tanks fire at each other are sprites as well, as are other game objects that the tanks may run into or be able to run over and destroy. Sprites can be programmatically moved around the screen under either player or computer control.

Displaying Bitmap Images

In Just BASIC, sprites are generated from bitmap or BMP files. A bitmap file is a collection of bits that represents a graphics image. You can add bitmaps to your Just BASIC applications by loading them from external graphics files into memory using the `loadbmp` command, which has the following syntax:

```
loadbmp "BitmapFileName", "PathFileName"
```

Here, `BitmapFileName` represents the name of the bitmap file to be loaded into memory. The following example demonstrates how to use this command to load and display a bitmap image named `BlueTank.bmp` that is stored in a `C:\images\` directory on the local computer:

```
nomainwin

loadbmp "tank", "C:\images\BlueTank.bmp"
open "Bitmap Demo" for graphics as #main
print #main, "drawbmp tank 1 1"

wait
unloadbmp("tank")
```

Once loaded into memory by the loadbmp command, the drawbmp command is used to display the bitmap in the upper-left corner of the graphics window. This command has the following syntax:

```
print #handle, "drawbmp bmpname x y"
```

Here, *bmpname* represents the name of the bitmap file image to be displayed (drawn) at the specified x and y coordinates. Figure 10.4 shows the output generated when the previous example is executed.

Figure 10.4 Using the loadbmp and drawbmp commands to load and display a bitmap image.
© 2016 Cengage Learning®

Hint

Note the use of the unloadbmp command in the previous example. This command removed the specified bitmap file from computer memory, freeing memory resources. It is a good programming practice to free up resources in this manner. This command has the following syntax:

```
UNLOADBMP "name"
```

Here, *name* represents the name assigned to the bitmap image.

Creating New Bitmap Images from Existing Ones

Another way of working with bitmap files is to create them yourself from images already displayed in the graphics windows or graphicbox control. This is accomplished using the getbmp command, which has the following syntax:

```
print #handle, "getbmp filename x y w h"
```

Here, *filename* represents the name of the bitmap file to be loaded into memory. *x* and *y* represent the coordinate location where the bitmap is to be placed, and *w* and *h* represent the width and height (in pixels) that the bitmap is to be drawn. As an example, consider the following statement, which loads a bitmap image and displays it in the upper-left corner of the graphics window of the graphics control and then uses the getbmp command to make a copy of the bitmap. Each copy is drawn on the graphics window at staggered intervals, creating a row of four identical images, as demonstrated in Figure 10.5:

```
nomainwin

loadbmp "brick1", "C:\images\brick.bmp"
open "Bitmap Demo" for graphics as #main
print #main, "drawbmp brick1 20 40"

print #main, "getbmp brick2 20 40 40 20"
print #main, "drawbmp brick2 80 40"

print #main, "getbmp brick3 20 40 40 20"
print #main, "drawbmp brick3 140 40"

print #main, "getbmp brick4 20 40 40 20"
print #main, "drawbmp brick4 200 40"

wait

unloadbmp("brick1")
unloadbmp("brick2")
unloadbmp("brick3")
unloadbmp("brick4")
```

Figure 10.5 Using the getbmp command to generate new bitmap images in computer memory.
© 2016 Cengage Learning®

Creating a Sprite

Sprites, which are key elements in arcade games, are generated from bitmaps. Just BASIC offers a large number of commands for managing and controlling sprites. These commands are listed here:

- **addsprite.** Generates a sprite based on a specified bitmap.
- **background.** Generates a background for a graphics window or graphicbox control.
- **cyclesprite.** Cycles a sprite through its image list. Refer to Just BASIC Help for additional information.
- **drawsprite.** Displays all visible sprites on a graphics windows or graphicbox control.
- **removesprite.** Deletes a specified sprite.
- **spritecollides.** Generates a list of sprites with which a specified sprite has collided.
- **spriteimage.** Displays one of a list of images stored in a sprite image list. Refer to Just BASIC Help for additional information.
- **spritemovexy.** Moves a sprite a specified number of pixels along the x and y coordinates.
- **spriteorient.** Orientates a sprite in one of four directions (normal, flip, mirror, or rotate 180).
- **spritescale.** Scales the displayed size of a sprite based on a specified percentage.
- **spritevisible.** Controls the visibility or invisibility of a sprite.
- **spritexy.** Moves a sprite to the specified coordinates.
- **spritexy?.** Retrieves the current x and y coordinates of the specified sprite.

You will learn how to work with many of these commands in this chapter. For those that are not covered, you can learn more about them using Just BASIC Help. You will want to review the syntax requirements for each of the commands in Just BASIC Help. The following example demonstrates how to add a sprite to an application using the addsprite, spritexy, and drawsprites commands:

```
nomainwin

open "Create Sprite Demo" for graphics as #main

print #main, "down"
print #main, "place 1 1; backColor darkgreen; boxfilled 42 84"
print #main, "getbmp ball 1 1 42 84"

print #main, "addsprite gameBall ball"
print #main, "spritexy gameBall 100 100"

print #main, "drawsprites"

wait

unloadbmp("ball")
```

In this example, a bitmap file is drawn from scratch using Just BASIC graphics commands. These commands use the down and place drawing commands (covered in Chapter 9, "Working with Sound and Graphics") to draw a dark green box on the graphics window. The getbmp command is then used to generate a bitmap image in memory, consisting of a copy of the image that was previously drawn. The addsprite command is then used to generate a sprite named gameBall, which is a copy of the ball bitmap. The spritexy command places the sprite on the graphics window at coordinates 100, 100. Finally, the drawsprites command makes the sprite visible. Figure 10.6 shows the output that is generated when this example is executed.

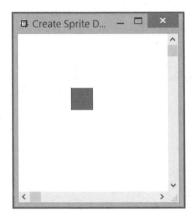

Figure 10.6 An example of a sprite displayed on a graphics window.
© 2016 Cengage Learning®

Using Sprites Within a Graphicbox Control

As the following example demonstrates, sprites are also supported by the graphicbox control. This allows you to use sprites in applications whose window does not have to be completely dedicated to graphics support. In other words, you can take a regular window, add any controls you want to it, and then work with sprites on a portion of that window where a graphicbox control has been placed:

```
nomainwin

WindowWidth = 305
WindowHeight = 330

graphicbox #main.draw, 10, 10, 280, 280
open "Graphic Demo" for window_nf as #main

print #main.draw, "down"
print #main.draw, "place 1 1; backColor darkgreen; boxfilled 42 84"
print #main.draw, "getbmp ball 1 1 42 84"
```

```
print #main.draw, "addsprite gameBall ball"
print #main.draw, "spritexy gameBall 100 100"

print #main.draw, "drawsprites"

wait

unloadbmp("tank")
```

In this example, a window with no frame is opened, and a graphicbox control is placed on it. A sprite is then created and displayed within the graphicbox control.

Providing a Background

In addition to drawing images and adding sprites to graphics windows and graphicbox controls, you can spice up your games by adding colorful and creative backgrounds. One way of doing this is to take a suitable bitmap graphics file and use it to draw a background, as demonstrated here:

```
nomainwin

loadbmp "tank", "C:\images\BlueTank.bmp"
open "Bitmap Demo" for graphics as #main

print #main, "background tank"
print #main, "drawsprites"

wait

unloadbmp("tank")
```

Here, a bitmap image named tank is loaded into memory using the loadbmp command to access a bitmap file located in C:\images\BlueTank.bmp, and then a graphics windows is opened. Next, the background command uses the tank bitmap as the background for the application window.

Another way of spicing up a graphics window or graphicbox control background is to paint the background a certain color, as demonstrated in the following example:

```
nomainwin

graphicbox #main.draw, 10, 10, 295, 310

open "Bitmap Demo" for window_nf as #main
```

```
print #main.draw, "down"
print #main.draw, "color 255 255 204"
print #main.draw, "line 0 0 1 1"

print #main.draw, "getbmp windowBackground 0 0 1 1"
print #main.draw, "background windowBackground"
print #main.draw, "drawsprites"

wait
```

Here, a graphicbox control has been added to the application window. Next, a pixel-sized line is drawn. The color of the line is set using the `color` command. Lastly, the `getbmp` command is used to generate a bitmap image of the line, and the `background` command is used to draw that image as the graphicbox control's background, stretching it as necessary to fill the control.

Managing Game State

Computer games typically have different states. They often start by displaying a welcome screen with instructions or a series of menu options. Games may transition between states when players click on a menu item, keyboard key, or sprite. Many computer games also support a paused state, which allows players to temporarily halt gameplay and then resume play when ready. These are just a few examples of the different types of states that computer games often support.

The following example demonstrates how you can implement and control game state within a Just BASIC gaming application:

```
nomainwin

MENU #main, "File", "New Game", ResetGame, "Exit", EndGame 'Create File menu
MENU #main, "Help", "Help", GameHelp, "About", AboutGame  'Create Help menu

graphicbox #main.draw, 10, 10, 762, 450
button #main.startButton, "&Launch Ball", StartGameLoop, UL, 672, 470, 100, 25

open "Bricks" for window_nf as #main

print #main, "trapclose ExitGame"

print #main.draw, "when characterInput ManagePaddleMovement"

'Add call to subroutines that further initialize the game

wait
```

In this example, the opening statements of a small Just BASIC game are displayed. This particular game begins by drawing the game board and then entering into a paused state. Gameplay is begun when the player clicks on a button control and pauses at the end of each round of play. Only a portion of the game's source code is shown in this example, but it is sufficient to demonstrate the management and control of game state.

This example begins by defining a series of menus for the application window. Menus, when clicked during gameplay, pause the game and thus change game state. Next, a graphicbox control and a button control are added to the application. Gameplay occurs as sprites, added later in the program, interact with one another. Gameplay does not begin when the application is started. Instead, the game board is displayed. Gameplay itself is initiated by clicking on the button control labeled Launch Ball. Clicking on the button control therefore changes game state by setting gameplay into motion, which it accomplishes when the button control executes the StartGameLoop subroutine. As already stated, the player can pause game state at any time by clicking on a menu command. In addition, game state can be changed by instructing the game to terminate. This is achieved by executing the trapclose command, which in turn executes a subroutine named ExitGame. The trapclose command was introduced and demonstrated in Chapter 9.

You can also programmatically control game state during gameplay. For example, you can pause gameplay between different rounds of play in an arcade game. You can also terminate it if a player is killed. For example, in a game in which the player is assigned a certain number of lives, you can track the lives using a variable; when the value of the variable becomes zero, you can terminate gameplay.

Finally, you can restore a terminated game's state back to initial start-up mode by giving the player a way of starting a new game. You can do this via a menu command or an interface control. You will see examples of all these game state management techniques employed later in this chapter's game project: the Bricks game.

Controlling Gameplay with Loops

Computer games are interactive computer applications. Games must be able to collect and process player input. For example, in a tank versus tank game that pits one player against another, the game has to be able to collect and process a constant flow of player input directing where players want to move their tanks. The game must also capture player input that tells it when each player wants to shoot. The game must continually integrate player input to keep the game updated and display any changes on the graphics windows or graphicbox control. The key to making everything work is the game's main game loop.

The following example shows the statements that make up a small game loop:

```
do until noOfBricks = 30

    call MoveTheBall
    call CollisionCheck
    call AnalyzeAndUpdateBallLocation
    call RegulateGameSpeed

loop
```

In this example, a do…until loop is used to control gameplay. It has been configured to execute until the value assigned to a variable named noOfBricks is set to 30. Within the game loop, a series of calls is made to subroutines that perform repetitive procedure calls, which in this case control game ball movement, check for sprite collisions, change ball direction in the event of a collision, and manage a process that controls the rate of gameplay.

As this example demonstrates, game loops are typically set up to run until a specific condition occurs, terminating only when a player wins or loses or when the player has signaled a decision to stop gameplay. You will see another example of how to set up a game loop when you work on the Bricks game.

Moving Things Around

As has been stated, arcade-style computer games developed using Just BASIC involve the movement and interaction of sprites on the graphics window or a graphicbox control. For example, in an arcade game like Pong, three sprites are used. Two sprites represent player paddles, and a third sprite represents the game ball. Once the game loop starts gameplay, the ball begins moving. In addition, it must be made to bounce around in different directions as it collides with player paddles and the edges of the game field.

The following example demonstrates how to programmatically move a sprite from the left side to the right side of a graphicbox control:

```
nomainwin

WindowWidth = 305
WindowHeight = 330

graphicbox #main.draw, 10, 10, 250, 250
open "Graphic Demo" for graphics as #main
```

```
print #main.draw, "down"
print #main.draw, "place 1 1; backColor darkgreen; boxfilled 42 84"
print #main.draw, "getbmp ball 1 1 42 84"

print #main.draw, "addsprite gameBall ball"

print #main.draw, "drawsprites"

for i = 1 to 205
  call RegulateTiming
  print #main.draw, "spritexy gameBall "; i; " "; 100
  print #main.draw, "drawsprites"
next i

wait

unloadbmp("ball")

sub RegulateTiming

  scan
  timeStamp = time$("milliseconds")

  do
  loop until time$("milliseconds") > timeStamp + 20
end sub
```

In this example, a small window is created that has a single control: a graphicbox that takes up most of the space in the window. Then a dark green bitmap image is created and used as the basis for creating a sprite. A for...next loop is then used to place and move the sprite from one side of the graphicbox control to the other. As you can see, the sprite is moved by repeatedly redrawing it using the spritexy and the drawsprite commands. Each time the spritexy command is executed, the value assigned to its x coordinate is increased by a value of 1, thus moving it in a straight line across the graphicbox control.

Note the call to the RegulateTiming subroutine that occurs at the beginning of each iteration of the loop. The addition of this subroutine is required to slow down or throttle the speed at which the application executes. Without this subroutine, Just BASIC executes the for...next loop as fast as possible—so fast that you cannot see the animated movement of the sprite. Instead, the sprite moves so quickly to the right side of the graphicbox control that it appears to have started there and not been moved. Details regarding this subroutine are provided in the next section.

Managing Event Synchronization Controlling Animation Speed

As just mentioned, by default Just BASIC executes your applications as fast as your computer is capable of processing them. In the case of many applications, this is just what you want. But when it comes to games, sometimes you need to slow things down and keep events going at a steady pace. You can use the following subroutine as the basis for accomplishing this task:

```
sub RegulateTiming

    scan
    timeStamp = time$("milliseconds")

    do
    loop until time$("milliseconds") > timeStamp + 20

end sub
```

As you can see, this subroutine is not very large or complex. It begins by executing the scan command, which instructs Just BASIC to pause for an instance to collect and process any keyboard or mouse input that the user may have provided. Then the current time, in milliseconds, is retrieved using a special built-in Just BASIC function named time$. Next, a do...until loop is set up that loops until the current time, stored in a variable named timeStamp, becomes greater than the timeStamp plus 20 (that is, until 20 milliseconds have passed).

Hint

Although it's not part of the synchronization and control process that this section discusses, execution of the scan command is an essential part of any Just BASIC arcade-style game, and it is in a procedure like this where the scan command belongs.

The end result is that when this subroutine is executed, it slows down (or regulates) game speed, ensuring that 20 milliseconds pass before program code resumes execution. The end result is that the game executes at a consistent speed. It does not go faster than players can keep up with, regardless of the computer where it is being executed.

Detecting Collisions

In addition to managing game state, setting up a game loop, controlling game speed, and synchronizing events, another required programming technique required by many computer arcade games is collision detection. A *collision* is an event that occurs whenever two sprites run into one another. For example, a collision occurs in a tank versus tank game whenever one tank rams another or when one tank shoots and hits another tank.

The following example demonstrates how to incorporate collision detection in a Just BASIC game:

```
for i = 1 to 205
  call RegulateTiming
  print #main.draw, "spritexy gameBall2 200 100"
  print #main.draw, "spritexy gameBall "; i; " "; 100
  print #main.draw, "drawsprites"

  call CollisionCheck

  if demoOver = 0 then
    exit for
  end if

next i

playwave "Miss.wav", asynch

wait

sub CollisionCheck

  print #main.draw, "spritecollides gameBall collision$"

  if collision$ <> "" then
    demoOver = 0
  end if

end sub
```

Hint

Sound effects are another critical component of many computer games, as demonstrated in this example. You learned how to add sound effects to your Just BASIC application in Chapter 9.

In this example, the loop that was previously used to move a sprite from one side of a graphicbox control to the other has been modified so that, in addition to calling on the RegulateTiming subroutine and drawing and moving the sprite, it now includes a call to a new subroutine called CollisionCheck. In addition, a second sprite has been created and placed in the graphicbox control. As before, each time the loop iterates, the gameBall sprite is moved. Also, the CollisionCheck subroutine is called.

Each time the CollisionCheck subroutine is called, it executes the spritecollides command, which populates a list called collision$ with a list of any sprites that the gameBall sprite has collided with. A check is then made to see if the collision$ list contains any entries (that is, it is not empty), which if true indicates that the sprite has collided with another sprite. If a collision has occurred, the value assigned to demoOver is set to 0. Once the CollisionCheck subroutine has finished executing, the value of demoOver is examined and, if set to 0, the example terminates.

Because the second sprite was placed directly in the path of the gameBall sprite, the end result is that the gameBall sprite eventually collides with it and then immediately halts its movement.

Hint

In the case of a computer arcade game like Pong, collisions occur all the time, such as when the game ball collides with the player's paddle. When a collision occurs in a game like Pong, the direction at which the game ball is traveling is altered upon impact. For example, Figure 10.7 shows three possible directions that a ball might be deflected in a Pong game after colliding with the left player's paddle. Changing the game ball's direction in this manner involves reversing the values of the ball's x and y coordinates. For example, changing the value of the x coordinate from 3 to -3 or from -3 to 3 reverses its horizontal direction. Likewise, changing the value of the y coordinate from 3 to -3 or from -3 to 3 reverses its vertical direction. You will see a detailed example of how this is done when you complete the Bricks game.

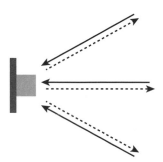

Figure 10.7 Examples of different types of directions that an object's directions might be set to after a collision.
© 2016 Cengage Learning®

Collecting Player Input

To play a game, players must be able to provide it with input. The type of input required will vary, of course, depending on the type of game. For example, while keyboard input is typically best used when playing a word guessing game, a strategy game might be better designed to incorporate mouse input, allowing players to select and control objects, and a computer arcade game may need to work with either the keyboard or a mouse.

In Chapter 9, you learned how to set up mouse and keyboard event handlers. In addition, through the creation of that chapter's drawing application, you received hands-on experience setting up a mouse event handler and using it to collect and process mouse input. In a similar fashion, the next example demonstrates how to set up a keyboard event handler and use it to collect and process keyboard input. To be specific, the example is designed to capture up, down, right, and left key events, which are keyboard keys commonly used to control computer games:

```
nomainwin

WindowWidth = 305
WindowHeight = 330

graphicbox #main.draw, 10, 10, 250, 250
open "Graphic Demo" for graphics as #main

print #main.draw, "when characterInput BallControl"

print #main.draw, "down"
print #main.draw, "place 1 1; backColor darkgreen; boxfilled 42 84"
print #main.draw, "getbmp ball 1 1 42 84"

print #main.draw, "addsprite gameBall ball"

print #main.draw, "drawsprites"

print #main.draw, "spritexy gameBall 100 100"

do
   call RegulateTiming
   print #main.draw, "drawsprites"
loop until i = 1
```

```
wait

unloadbmp("ball")

sub RegulateTiming

  scan
  timeStamp = time$("milliseconds")

  do
  loop until time$("milliseconds") > timeStamp + 50

end sub

sub BallControl handle$, Inkey$

  userInput$ = right$(left$(Inkey$,2),1)

  select case userInput$
    case "%"
      playwave "Miss.wav", asynch
      print #main.draw, "spritexy? gameBall x y"
      print #main.draw, "spritexy gameBall "; x - 10; " "; y;
    case "'"
      playwave "Miss.wav", asynch
      print #main.draw, "spritexy? gameBall x y"
      print #main.draw, "spritexy gameBall "; x + 10; " "; y;
  end select

end sub
```

Hint

Mouse and keyboard events, like graphics commands, are only valid when you use them within the confines of a graphics window or graphicbox control.

In this example, an event handler has been created to call on a subroutine named `BallControl` whenever `characterInput` (for example, keyboard) input is captured. The `BallControl` subroutine has been set up to process two arguments: `handle$` and `Inkey$`. The `handle$` argument represents the handle of the graphics window or graphicbox control, and the `Inkey$` argument specifies the character input that has been captured.

When pressed, most keyboard keys result in a single character being passed when a `characterInput` occurs. For example, pressing the 1 key passes a character of 1, and pressing the h key passes the h character. However, other key events pass multiple characters when their associated keys are pressed. The up, down, left, and right arrow keys pass two characters when pressed: a blank space followed by a character that indicates the arrow key that was pressed. When the up arrow key is pressed, a blank space and the & key are captured. The down arrow key generates a blank space followed by the (character. The left arrow key generates a blank space followed by the % character, and the right arrow key generates a blank space and the ' character.

Hint

In most keyboard-controlled computer games, the space bar and the up, down, left, and right arrow keys are the most common. However, some games, like first-person shooters, use w, a, s, and d keys instead of the arrow keys to allow the player to use his right hand to work with and control the mouse.

Therefore, the first thing the `BallControl` subroutine does is use the `right$` and `left$` functions to strip away the first (blank) character. Then a `select…case` statement is used to determine if either the left or the right arrow key has been pressed. If a match occurs, a wave file is played, and the location of the `gameBall` sprite is changed. Pressing the left arrow key therefore moves the sprite 10 pixels to the left, and pressing the right arrow key moves the sprite 10 pixels to the right. Using logic similar to this in this chapter's Bricks game, you will develop the programming logic required to control the game's paddle control.

Hint

In addition to keyboard input, Just BASIC supports the ability to capture and respond to both mouse and joystick input. For mouse input, Just BASIC can respond to both left and right mouse button clicks and retrieve mouse x and y coordinates. To learn more about Just BASIC's support for mouse input, access Just BASIC's "Reading Mouse Events and Keystrokes" Help file. Just BASIC can support up to two joysticks at a time, retrieving coordinate data as well as button input. To learn more about Just BASIC's support for joysticks, access Just BASIC's "READJOYSTICK" Help file.

Back to the Bricks Game

Okay, now that you have learned the fundamentals of arcade-style game development, it is time to put your newfound knowledge to the test through the development of the Bricks game. As you work on the different parts of this program, you will gain valuable game development experience managing sprites, controlling game state, setting up a game loop, and detecting and responding to collisions while also managing event synchronization, user input collection, and ultimately game termination.

Designing the Game

The Bricks game is considerably more complicated than the other game programs you have worked on so far in this book. The structure chart shown in Figure 10.8 has been provided to help you understand the organization of the programming logic that makes up the Bricks game.

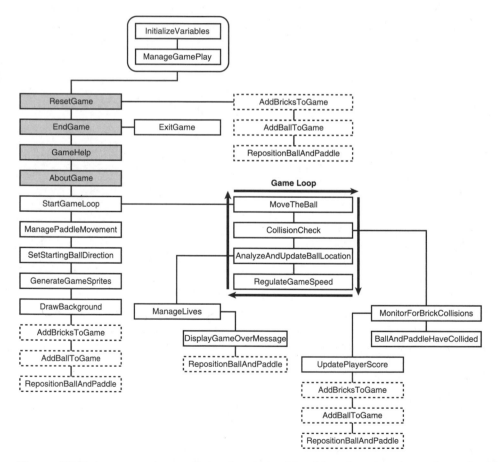

Figure 10.8 A structure chart outlining the relationship of the subroutines that make up the Bricks game.
© 2016 Cengage Learning®

> ## Hint
>
> A *structure chart* is a visual depiction of the organization of the computer application. Structure charts visually outline the relationship of the procedures that make up computer applications. In a structure chart, each procedure is represented by a box that shows the procedure's name and its relationship to other procedures.

In total, the Bricks game consists of 22 subroutines, several of which are called upon from different locations within the program file to execute. The reused subroutines are identified in Figure 10.8 by a dotted line box. In addition, the application's game loop is called out in the diagram, being surrounded by four arrows, highlighting the critical nature of its execution in controlling gameplay. Finally, four of the boxes in the structure chart have been filled in with light gray, which is intended to identify them as subroutines that are called on for execution exclusively through an application's menu commands.

The application's opening statements and its subroutines are covered one at a time in the sections that follow, where they are grouped based on their relationship to one another and common functionality.

Creating a Just BASIC Application File

As with previous chapter projects, begin the creation of the Bricks game by setting up a new BASIC file and adding the code statements that document its purpose, as shown here:

```
' ***********************************************************************
'
' Script Name: Bricks
' Version:     1.0
' Author:      Jerry Lee Ford, Jr.
' Date:        January 25, 2015
'
' Description: This is a breakout style computer game. The goal of the game
'              is to keep the ball in play as long as possible and to knock
'              out as many bricks as possible by using the game paddle to
'              deflect the bouncing ball and keep it from dropping out of
'              the play area. The player is given three game balls and an
'              unlimited number of bricks. Gameplay ends when the player
'              runs out of balls.
'
' ***********************************************************************
```

Next, add the following statement to the code file:

```
nomainwin    'Suppress the display of the default text window

call InitializeVariables 'Call subroutine that defines key game variables
call ManageGamePlay 'Call the subroutine responsible for managing gameplay

wait   'Pause the application and wait for the player's instruction
```

These statements execute the nomainwin command, suppressing the display of the application's default mainwin text window, and then execute two subroutines that initialize application variables and establish initial game state.

Initializing Game State

The first two subroutines of the Bricks application are responsible for initializing a variable's values and establishing initial game state. Instructions for developing these two subroutines are provided in the sections that follow.

Define and Assign Initial Values to Global Variables

The InitializeVariables subroutine, shown here, is responsible for defining global variables used throughout the application and for assigning initial values to most of the variables:

```
'This subroutine defines and assigns initial values for key variables
sub InitializeVariables

  'Define global variables
  global ballX         'Location of the game ball's x-axis current coordinate
  global ballY         'Location of the game ball's y-axis current coordinate
  global newX          'Location of the game ball's x-axis next coordinate
  global newY          'Location of the game ball's y-axis next coordinate

  global playerScore   'Keep track of the player's score
  global noOfBricks    'Count bricks for level change
  global noOfLives     'Keep count of the number of player lives
  global ballSpeed     'Change speed to make call go faster

  global ballStartX    'Location of the game ball's starting x-axis coordinate
  global ballStartY    'Location of the game ball's starting y-axis coordinate
  global paddleStartX  'Location of the game paddle's starting x-axis coordinate
  global paddleStartY  'Location of the game paddle's starting y-axis coordinate
```

```
'Assign initial variable values
playerScore = 0        'Set player score equal to zero
noOfBricks = 0         'Set number of bricks to zero
noOfLives = 3          'Set the number of player lives equal to three
ballSpeed = 20         'Set the number of pixels used when moving the ball

'Set game ball's starting coordinates
ballStartX = 362       'Set starting x-axis coordinate for the game ball
ballStartY = 380       'Set starting y-axis coordinate for the game ball

'Set game paddle's starting coordinates
paddleStartX = 338     'Set starting x-axis coordinate for the game paddle
paddleStartY = 410     'Set starting y-axis coordinate for the game paddle
```

end sub

Details regarding the purpose of each variable are documented in comments embedded in the code statements.

Create the Subroutine That Establishes Initial Game State

The ManageGamePlay subroutine, shown here, is responsible for establishing initial game state. This includes setting application window's size, setting up its menu system, and defining interface controls. This subroutine also establishes the application's trapclose event and sets up keyboard input data collection using the characterInput event. The subroutine then ends after making a series of procedure calls to subroutines that complete the establishment of game state by setting starting game ball direction, generating sprites, drawing the application background, adding game bricks and the game ball, and then finally setting ball and paddle starting location. Once again, additional explanation for each programming statement is provided in comments throughout the subroutine:

```
'This subroutine displays the game board and interaction with the player

sub ManageGamePlay

  WindowWidth = 790  'Special variable that sets window width (in pixels)
  WindowHeight = 570 'Special variable that sets window height (in pixels)

  MENU #main, "File", "New Game", ResetGame, "Exit", EndGame 'Create File menu
  MENU #main, "Help", "Help", GameHelp, "About", AboutGame   'Create Help menu
```

```
'Add a graphicbox control to be used to display the playing area
graphicbox #main.draw, 10, 10, 762, 450

'Add statictext controls to be used to display player lives and score
statictext #main.lives, ("Lives = "; str$(noOfLives)), 10, 470, 250, 20
statictext #main.score, ("Score = "; str$(playerScore)), 100, 470, 200, 25

'Add a button control to be used to initiate a round of play
button #main.startButton, "&Launch Ball", StartGameLoop, UL, 672, 470, 100, 25

'Open the window with no frame and a handle of #main
open "Bricks" for window_nf as #main

'Set up the trapclose event for the window
print #main, "trapclose ExitGame"

'Set the font type, size, and attributes for statictext controls
print #main.lives,"!font arial 11 bold"
print #main.score,"!font arial 11 bold"

'Instruct the window to process keyboard events
print #main.draw, "when characterInput ManagePaddleMovement"

'Put the graphicsbox in draw mode
print #main.draw, "down"

'Call subroutine that randomly sets ball direction
Call SetStartingBallDirection

'Call subroutine that generates sprites (bricks, paddle, game over message)
call GenerateGameSprites

'Call subroutine that draws the background for the graphicbox control
call DrawBackground

'Call subroutine that adds a new set of bricks to the game
call AddBricksToGame

'Call subroutine that adds the game ball to the game
```

```
call AddBallToGame

'Call subroutine that centers the game ball and paddle
call RepositionBallAndPaddle

end sub
```

Establishing and Maintaining Game State

The next 12 subroutines that make up the Bricks application work together to establish and maintain game state. Each of these subroutines performs a separate, discrete task and is covered in the sections that follow.

Create the Subroutine That Resets Gameplay

The first of the subroutines that help establish game state is ResetGame. It is executed whenever the player selects the New Game command located on the application's File menu:

```
'This subroutine resets variables, enables the Start button, and updates
'displayed text
sub ResetGame

  'Reset variables to their starting values
  noOfBricks = 0
  playerScore = 0
  noOfLives = 3

  'Enable the Start button
  print #main.startButton, "!enable"    'Enable the Start Button

  'Remove the End of Game message from view
  print #main.draw, "spritexy EndOfGameMsg 0 -50"

  'Update the display of player lives and score
  print #main.lives, "Lives = "; str$(noOfLives)
  print #main.score, "Score = "; str$(playerScore)

  'Call subroutine that adds a new set of bricks to the game
  call AddBricksToGame

  'Call subroutine that adds the game ball to the game
```

```
call AddBallToGame

'Call subroutine that centers the game ball and paddle
call RepositionBallAndPaddle
```

```
end sub
```

When called, this subroutine reinitializes the starting values assigned to variables that keep track of the total number of bricks that have been removed from the game window as well as player score and lives. The subroutine also enables the button control labeled Launch Ball and hides the end of game message (if it is visible) by moving it out of view of the graphicbox control. Next, this subroutine displays the value of the now-updated player score and live variables and calls upon three subroutines that refill the graphicbox control with bricks, add a ball to the game, and reposition the ball and paddle.

Create the Subroutine That Allows the Player to End the Game

The EndGame subroutine, shown here, comes next. It is run only when the player executes the ExitGame command, located on the application's File menu. When executed, this subroutine calls the ExitGame subroutine, passing it an empty string as an argument:

```
'This subroutine is executed when the player selects the Exit menu's Exit
'command. It then turns around and executes the ExitGame subroutine.
sub EndGame

   call ExitGame ""

end sub
```

The ExitGame subroutine, discussed here, ensures an orderly shutdown of the application. It is also called automatically by Just BASIC if the player closes the game by clicking on the game window's Close button. When called this way, the subroutine is passed an argument. Because the ExitGame subroutine has to be able to process an argument, an empty string satisfies this requirement. The empty string, other than allowing the ExitGame subroutine to be repurposed, has no other value.

Create the Subroutine That Displays Help

The GameHelp subroutine, shown here, displays a Help window using the Notice dialog, telling the user how to play the game. This subroutine is executed when the player clicks on the Help command located on the application's Help menu:

```
'This subroutine displays the game's Help menu
sub GameHelp

  notice "Bricks Help" + Chr$(13) + _
    "Use the left and right arrow keys to move the paddle." + Chr$(13) + _
    "Click on the Launch Ball button to begin gameplay. You " + Chr$(13) + _
    "have three lives at the end of which gameplay ends. " + Chr$(13) + _
    "Points are scored by clearing the screen of bricks." +  Chr$(13) + _
    Chr$(13) + "Click on File > New Game to play again or " + Chr$(13) + _
    "click on File > Exit to end the game."

end sub
```

Create the Subroutine That Displays Information About the Game

The AboutGame subroutine, shown here, uses the Notice dialog to display additional information about the game. It is called when the player clicks on the About command located on the Help menu:

```
'This subroutine displays the game's About menu
sub AboutGame

  notice "About" + Chr$(13) + _
    "Bricks Version 1" + Chr$(13) + _
    "Copyright Cengage, 2015"

end sub
```

Create the Subroutine That Manages Overall Gameplay

The StartGameLoop subroutine, shown here, comes next. It is executed when the player clicks on the button control labeled Launch Ball. The first thing it does is disable the button control, preventing it from being clicked again. The subroutine then sets the game ball's starting direction back to its initial default settings. The rest of the subroutine consists of a loop that iterates until all 30 of the game bricks have been cleared from the play area. The four procedure calls that make up this loop constitute the application's game loop. Together, they keep the game ball in continuous motion, monitoring for collisions and player misses, while also regulating the speed at which gameplay occurs and ensuring that the game has sufficient time to collect and process keyboard input:

```
'This subroutine manages overall gameplay
sub StartGameLoop handle$
```

```
   print #main.startButton, "!disable"    'Disable the Start Button

   'Set the ball's starting x-axis coordinate to the default starting location
   ballX = ballStartX
   ballY = ballStartY

   'Execute this loop until all the game bricks have been eliminated
   do until noOfBricks = 30

      call MoveTheBall   'Move and update the position of the ball

      call CollisionCheck   'Check for collisions

      'Call subroutine that manages nonball/paddle collisions and player misses
      call AnalyzeAndUpdateBallLocation

      call RegulateGameSpeed   'Call subroutine that pauses game execution just
                               'long enough to allow the game to collect and
                               'process keyboard input
   loop

end sub
```

Create the Subroutine That Manages Paddle Movement

The next subroutine to be added to the application is the ManagePaddleMovement subroutine, shown here. It is called whenever keyboard input is captured, and its job is to parse through that input and then move the player paddle right or left based on the player's instruction:

```
'This subroutine processes paddle movement when the player presses
'the left and right arrow keys
sub ManagePaddleMovement handle$, Inkey$   'Inkey$ is a special
                                           'variable containing
                                           'information on the last
                                           'key pressed

   'Inkey$ contains multiple characters. The key pressed is specified
   'in the second character stored in Inkey$. A value of % indicates
   'that the left arrow has been pressed. A value of ' indicates that
   'the right arrow has been pressed.
   userInput$ = right$(left$(Inkey$,2),1)
```

```
select case userInput$   'Process keyboard input
  case "%" 'Execute if the left arrow key was pressed
    'Retrieve current sprite location coordinates
    print #main.draw, "spritexy? playerPaddle x y"
    'Determine if paddle still has space to move left (e.g., make
    'sure it has not reached the left side of the graphics window)
    if x > 0 then
      x = x - 8    'There is room, so move paddle left by 8 pixels
      print #main.draw, "spritexy playerPaddle "; x; " "; y; 'Redraw paddle
    end if


  'If player has pressed right arrow key, make sure the paddle has
  'not gone past the right edge of the window
  case "'" 'Execute if the right arrow key was pressed
    'Retrieve current sprite location coordinates
    print #main.draw, "spritexy? playerPaddle x y"
    'Determine if paddle still has space to move right (e.g., make
    'sure it has not reached the right side of the graphics window)
    if x < 680 then
      x = x + 8    'There is room, so move paddle right by 8 pixels
      print #main.draw, "spritexy playerPaddle "; x; " "; y; 'Redraw paddle
    end if
  case else

  end select
end sub
```

Any captured keyboard data is passed to the subroutine's Inkey$ argument and then analyzed. If the left arrow key is pressed and the location of the game paddle is greater than zero (meaning that it has not started to move off the left side of the graphicbox control, the paddle is moved 8 pixels to the left. If the paddle has reached the left side of the graphicbox control, its position will remain unchanged. A similar process is followed if the right arrow key is pressed. This time the value of the game ball's x coordinate is checked to see if it is less than 680, in which case it is moved 8 pixels to the right. Anything above 680 indicates that the paddle has reached the right side of the graphicbox control.

Create the Subroutine That Sets Starting Ball Direction

The SetStartingBallDirection subroutine, shown here, is responsible for setting the direction that the game ball moves when the player initiates gameplay. It does so by randomly setting the direction of the game ball on both its x- and its y-axis. By varying the value of the game ball's coordinates, the subroutine effectively sets ball direction randomly across a range of different angles:

```
'This subroutine randomly sets ball direction left or right at different angles
sub SetStartingBallDirection

  verticalDirection = int(rnd(1) * 2) 'Generate a random number from one to two

  'Use the random number to set the game ball's initial vertical axis direction
  if verticalDirection = 1 then
    newX = (int(rnd(1) * 3) + 2) 'Set direction of ball on the x-axis
  else
    newX = (int(rnd(1) * 3) + 2) * -1 'Set direction of ball on the x-axis
  end if

  'Generate another random number and use it to set the ball's direction
  'on its y-axis
  newY = (int(rnd(1) * 3) + 2) * -1


end sub
```

Create the Subroutine That Generate Sprites

The GenerateGameSprites subroutine, shown here, generates sprites used to play the game, including the game paddle and the sprite used to display the game's GAME OVER message. Note that the game ball sprite is generated elsewhere:

```
'This subroutine generates sprites (bricks, paddle, GAME OVER message)
sub GenerateGameSprites

  open "temp" for graphics as #tempSprites  'Create temporary graphics object
  print #tempSprites, "down"                'Start drawing mode

  'Create a dark green colored brick to be used when creating game bricks
  print #tempSprites, "place 0 1; backColor darkgreen;  boxfilled 42 42"

  'Create red colored, filled brick to be used to create the game paddle
  print #tempSprites, "place 42 1; backColor blue; boxfilled 117 42"

  'Create black colored, filled ball to be used to create the game ball
```

```
   print #tempSprites, "place 118 1; backColor black; boxfilled 148 60"

   'Create text-based sprites to be used to display a GAME OVER message
   print #tempSprites, "place 149 20; font arial bold"
   print #tempSprites, "|G A M E   O V E R "
   print #tempSprites, "place 149 40; backColor red; color yellow"
   print #tempSprites, "|G A M E   O V E R "

   'Use the sprites to establish bitmaps to be used in sprite animation
   print #tempSprites, "getbmp brick 0 1 42 42"
   print #tempSprites, "getbmp paddle 42 1 75 42"
   print #tempSprites, "getbmp game_ball 118 1 25 50"
   print #tempSprites, "getbmp EndOfGameMsg 149 1 170 45"

   'Create sprites using the now established bitmaps
   print #main.draw, "addsprite playerPaddle paddle"
   print #main.draw, "addsprite EndOfGameMsg EndOfGameMsg"
   print #main.draw, "spritexy EndOfGameMsg 0 -50" 'Hide this sprite from view

   close #tempSprites   'Remove the temporary sprites after creating the bitmaps

end sub
```

The subroutine ends by using the addsprite command to generate the playerPaddle and EndOfGameMsg sprites. It then hides the EndOfGameMsg sprite from view. Note that the brick sprites are added later in the AddBricksToGame subroutine.

Create the Subroutine That Draws the Window's Background

The DrawBackground subroutine, shown here, is responsible for drawing and displaying the background displayed in the graphicbox control. It accomplishes this by drawing a small cream colored line, which it then uses as the basis for creating a bitmap in computer memory. The background command is then executed, setting the bitmap image as the background.

```
'This subroutine creates a bitmap image in memory to be used as the
'background in the game window
sub DrawBackground

   'Draw a suitable background for the game
   print #main.draw, "color 255 255 204"        'Make it cream colored
   print #main.draw, "line 0 0 1 1"              'Draw a small line
```

```
'Take what was just drawn, name it, and make a bitmap of it in memory
print #main.draw, "getbmp gameBackground 0 0 1 1"

print #main.draw, "background gameBackground"  'Set bitmap as the background
print #main.draw, "cls"    'Clear the mainwin of any text

end sub
```

Create the Subroutine That Adds Bricks to the Game

The AddBricksToGame subroutine, shown here, is responsible for drawing and displaying the three rows of bricks across the top of the play area. It accomplishes this by executing a for…next loop 30 times while executing the addsprite command upon each iteration. Note that each time the addsprite command is executed, a new sprite is created and incrementally named by appending the numeric value assigned to the local *i* variable to the end of the brick string.

Next, a second for…next loop is used to place the brick sprites, three at a time (one per row), along the top of the play area. The drawsprites command is then executed to draw and display the brick sprites. Finally, the button control labeled Launch Ball is enabled, allowing the player to start a new round of play:

```
'This subroutine draws three rows of bricks across the top of the game window
sub AddBricksToGame

  noOfBricks = 0  'Reset variable value to zero

  'Add 30 sprites named brick0, brick1,... brick29 using the brick bitmap
  for i = 0 to 29
    print #main.draw, "addsprite brick"; i; " brick"
  next i

  for i = 0 to 9
    upperRow = (80 + i * 62)
    print #main.draw, "spritexy brick"; i; " "; upperRow; " 50"
    middleRow = (80 + i * 62)
    print #main.draw, "spritexy brick"; 10 + i; " "; middleRow; " 80"
    lowerRow = (80 + i * 62)
    print #main.draw, "spritexy brick"; 20 + i; " "; lowerRow; " 110"
  next i

  'Draw all the sprites on the background and update the display
```

```
print #main.draw, "drawsprites"

print #main.startButton, "!enable"    'Enable the Start button

end sub
```

Create the Subroutine That Adds the Ball to the Game

The AddBallToGame subroutine, shown here, executes the addsprite command to create a new sprite representing the game ball. As with the creation of the brick sprites, the game ball sprite is created using a bitmap image that was created earlier in the application:

```
'This subroutine adds the game ball to the game
sub AddBallToGame

    'Add a sprite representing the game ball using the game_ball bitmap
    print #main.draw, "addsprite ball game_ball"

end sub
```

Create the Subroutine That Repositions the Ball and Paddle

The RepositionBallAndPaddle subroutine, shown here, is responsible for positioning the game ball and paddle at the bottom, center of the play area. This is done using the spritexy command and prespecified x and y coordinate values (stored in global variables). Both sprites are then drawn and displayed using the drawsprites command, and a value of −3 is assigned to newY to ensure that the game ball's starting direction is set upward:

```
'This subroutine places the game ball at the bottom center of the play
'area just above the paddle, readying it for a new round of play
sub RepositionBallAndPaddle

    'Draw the game ball
    print #main.draw, "spritexy ball "; ballStartX; " "; ballStartY

    'Place the game paddle just beneath the game ball and draw it
    print #main.draw, "spritexy playerPaddle "; paddleStartX; " "; paddleStartY

    'Update the display
    print #main.draw, "drawsprites"

    'Make sure the ball's direction on the y-axis is upward
```

```
newY = -3

'Halt the game and wait for the user to provide input
wait
```

end sub

Create the Subroutine That Manages Ball Movement

The MoveTheBall subroutine, shown here, moves the game ball around the play area. Each time the subroutine is called, it updates the game ball's location by adding the values of newX and newY to ballX and ballY, respectively. The drawsprites command is then executed, drawing and displaying the ball sprite at its new location (new coordinates):

```
'This subroutine is responsible for moving the ball around the screen
sub MoveTheBall

  'Update the position of the ball
  ballX = ballX + newX
  ballY = ballY + newY

  'Draw the ball at its new location
  print #main.draw, "spritexy ball "; ballX; " "; ballY;
  print #main.draw, "drawsprites"

end sub
```

Create the Subroutine That Checks for Collisions

The CollisionCheck subroutine, shown here, monitors for collisions between the game ball and other sprites (excluding the paddle) and then calls on other subroutines that are designed to process and handle collisions. It begins by using the spritecollides command to capture a list named collision$ made up of the names of any sprites that the ball sprite is in contact with.

The collision$ list is then analyzed to see if it contains any entries. If the ball sprite has collided with a sprite other than the playerPaddle sprite, it has collided with a brick, and a call is made to the MonitorForBrickCollisions subroutine, passing it the name of the sprite that the ball sprite has come into contact with. If the ball sprite has instead come into contact with the playerPaddle sprite, a call is made to the BallAndPaddleHaveCollided subroutine. There is no need to pass an argument to the BallAndPaddleHaveCollided subroutine because it has already been determined that the ball sprite has collided with the playerPaddle sprite:

```
'This subroutine determines if the ball has collided with anything
sub CollisionCheck

  'Retrieve a list that contains the names of any sprites that may be overlap-
ping
  'the ball sprite, and store that list in the collision$ variable
  print #main.draw, "spritecollides ball collision$"

  'This statement executes when the ball collides with anything other than
  'the paddle
  if (collision$ <> "") and (instr(collision$, "playerPaddle")= 0) then

    'Call subroutine that handles collisions with bricks
    call MonitorForBrickCollisions collision$

  else

    'This statement executes when the ball collides with the player paddle
    if instr(collision$, "playerPaddle") > 0 then call BallAndPaddleHaveCollided

  end if

end sub
```

Create the Subroutine That Changes Ball Direction After a Collision

The AnalyzeAndUpdateBallLocation subroutine, shown here, changes the direction that the ball sprite is traveling when it reaches the right, left, or top of the play area. It determines if the ball sprite has reached the top of the play area (for example, graphicbox control) by checking to see if its y coordinate, stored in ballY, is less than or equal to zero. In similar fashion, the value of ballX is checked to determine if the ball sprite has reached the left or right side of the play area. Any time one of the preceding cases evaluates as true, an audio file named Collision.wav is played. In addition, the direction that the ball is traveling is modified to deflect the ball's movement away from its current location.

Hint

The Collision.wav file is a small audio file that makes a short ping-like sound when played. A copy of the wave file can be downloaded along with a copy of the Bricks application source code from the book's companion website, located at www.cengageptr.com/downloads.

A fourth check is made to see if the ball sprite's y coordinate is greater than or equal to 400, which indicates that it has dropped below the height of the playerPaddle sprite. If this turns out to be the case, the current round of play has ended. An audio file named Miss.wav is played, and a call is made to the ManageLives subroutine:

```
'This subroutine changes ball direction when the ball reaches the right, left,
'or top wall; it also manages player misses
sub AnalyzeAndUpdateBallLocation

  'Check to see if the ball has reached the top of the window (thus colliding
  'with the top wall)
  if (ballY <= 0) then  'Has the top of the window been reached?
    newY = 3  'Move the ball's y coordinate three pixels downward
    playwave "Collision.wav", asynch  'Play the Collision.wav wave file
  end if

  'Check to see if the ball has reached the left side of the window (thus
  'colliding with the left wall)
  if (ballX <= 0) then  'Has the left side been reached?
    newX = 3  'Move the ball's x coordinate three pixels to the right
    playwave "Collision.wav", asynch  'Play the Collision.wav wave file
  end if

  'Check to see if the ball has reached the right side of the window (thus
  'colliding with the right wall)
  if (ballX >= 736) then  'Has the right side been reached?
    newX = -3  'Move the ball's x coordinate three pixels to the left
    playwave "Collision.wav", asynch  'Play the Collision.wav wave file
  end if

  'Check to see if the ball has dropped below the height of the game paddle
  if (ballY >= 400) then  'Has the ball dropped below the paddle?
    playwave "Miss", asynch    'Play the Miss.wav wave file
    call ManageLives           'Call subroutine that keep track of player lives
  end if

end sub
```

Create the Subroutine That Controls Game Pace

The RegulateGameSpeed subroutine, shown here, facilitates the collection of keyboard input and regulates game speed to ensure it runs at an acceptable pace. This is achieved by executing the scan command to allow for input collection followed by the execution of a do…until loop that moderates the speed of the game:

```
'This subroutine pauses game execution just long enough to allow the
'game to collect and process mouse and keyboard input and ensure the
'game executes at an appropriate pace
sub RegulateGameSpeed

    scan   'Briefly pause execution to allow collection of keyboard/mouse input

    timeStamp = time$("milliseconds") 'Get number of milliseconds since midnight

    'Loop until an amount of time greater than the speed of the ball has passed
    do
    loop until time$("milliseconds") > timeStamp + ballSpeed


end sub
```

Create the Subroutine That Processes Collisions with Bricks

As mentioned earlier, the MonitorForBrickCollisions subroutine is called whenever the ball sprite collides with an object other than the playerPaddle sprite. The name of the sprite that the ball sprite has collided with is passed to the subroutine as an argument. The subroutine changes the direction the ball sprite is moving based on whether it comes into contact with the left, right, top, or bottom of the other sprite. Bricks involved in collision are deleted from the game using the removesprite command, and the Collision.wav file is played, adding an essential sound effect to the game. Every time a brick is eliminated, the player's score must be increased. This is accomplished by calling the UpdatePlayerScore subroutine:

```
'This subroutine processes collisions between the ball and bricks
sub MonitorForBrickCollisions object$

  'Retrieve the x, y coordinates of the sprite that has collided with the ball
  print #main.draw, "spritexy? "; object$; " objectX objectY"

  'Change the ball's direction on its x-axis when it collides with the
  'left side of the other object
  if ballX < (objectX - 12) then newX = -5
```

```
'Change the ball's direction on its x-axis when it collides with the
'right side of the other object
if (ballX > (objectX + 20)) and (ballX < (objectX + 40)) then newX = 3

'Change the ball's direction on its y-axis depending on whether it collides
'with the top or bottom of the other object
if (ballY + 12) > (objectY + 5) then
   newY = 3
else
   newY = -3
end if

'The ball has collided with a brick, so remove the brick
print #main.draw, "removesprite "; object$

playwave "Collision.wav", asynch  'Play wave file that signals a player miss

call UpdatePlayerScore  'Call the subroutine that updates the player's score

end sub
```

Create the Subroutine That Processes Collisions with the Paddle

The BallAndPaddleHaveCollided subroutine, shown here, is called whenever the ball sprite collides with the playerPaddle sprite. When this occurs, the ball sprite direction on its y-axis is reversed. This deflects the ball sprite away from the playerPaddle. Lastly, the Collision.wav file is played:

```
'This subroutine manages collisions between the player paddle and the game ball
sub BallAndPaddleHaveCollided

   if newY = 3 then
      newY = -3
   else
      newY = 3
   end if

   playwave "Collision.wav", asynch 'Play wave file when ball collides
                                    'with the paddle
end sub
```

Create the Subroutine That Updates the Player's Score

The UpdatePlayerScore subroutine is responsible for incrementing the value assigned to the player's score, stored in the playerScore variable, by one every time the subroutine is called. The subroutine is also responsible for keeping count of the number of bricks removed from the game. Every time it is called, the subroutine also refreshes the display of both the playerScore and noOfLives variables. If the subroutine determines that all 30 bricks have been removed from the screen, the current round of play has ended and calls are made to the AddBricksToGame, AddBallToGame, and RepositionBallAndPaddle subroutines to ready the game for a new round of play:

```
'This subroutine is called whenever the player scores a point
sub UpdatePlayerScore

  playerScore = playerScore + 1 'Increment player score by one
  noOfBricks = noOfBricks + 1    'Increment variable value by one

  'Display the number of lives remaining and the player's score
  print #main.lives, "Lives = "; str$(noOfLives)
  print #main.score, "Score =  "; str$(playerScore)

  if noOfBricks = 30 then  'If all 30 bricks have been eliminated

    'Call subroutine that adds a new set of bricks to the game
    call AddBricksToGame

    'Call subroutine that adds the game ball to the game
    call AddBallToGame

    'Call subroutine that centers the game ball and paddle
    call RepositionBallAndPaddle

  end if

end sub
```

Create the Subroutine That Keeps Track of Player Lives

The ManageLives subroutine is responsible for keeping track of the number of lives the player has left in the game and for decrementing that value, stored in the noOfLives variable, by one every time the subroutine is called. Every time it is called, the subroutine also refreshes the display of both the playerScore and noOfLives variables. The subroutine is also responsible for determining when the game has ended, which occurs when the value of noOfLives becomes zero.

When this occurs, the DisplayGameOverMessage subroutine is called. Otherwise, while a round of play has just ended, the game continues because the player still has at least one life remaining. If this is the case, the button control labeled Launchl Ball is re-enabled, and the RepositionBallAndPaddle subroutine is called:

```
'This subroutine is called whenever the player loses a life
sub ManageLives

  noOfLives = noOfLives - 1  'Take away one of the player's lives

  'Display number of lives remaining
  print #main.lives, "Lives = "; str$(noOfLives)
  print #main.score, "Score = "; str$(playerScore)

  'Analyze the number of lives that the player has remaining
  if noOfLives = 0 then
    call DisplayGameOverMessage    'Call game over if there are no lives left
  else
    print #main.startButton, "!enable"   'Enable the Start button
    call RepositionBallAndPaddle  'Continue play if player has any lives left
  end if

end sub
```

Create the Subroutine That Displays the Game Over Message

The DisplayGameOverMessage subroutine is called at the end of gameplay, after the player has lost all three of his lives. The subroutine repositions the EndOfGameMsg sprite in the play area (in the graphicbox control) and then draws and displays it. It then disables the button control labeled Launch Ball, preventing the current game from continuing:

```
'This subroutine displays the End of Game message
sub DisplayGameOverMessage

  print #main.draw, "spritexy EndOfGameMsg 300 250" 'Draw End of Game sprite
  print #main.draw, "drawsprites"                    'Display the sprite
  print #main.startButton, "!disable"               'Disable the Start button
  wait   'Stop program execution

end sub
```

Create the Subroutine That Terminates Game Execution

The last subroutine that makes up the Bricks application is the ExitGame subroutine. Its job is to display a pop-up dialog window that requests the player confirm his intention to terminate gameplay. If the player responds in the affirmative, the game's bitmap files are unloaded from memory, the game window is closed, and the application ends:

```
'This subroutine prompts for confirmation and handles game termination
sub ExitGame handle$
  'Display confirmation message in pop-up dialog window
  confirm "Are you sure you wish to stop playing?"; userResponse$

  if userResponse$ = "yes" then  'User has provided confirmation
    'Keep things clean and free up resources by unloading graphics files
    'from memory

    unloadbmp "paddle"
    unloadbmp "game_ball"
    unloadbmp "brick"
    unloadbmp "gameBackground"
    close #main   'Close the game window
    wait  'Stop program execution
  end if

end sub
```

The Final Result

Okay, assuming that you followed all the steps that have been outlined without making typos, your copy of the Bricks game should be ready to go. Take a little time to test the game and put it through its paces. While you are at it, make sure that you enter both valid and invalid data to ensure the game handles it correctly. Keep an eye on the player score and live data that is displayed at the bottom of the game window and validate that it is being tabulated correctly. Last but not least, make sure that the game window's menus and the button control labeled Launch Ball are operating and that the Help and About windows display correctly.

Summary

In this chapter, you learned the basics of arcade-style game development. This included creating and managing sprites, managing game state, and controlling gameplay using loops. You also learned how to control the timing of events and to incorporate the collection and processing of keyboard input. Finally, you discovered how to perform collision detection and to execute a controlled termination of gameplay.

Before you move on to Chapter 11, "Debugging Your Applications," consider setting aside a little time to improve the Bricks game by addressing the following list of challenges.

Challenges

1. As currently designed, the game ball travels at a consistent pace during gameplay. Consider modifying the application to slowly increase ball speed as the player's score increases.

2. To make gameplay more challenging, consider modifying it by adding additional layers of bricks to the game, making it more difficult to clear the game board.

3. Consider adding a menu option to the game that allows the player to specify paddle sizes of small, medium, and large and them modify the game accordingly to provide paddles of these sizes. In this manner, you can add different levels of game difficulty.

4. Finally, to spice things up a bit, consider randomly changing brick color each time the screen is cleared of bricks.

11

Debugging Your Applications

In this final chapter of the book, you will learn how to track down and deal with the errors that inevitably occur when developing a new software application. Program errors can occur for any number of reasons, including typos, inappropriately applied command syntax, and faulty programming logic. This chapter is designed to help teach you the fundamental steps involved in identifying and correcting these types of errors. Discussion will also include the development of error-handling procedures as well as the use of Just BASIC's debugger as a means of keeping an eye on the internal operation of your programs, allowing you to track down and spot errors that might otherwise be difficult to locate. In addition to all this, you will get the chance to develop the book's final application: the Hangman game.

Specifically, you will learn the following:

- The differences between syntax, logical, and runtime errors
- How to execute a program using a debugger
- How to control program execution and monitor variable values when debugging applications
- How to set up error handlers

Project Preview: The Hangman Game

In this chapter, you will learn how to develop the book's final Just BASIC application: the Hangman game. In this game, the player is challenged to try to guess a mystery word without making more than five incorrect guesses. Figure 11.1 shows how the game looks when it's started.

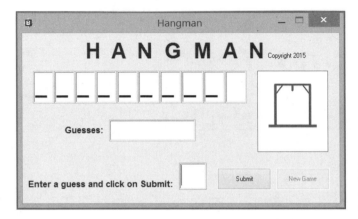

Figure 11.1 Underscore characters are used to represent the letters that make up the mystery word.
© 2016 Cengage Learning®

The player submits guesses by typing a letter into the Enter a Guess and Click on Submit field and then clicking on the Submit button. If the letter that is guessed is used in the mystery word, the letter is displayed in the appropriate textbox control at the top of the window, as demonstrated in Figure 11.2.

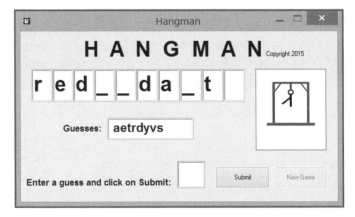

Figure 11.2 The player has made six correct guesses so far.
© 2016 Cengage Learning®

Each time the player enters a guess, whether it is right or wrong, the letter is added to the list of letters shown in the Guesses field, making it easy for the player to keep track of the guesses made so far. A graphical depiction, located on the right side of the window, shows how many misses the player has made so far.

Each guess submitted by the player is validated. First, the game prevents the player from entering the same letter twice. Second, it prevents the player from entering a number or a special character. Third, it prevents the player from entering more than one character at a time. For example, Figure 11.3 shows an example of the message that the game displays if the player clicks on the Submit button without first keying in a guess.

Figure 11.4 shows an example of a game that has been won by the player. As you can see from the Guesses field, it took the player several guesses to determine the game's mystery word. However, the player made only three incorrect guesses, as depicted by the partially drawn hangman image.

Figure 11.3 Invalid guesses are not counted against the player.
© 2016 Cengage Learning®

Figure 11.4 Mystery words are randomly selected from an array of words stored inside the game.
© 2016 Cengage Learning®

Figure 11.5 shows an example of a game in which the player has lost and the hangman is complete. As the figure shows, the Submit button is disabled at the end of each game to stop gameplay. At the same time, the New Game button is enabled, allowing the player to start a new game.

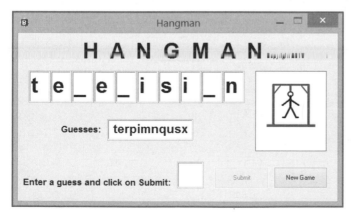

Figure 11.5 The player failed to guess the game's mystery word.
© 2016 Cengage Learning®

Coping with Errors in Your Applications

Every programmer, no matter how proficient and talented he may be, runs into errors when developing computer applications. The number of errors and problems that you run into grows based on the size and complexity of your applications. Unfortunately, there is no way around this inevitability. Errors will happen. The purpose of this chapter is to give you an overall understanding of the types of errors that you will run into and offer guidance on how to go about finding, fixing, and handling them.

Computer applications are subject to different types of errors. Errors can wreak havoc on an application and result in unpredictable results. Sometimes the bugs are easy to find and eliminate. Other times, they are hidden deep within your program code and surface only on rare occasions to drive both programmers and users crazy. Many programmers refer to errors as *bugs*. Your job as a programmer is to seek out and exterminate or *debug* all the errors from your applications.

As this chapter demonstrates, there are a number of steps that you can take to reduce errors in your applications. One of the most obvious steps is to take time before you start writing your program to plan out its overall organization and design as opposed to just sitting down at the keyboard and making things up as you go along. You should also make liberal use of subroutines and functions to develop modular program code that can be created and tested a section at a time. Another step that you should always include is properly testing your applications. This includes testing to make sure they operate as expected as well as trying to feed your application inappropriate data to see if the program handles it correctly.

Along with these programming practices, there are additional steps you can take to ensure that your applications will operate as expected, including these:

- Carefully laying out a clear and easy-to-use user interface
- Making sure that you provide users with access to clear instructions and help information so that they will know how to properly operate the application
- Adding program code to your application that will validate all input, whether it is supplied from an external file or directly from the user
- Using a consistent naming scheme for all your variables, arrays, subroutines, and functions, and ensuring that names are as descriptive as possible

In addition to following the preceding advice, you should determine which parts of your applications are most subject to errors and add programming logic to attempt to deal with them. As previously discussed, one way of doing this is through data validation. Another way of handling errors is to develop error-handling routines, as discussed later in this chapter.

Regardless of which programming language you are working with, you will run into three distinct types of programming errors, as listed here:

- Syntax errors
- Logical errors
- Runtime errors

Understanding Syntax Errors

The most obvious and common type of error that you will come across is a syntax error. A *syntax error* occurs when the programmer fails to write a code statement that follows the syntax rules specified by the programming language. The most common cause of syntax errors is typos. For example, a syntax error will occur if you misspell a command or inappropriately format a code statement, which would be the case if you left out a key parameter.

Programming languages notify programmers of errors in many different ways. A text-based scripting language like Perl, Python, or Ruby will display a text error message. *Rapid Application Development (RAD)* programming languages like Visual Basic and Liberty BASIC will sometimes display error messages in the code editor's status bar or in pop-up dialogs. Regardless of the programming language used, error messages generally provide the same type of information, which includes a brief description of the error and an error number. A text-based scripting language may also supply the line number where the error was detected, and RAD programming languages often highlight the offending programming statement in the *integrated development environment (IDE)*.

Syntax errors prevent an application from compiling. In Just BASIC, the compiler stops executing if it comes across a syntax error. To see an example of a syntax error, take a look at the following statement:

```
print "Hello world!
```

There is a double-quote missing from the end of the text string in this statement. In addition to halting the compile process, Just BASIC highlights the statement that contains the syntax error in the code editor and displays a text message describing the error in the status bar at the bottom of the code editor window, as demonstrated in Figure 11.6.

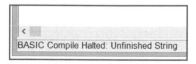

Figure 11.6 An example of a syntax error caused by an unfinished string.

© 2016 Shoptalk Systems

As you can see, the text message displayed in the status bar clearly identifies the problem as being an unfinished string (that is, it's missing its closing double-quotation mark). To fix this error, all you have to do is add the closing quotation mark to the end of the string being displayed, as shown here:

```
print "Hello world!"
```

Upon fixing the syntax error, you can perform the compile process again. Just BASIC will either compile your program or, if it comes across another syntax error, pause and display information about the error.

An example of another common type of syntax error is shown here:

```
sampleString = "Hello world!"
```

Here a type mismatch syntax error has occurred because a string is being assigned to a numeric variable. Remember that string variable names must end with the $ character, as shown here:

```
sampleString$ = "Hello world!"
```

Because Just BASIC clearly identifies the program statement that generates a syntax error and provides a descriptive error message, it is generally easy to identify and fix syntax errors. If, after examining the statement in question, you are unable to locate the source of the error, you can always use Just BASIC's Help file to look up the syntax of the command in question and double-check your syntax usage that way.

Coping with Logical Errors

Sometimes errors occur because of a mistake on your part in the logic being applied to solve a problem or to perform a particular task. These types of errors are usually referred to as *logical errors*. For example, you may have meant to take two numbers provided by the user and multiply them together to create a third number. However, when you sat down and wrote the program, you may have inadvertently added these two numbers together. As a result, your application might run just fine, doing exactly what it was told to do. The problem is that this is not what you wanted the program to do.

The best way to guard against logical errors is to carefully outline and review the programming logic required to develop a program before you write it and then extensively test your application once it has been written to ensure that it is operating as expected. One way of executing your program is to use the Just BASIC debugger, covered later in this chapter, to keep an eye on the execution flow of program statements and to monitor the values being assigned to program variables and arrays.

Unfortunately, because Just BASIC does not see any problems with the programming logic, it is not able to flag logical errors. But don't fret; all hope is not lost. There are ways to track down and fix logical errors. The first step is to realize that your program is not operating as expected. You can then sit down and review your application's source code to see if you can spot the error that way. If you cannot find the error this way, your next step might be to embed a few `print` statements or `notice` commands at different locations within your program to identify when particular parts of the program are being executed. This gives you a rudimentary way of keeping track of the logical execution flow of your program. You can even expand the usefulness of the `print` statements and `notice` commands by displaying the values of any variables that you think are relevant to the problem you are trying to track down. In the case of the previous example, you would want to display the value of the three variables at different locations within the application to keep an eye on them. In this manner, you'd be able to identify the problem as soon as you saw the two values were being added together instead of being multiplied.

Embedding extra `print` statements and `notice` commands inside your programs is a sufficient approach for debugging and finding problems in small programs. However, as your programs grow in size, this debugging technique becomes difficult to implement. This is where Just BASIC's built-in debugger comes into play. Using the debugger, as described later in this chapter, you can trace program execution flow and monitor variable values while also exercising detailed line-by-line control over the execution of your program.

Eliminating Runtime Errors

To run your application, it must be free of syntax errors. However, your application is still susceptible to another type of error, referred to as a runtime error. *Runtime errors* occur when a program statement attempts to perform an illegal action. For example, your program might attempt to access a local disk drive that has crashed or become full, in which case the access attempt will fail and the program will stop running and crash. If this happens, the application may generate an ugly error message that is sure to confound your users, or it may simply shut down without an explanation of what has happened.

Application compilers are not able to detect and notify you of runtime errors. To detect them, you need to extensively test your applications. This is especially true if your application contains subroutines or functions that may not be executed except on rare occasions. Failure to test every procedure in an application and to attempt to validate the application's execution in every possible scenario means that your users will be left to discover runtime errors on their own. The result may be a loss of faith in the quality of the application or, even worse, their belief in the quality of your work.

If a runtime error occurs when you are executing a program using Just BASIC's code editor, Just BASIC displays an error message in a pop-up dialog informing you of the error before terminating your program's execution. For example, the following statement is guaranteed to produce a runtime error. (It is illegal in any programming language to divide a number by zero.)

```
x = 10 / 0
```

As soon as it comes across this statement, Just BASIC displays the pop-up error message shown in Figure 11.7.

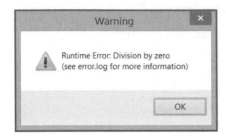

Figure 11.7 An example of a runtime error being reported by Just BASIC.
© 2016 Cengage Learning®

Runtime errors can occur for all sorts of reasons. The user may, for example, provide your application with invalid input. You can deal with this by adding input validation logic to your program. Your program may need to work with a specific file. Because files have a tendency to disappear for all kinds of reasons, it is a good idea to add logic to your program to check for the existence of a file prior to trying to access it. This way if the file is not found, you can take corrective action. This action might be to re-create the file, or it might be to display a message informing the user of the problem and stating that until it has been fixed, your application will not be able to perform a particular task.

Nothing is ever perfect, including computer programs. Therefore, try as you might, there is no way to ever be 100-percent certain that all runtime errors have been eliminated from your applications. However, even in this worst-case scenario, you still have options. Specifically, you can add error-handling logic to your applications, as discussed later in this chapter, to recover from errors or at the very least to gracefully handle them (for example, by displaying a user-friendly error message and by closing any open files in use by the program).

What Is Just BASIC's Error.log File?

As was demonstrated in Figure 11.7, sometimes error messages reference Just BASIC's `Error.log` file. Just BASIC writes internal information to the file as it executes. Sometimes you can get helpful bits and pieces of information that provide insight as to why a particular error occurred by examining this file. However, more often than not, you probably will not find this file overly helpful.

Hint

If you run into a problem that you cannot figure out and you think it might be the result of a problem with Just BASIC, you can send an email to support@justbasic.com explaining your problem in as much detail as possible. In addition, you might want to include a copy of the program in which the error is occurring, as well as a copy of the `Error.log` file.

Debugging Your Just BASIC Applications

Most modern-day programming languages, including Just BASIC, Visual Basic, and Liberty BASIC, give programmers access to a built-in program debugger. A *debugger* is a utility program that runs an application in a special mode that allows the programmer to pause application execution to view variable values and to then execute line-by-line control over program statements.

Just BASIC also includes a debugger that you can use to debug your Windows application to trace its execution flow, thus validating that things are occurring in the order you expect them to. In addition, because you can see and keep an eye on the values assigned to application variables, you can also use the debugger to ensure that your program is correctly calculating and updating variable values.

To run a program using the Just BASIC debugger, open your program in the Just BASIC editor and then click on the Run menu and select Debug or click on the Debug button, which looks like a small ladybug. In response, Just BASIC loads—but does not run—your application into the debugger and displays the debugger window, as demonstrated in Figure 11.8.

Figure 11.8 Using Just BASIC's built-in debugger to execute a Windows application.

Working with the Debugger Toolbar

Just BASIC's debugger consists of a toolbar and two window panes. The toolbar, shown in Figure 11.9, contains buttons that give you detailed control over how your program is executed.

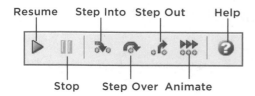

Figure 11.9 Just BASIC's debugger toolbar gives the programmer control over program execution.
© 2016 Shoptalk Systems

The function of each of the toolbar buttons is explained here:

- **Resume.** Continues the normal execution of the program and does not display information about variable values while executing.
- **Stop.** Stops program execution and highlights the line where execution has been paused.
- **Step Into.** Executes the next statement in the program and then pauses the program. If the next statement is a subroutine or a function, execution pauses at the opening subroutine statement.
- **Step Over.** Executes the next statement in the program and then pauses the program unless the next statement is a subroutine or a function, in which case the entire procedure is run before program execution pauses.
- **Step Out.** Executes any statements remaining in a subroutine or function and then pauses program execution. Resumes the execution of the program, allowing it to run normally.
- **Animate.** Executes the program normally while also displaying variable values in the upper pane as the program runs.
- **Help.** Displays information about the debugger and its operation.

Examining Variable Values

When it's started, the debugger highlights the first statement in your application and waits for you to tell it what to do. By default, only the variables explicitly defined within your application are displayed in the upper window pane. However, Just BASIC automatically generates additional variables for every application. You can view these variables by selecting the Show Default Variables checkbox control located in the space between the upper and lower window pane. When selected, this option instructs the debugger to show all program variables, as demonstrated in Figure 11.10.

As you use the debugger to execute your application, the value of variables displayed in the upper pane is constantly updated as changes are made to them. As such, you can keep an eye on your application's variables to determine if their values are being correctly modified as the application executes.

Figure 11.10 Viewing all the variables being managed by Just BASIC as your program executes.

© 2016 Shoptalk Systems

A Quick Demonstration of How to Use the Debugger

The best way to learn how to work with any programming language's debugger is to spend some time getting comfortable with its operation. Let's take Just BASIC's debugger for a quick test drive. For starters, you need a program to execute, so begin by keying the following program into the Just BASIC code editor:

```
print "It is time to count to 5." + chr$(13) + chr$(13)

x = 5

for i = 1 to 5
  print i
  x = x + i
next i

call DisplayMessage

end

sub DisplayMessage
  notice "All done!"
end sub
```

When executed, this program displays a list of numbers from 1 to 5 and then displays a pop-up dialog announcing the end of the program's execution. Rather than running the program normally, click on the Debug (ladybug) button located on Just BASIC's toolbar. In response, Just BASIC opens the debugger window, loads your application, and then pauses. In addition, the application's mainwin text window appears. To run your program at normal speed, click on the debugger's Resume button. When run this way, the debugger does not keep track of statement execution flow or variable values and is not much help in tracking down an error.

Now close the debugger window and click on the Debug button again. Note that when the debugger reappears, the first statement in your program is highlighted, identifying it as the next line of code to be executed. Also note that the value of both x and i are set to zero. Click on the Step Into button. In response, the debugger processes the highlighted statement and pauses execution again. If you look at the mainwin text window, you see a line of text has been printed to it. Click on the Step Into button again. Note that the value of x has been set equal to 5. If you continue to click on the Step Into button, you see that the statements that make up the program's for...next loop are repeatedly executed five times and that the values assigned to x and i are continuously updated.

Once the loop has executed for the fifth and final time, the Call DisplayMessage statement is highlighted. If you click the Step Into button a few more times, you step through the execution of the DisplayMessage subroutine a line at a time. Alternatively, you can click on the Step Over button, in which case the entire subroutine executes without pausing. However, execution pauses again at the end statement. You can also Step Into the subroutine and then decide to click on the Step Out button, in which case the rest of the subroutine is executed and pauses again at the end statement. Lastly, you can click on the Animate button at any time, in which case the debugger executes the rest of the program at normal speed while updating the value of x and i in the upper pane and showing in the lower pain the order in which statements are being executed. Because this example loops only five times, the animate feature is of little help. But if you modify the program to loop 1,000 times, you're able to get a better understanding of how the animate option works.

All in all, the debugger can be a great tool for tracking down a particularly pesky bug because it allows you to run your program and control the pace at which things occur while easily keeping an eye on variable values.

Hint

One major feature not found in Just BASIC's debugger is the ability to set breakpoints. A *breakpoint* is a marker that tells the debugger to pause execution at a specified location in a program. By setting breakpoints at different points within a program, you have an additional means of controlling and pausing program execution.

Developing a Runtime Error Handler

As previously discussed, runtime errors can occur for different reasons. As a programmer, it is your job to anticipate and deal with runtime errors. Your goal is to develop bug-free applications that never crash and that handle any unavoidable errors as gracefully as possible. The end result should be an application that meets user needs and minimizes potential confusion in the event of a runtime error.

Your first step in meeting this challenge is to anticipate the places within your applications where errors are most likely to occur and try to programmatically deal with them. You should, for example, validate any user input and ensure that files exist before attempting to open them.

For situations that may be out of your control, you can set up a runtime error handler to deal with errors. Examples of these types of situations include an unavailable disk drive or a missing file. Using a runtime error handler, you set up your program to gracefully handle the situation using any of the following options:

- Presenting user-friendly error messages
- Closing any open files and resources in use by the applications
- Providing the user with additional instruction on how to fix the problem
- Apologizing for any inconvenience
- Requesting that the user report the error

Whenever an error occurs in a Just BASIC application, the Err special variable is populated with an error number. Likewise, the Err$ special variable is populated with a string that describes the error.

Trap

Both Err and Err$ are case sensitive, so when you use them, be sure to type them exactly as shown here.

Using the information provided by the Err and Err$ special variables, you can capture and identify the cause of a runtime error. Using this information, you can add an error-handling routine to your program that attempts to recover from or gracefully deal with the error. To set up an error handler within your Just BASIC program, you need to use the On Error GoTo statement.

Use of the On Error GoTo statement as a means of setting up an error handler is supported in many different programming languages. This approach to error handling is sometimes referred to as *unstructured error handling*. *Structured error handling* is an alternative approach that many programming languages provide, including C++ and Visual Basic. In structured error handling, you use a Try…Catch…Finally statement to build error-handling routines. Specifically, Try statements are inserted into locations within the application where exceptions are most likely to occur, and Catch statements are then added that are designed to handle the exception. To handle different types of exceptions, you can add additional Catch blocks. Programmers can also add an optional Finally block. If included, the Finally block executes and runs program statements that need to be executed in response to any error.

The On Error GoTo statement instructs Just BASIC to redirect program flow to a specified label if an error occurs. This statement has the following syntax:

```
On Error GoTo [label]
```

To better understand how the On Error GoTo statement works, take a look at the following example:

```
On Error GoTo [ErrorHandler]

open "C:\Sample.log" for input as #logFile

line input #logFile, variableName$
print variableName$

close #logFile


wait

[ErrorHandler]

  print "The following error occurred during program execution:" _
    + chr$(13) + chr$(13)

  print "————————————————————————"
  print "Error Code: "; Err
  print "Error Message: "; Err$
```

```
print "————————————————————————————"
print
print "An error code of 0 indicates that the Sample.log file is empty."
print
print "An error code of 53 indicates that Sample.log has been removed "
print "from this computer."
print
print "Please report this error message to Technical Support."

if Err = 0 then
  close #logFile
end if

end
```

Here, an On Error GoTo statement has been added as the first statement at the beginning of a small application. As a result, if an error occurs, execution flow is redirected to a label named [ErrorHandler]. The code statements that follow the label are then executed.

The code statements that make up the actual application have been inserted after the On Error GoTo statement and before [ErrorHandler]. The first of these statements attempts to open a file named Sample.log that should be found in the root of the computer's C: drive. If the file is found, it is opened, and the first line of the file is read and then displayed. The file is then closed.

The application's error handler has been designed to handle two possible runtime errors. First, if the file exists but is empty, leaving nothing to be retrieved and displayed, when the line input command is executed, an error occurs. In response, the execution flow is immediately passed to [ErrorHandler]. Within the handler, the values of Err and Err$ are used to display a user-friendly error message. In addition, because Err will be equal to 0, the close command is used to close the Sample.log file. Figure 11.11 shows the result that is produced when this example is executed.

If, on the other hand, the program is run and it turns out that somebody has deleted the Sample.log file, a different error occurs. In response, execution flow jumps to [ErrorHandler], where a user-friendly error message is displayed. Because the value of Err is 53 this time, there is no need to close the Sample.log file; it was never opened.

Regardless of the type of error that occurs, once executed, the last statement following the [ErrorHandler] executes, terminating the execution of the program.

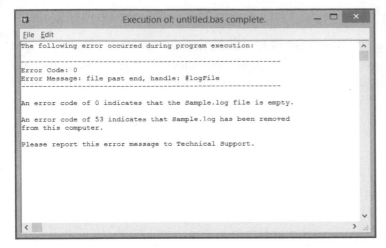

Figure 11.11 Using a custom error handler to gracefully handle a runtime error.
© 2016 Shoptalk Systems

To see the benefit of including an error handler within your Just BASIC applications, consider what would happen if you were to remove the `On Error GoTo` statement and its corresponding error handler from the application, leaving only the statements shown here:

```
open "C:\Sample.log" for input as #logFile


line input #logFile, variableName$
print variableName$

close #logFile


wait
```

This time, if you execute the application, instead of displaying a user-friendly error message and gracefully terminating the application, the two pop-up dialog error messages shown in Figure 11.12 are displayed, and the application abruptly terminates.

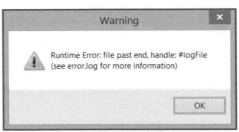

Figure 11.12 An example of the type of errors that users may see when a runtime error is not programmatically handled.
© 2016 Shoptalk Systems

Back to the Hangman Game

Now it is time to turn your attention back to this book's final application development project: the Hangman game. This game serves as an excellent capstone project for this book, giving you the chance to put together everything you have learned. You'll need to work with both variables and arrays. You'll use loops and conditional logic. You'll also need to work with both subroutines and functions. And, of course, you'll have to design and develop the game's GUI.

Designing the Game

As has already been stated, the design of the Hangman game relies on subroutines and functions. In total, the game will be created in nine steps, as outlined here:

1. Create a new BASIC file and add initial comment statements.
2. Define an array and global variables, and initiate gameplay.
3. Create the ManageGamePlay subroutine.
4. Create the StartNewGame subroutine.
5. Create the GetNewWord$() function.
6. Create the ProcessGuess subroutine.
7. Create the ValidateInput$() function.
8. Create the PlayAgain subroutine.
9. Create the ClosePlay subroutine.

Creating a Just BASIC File Script

The first step in the creation of the Hangman game is to create a new BASIC file named Hangman.bas and add the following statements to it:

```
' ***************************************************************************
'
' Script Name:  Hangman.bas (The Hangman Game)
' Version:      1.0
' Author:       Jerry Lee Ford, Jr.
' Date:         February 5, 2015
'
' Description: This is a computerized version of the classic
'              Hangman game. The objective of the game is for the player to
'              try to guess mystery words one letter at a time in as
'              few guesses as possible without getting hung.
'
```

```
' **************************************************************************
```

```
nomainwin    'Suppress the display of the default text window
```

As you can see, there is nothing new here beyond the addition of standard opening comment statements and the execution of the nomainwin command.

Defining Global Variables and an Array

The next step in the development of the Hangman game is to declare a few global variables used to store the game's mystery word and to keep track of the total number of incorrect and correct player guesses. In addition, you will define an array named words$() and populate it with 10 mystery words. Lastly, the ManageGamePlay subroutine, which generates the game's user interface, is called. To accomplish all this, add the following statements to the end of the program file:

```
'Define global variables
global secretWord$, totalMissed, totalCorrect

'Define an array capable of storing 10 words
dim words$(9)

'Load the array with words (limit word size to a maximum of 10 letters)
words$(0) = "piano"
words$(1) = "article"
words$(2) = "television"
words$(3) = "musical"
words$(4) = "redundant"
words$(5) = "remarkable"
words$(6) = "experience"
words$(7) = "adventure"
words$(8) = "discover"
words$(9) = "military"


call ManageGamePlay 'Call the subroutine responsible for managing gameplay

wait   'Pause the application and wait for the player's instruction
```

Designing the Game's User Interface

The code statements that compose the ManageGamePlay subroutine are shown next and should be added to the end of the program file. When executed, this subroutine generates the game's user interface and is responsible for managing overall gameplay:

```
'This subroutine displays the game board and controls interaction with the
'player
sub ManageGamePlay

  WindowWidth = 600    'Set the width of the window to 600 pixels
  WindowHeight = 350   'Set the height of the window to 350 pixels

  loadbmp "blank", "C:\images\blank.bmp"        'Load the specified bitmap
                                                'file into memory
  loadbmp "head", "C:\images\head.bmp"          'Load the specified bitmap
                                                'file into memory
  loadbmp "body", "C:\images\body.bmp"          'Load the specified bitmap
                                                'file into memory
  loadbmp "leftarm", "C:\images\leftarm.bmp"    'Load the specified bitmap
                                                'file into memory
  loadbmp "rightarm", "C:\images\rightarm.bmp" 'Load the specified bitmap
                                                'file into memory
  loadbmp "leftleg", "C:\images\leftleg.bmp"    'Load the specified bitmap
                                                'file into memory
  loadbmp "rightleg", "C:\images\rightleg.bmp" 'Load the specified bitmap
                                                'file into memory

  'Define the format of statictext controls displayed on the window
  statictext #play.statictext1, "H  A  N  G  M  A  N", 120, 10, 340, 50
  statictext #play.statictext2, "Copyright 2015", 460, 35, 80, 20
  statictext #play.statictext3, "Enter a guess and click on Submit:", _
    10, 270, 280, 20
  statictext #play.statictext4, "Guesses:", 80, 170, 80, 20

  'Add a graphicbox control to be used to display hangman image files
  graphicbox #play.pic1, 440, 70, 133, 150

  'Add textbox controls to be used to display the letters of each word
  textbox #play.letter1 20, 70, 40, 60
  textbox #play.letter2 60, 70, 40, 60
  textbox #play.letter3 100, 70, 40, 60
  textbox #play.letter4 140, 70, 40, 60
  textbox #play.letter5 180, 70, 40, 60
  textbox #play.letter6 220, 70, 40, 60
```

```
textbox #play.letter7 260, 70, 40, 60
textbox #play.letter8 300, 70, 40, 60
textbox #play.letter9 340, 70, 40, 60
textbox #play.letter10 380, 70, 40, 60

'Display a list of guessed letters
textbox #play.guesses 165, 160, 160, 40

'Add textbox control used to collect player guesses
textbox #play.guess 295, 240, 50, 50

'Add button controls for submitting guesses and starting new games
button #play.button1 "Submit", ProcessGuess, UL, 365, 250, 100, 40
button #play.button2 "New Game", PlayAgain, UL, 475, 250, 100, 40

'Open the window with no frame and a handle of #play
open "Hangman" for window_nf as #play

print #play.button1, "!enable"  'Enable the Submit button
print #play.button2, "!disable" 'Disable the New Game button

'Set up the trapclose event for the window
print #play, "trapclose ClosePlay"

'Set the font type, size, and attributes
print #play.statictext1, "!font Arial 24 bold"
print #play.statictext3, "!font Arial 10 bold"
print #play.statictext4, "!font Arial 10 bold"
print #play.guesses, "!font Arial 14 bold"
print #play.letter1, "!font Arial 24 bold"
print #play.letter2, "!font Arial 24 bold"
print #play.letter3, "!font Arial 24 bold"
print #play.letter4, "!font Arial 24 bold"
print #play.letter5, "!font Arial 24 bold"
print #play.letter6, "!font Arial 24 bold"
print #play.letter7, "!font Arial 24 bold"
print #play.letter8, "!font Arial 24 bold"
print #play.letter9, "!font Arial 24 bold"
print #play.letter10, "!font Arial 24 bold"
```

```
print #play.guess, "!font Arial 20 bold"

print #play.guess, "!setfocus"   'Set focus to the button control

call StartNewGame   'Call on the subroutine that gets things started

'Pause the application and wait for the player's instruction
wait

end sub
```

This subroutine begins by assigning values to the WindowWidth and WindowHeight special variables to set the window's width and height. Then a series of loadbmp commands are executed to preload bitmap images representing different graphical depictions of a hangman character. A series of statictext controls is defined next, displaying the name of the game and its copyright statement and providing labels for other controls. A graphicbox control is then added to the right side of the window.

The game is designed to display mystery words that are ten letters or less in length. To display the letters that make up each word, 10 textbox controls are added next, each of which is 40 pixels wide by 60 pixels tall. Two additional textbox controls are then added. The first textbox control is used to display a list of all the letters guessed by the player, making it easy for the player to keep track of things. The second textbox control is used to collect player guesses.

Next, two button controls are added. The first button control is labeled Submit. When clicked, it calls on a subroutine named ProcessGuess, which is responsible for ensuring that the player's guess is valid and for displaying letters that are correctly guessed. The second button control is labeled New Game. When clicked, it calls on a subroutine named PlayAgain. This subroutine is responsible for preparing the game for a new round of play.

At this point, the user interface is complete and the open command is used to display the window and assign it a handle of #play. Next, two print statements are executed to enable the Submit button and disable the New Game button. Another print statement is used to set up the trap-close event for the window. Additional print statements are then executed to specify the font type, size, and attributes for various interface controls. A final print statement is executed to set focus to the textbox control used to collect player guesses, and then the StartNewGame subroutine is called. The last statement in the ManageGamePlay subroutine executes the wait command to pause the game and wait for the player to make a guess.

Starting a New Game

The StartNewGame subroutine, shown next, is responsible for setting up the game window to play a new game. This subroutine starts off by clearing out the textbox control used to collect the player's guesses. Next, a bitmap showing an empty hangman gallows is loaded into the window's graphicbox control using the drawbmp command.

Next, the GetNewWord$() function is called. This function returns a randomly selected word from the words$() array, which is then stored in the secretWord$ variable.

To clear out anything displayed in the textbox controls representing the letters of the secret word, print statements are used to display an empty string in each control. A for...next loop is then set up that loops once for each letter in the game's mystery word and displays an underscore character in the corresponding textbox controls:

```
'This subroutine starts a new round of play
sub StartNewGame

  print #play.guesses, ""  'Clear out any previous guesses

  'Load a blank bitmap image into the game's graphicbox control
  print #play.pic1, "flush"  'Flush the previous image
  print #play.pic1, "drawbmp blank 1 1" 'Display the bitmap image
  print #play.pic1, "flush"  'Flush the new image

  'Call on the function responsible for selecting a new word
  secretWord$ = GetNewWord$()

  'Clear out anything displayed in the textbox controls used to
  'represent the letters of the word
  print #play.letter1, ""
  print #play.letter2, ""
  print #play.letter3, ""
  print #play.letter4, ""
  print #play.letter5, ""
  print #play.letter6, ""
  print #play.letter7, ""
  print #play.letter8, ""
  print #play.letter9, ""
  print #play.letter10, ""
```

```
i = 1   'Define a variable to be used as a counter

'Loop through each letter in the word and display an underscore
'character for each letter in the appropriate textbox control
for i = 1 to len(secretWord$)
  if i = 1 then print #play.letter1, "_"
  if i = 2 then print #play.letter2, "_"
  if i = 3 then print #play.letter3, "_"
  if i = 4 then print #play.letter4, "_"
  if i = 5 then print #play.letter5, "_"
  if i = 6 then print #play.letter6, "_"
  if i = 7 then print #play.letter7, "_"
  if i = 8 then print #play.letter8, "_"
  if i = 9 then print #play.letter9, "_"
  if i = 10 then print #play.letter10, "_"
next i

end sub
```

Hint

Take note of the use of the len() function in the for…next loop. This function returns a numeric value representing the number of characters in the specified string.

Retrieving a Mystery Word

The code statements that make up the GetNewWord$() function are shown here and should be added to the end of the program file:

```
'This function is responsible for retrieving a word for the player
'to guess
function GetNewWord$()

  RandomNumber = int(rnd(1)*10)   'Retrieve a number between 0 and 9

  'Use the random number to retrieve a word from the array and return
  'the word to the calling statement
  GetNewWord$ = words$(RandomNumber)

end function
```

The function begins by retrieving a random number in the range of 0–9. Next, using this number, a mystery word is selected from the words$() array and assigned to a local variable named Get-NewWord$. GetNewWord$ is also the name of the function. In Just BASIC, any time you assign a value to a variable that is named after the function in which it resides, the assigned value is returned to the statement that called the function. As such, the word retrieved from the words$() array is passed back to the StartNewGame subroutine, where it is assigned to the secretWord$ variable.

Processing Player Guesses

The code statements that make up the ProcessGuess subroutine are shown next and should be added to the end of the program file:

```
'This subroutine processes player guesses
sub ProcessGuess handle$

  print #play.guess, "!contents? letterGuessed$" 'Get the player's guess

  letterGuessed$ = lower$(letterGuessed$) 'Convert all input to lowercase

  print #play.guess, ""   'Clear out the textbox control used to collect
                          'player input

  'Call the function responsible for validating player guesses
  result$ = ValidateInput$(letterGuessed$)

  if result$ = "Invalid" then 'Exit the subroutine if the guess is invalid
     exit sub
  end if

  print #play.guesses, "!contents? guesses$" 'Get the player's guess

  guesses$ = guesses$ + letterGuessed$ 'Add the current guess to the list
                                       'of letters already guessed

  print #play.guesses, guesses$  'Display the list of guessed letters

  'Determine if the letter that was guessed is part of the word
  if instr(secretWord$, letterGuessed$) = 0 then

     'The letter is not part of the word, so increment the variable used to
     'keep track of the total number of misses
     totalMissed = totalMissed + 1
```

```
    notice "Sorry: Your guess was wrong!"  'Inform the player

    print #play.guess, "!setfocus"  'Set focus to the button control

    'Update the display of the hangman image based on how many misses
    'the player has made so far
    if totalMissed = 1 then print #play.pic1, "drawbmp head 1 1"
    if totalMissed = 2 then print #play.pic1, "drawbmp body 1 1"
    if totalMissed = 3 then print #play.pic1, "drawbmp leftarm 1 1"
    if totalMissed = 4 then print #play.pic1, "drawbmp rightarm 1 1"
    if totalMissed = 5 then print #play.pic1, "drawbmp leftleg 1 1"
    if totalMissed = 6 then   'At 6 misses the game is over
      print #play.pic1, "drawbmp rightleg 1 1"  'The player is hung
      notice "Game over. You Lose!"  'Notify the player
      print #play.button1, "!disable" ' Disable the Submit button
      print #play.button2, "!enable"  'Enable the New Game button
      print #play.button2, "!setfocus"  'Set focus to the New Game button
    end if

    print #play.pic1, "flush"  'Make the bitmap image stick

else 'The letter is part of the word

    'Replace the underscore character for each occurrence of the letter
    'in the word
    for i = 1 to len(secretWord$)

      'Retrieve a letter from the word
      letter$ = mid$(secretWord$, i, 1)

      'See if the letter matches the player's guess and display it if it
      'matches
      if letter$ = letterGuessed$ then
        if i = 1 then print #play.letter1, letterGuessed$
        if i = 2 then print #play.letter2, letterGuessed$
        if i = 3 then print #play.letter3, letterGuessed$
        if i = 4 then print #play.letter4, letterGuessed$
        if i = 5 then print #play.letter5, letterGuessed$
        if i = 6 then print #play.letter6, letterGuessed$
        if i = 7 then print #play.letter7, letterGuessed$
        if i = 8 then print #play.letter8, letterGuessed$
        if i = 9 then print #play.letter9, letterGuessed$
```

```
        if i = 10 then print #play.letter10, letterGuessed$

        totalCorrect = totalCorrect + 1  'Increment the variable used to
                                         'keep track of correct guesses
      end if

    next i

    print #play.guess, "!setfocus"  'Set focus to the button control

    'The player wins when the total number of correct guesses equals the
    'number of letters in the word
    if totalCorrect = len(secretWord$) then
       notice "Game Over. You have won!"  'Notify the player
       print #play.button1, "!disable"    'Disable the Submit button
       print #play.button2, "!enable"     'Enable the New Game button
       print #play.button2, "!setfocus"   'Set focus to the button control
    end if

  end if

end sub
```

This subroutine begins by retrieving the contents of the textbox control into which player guesses are entered and assigns this value to a variable named letterGuessed$. Once its value has been retrieved, the contents of the #play.guess textbox control are replaced with an empty string.

Next, the ValidateInput$ function is called and passed letterGuessed$ as an argument. The ValidateInput$ function analyzes the player's guess and returns a string of "Invalid" if a problem is found. If this is the case, no additional tasks need to be performed in the ProcessGuess subroutine, and the exit sub command is executed. If this is not the case, a valid guess has been entered, so the next few statements retrieve the list of guesses that have been already made (from the #play.guesses textbox control), add the player's current guess to this list, and then redisplay the updated list of guesses back in the textbox control.

Next, an if…then…else code block is set up to determine whether the player's guess is part of the mystery word. This is accomplished by first using the lower$() function to convert the player's guess to all lowercase characters and then using the instr() function to search secretWord$ and see if it contains the letter the player guessed. If instr() returns a value of 0, the player has guessed a letter that is not in the word. In this case, the value of totalMissed is incremented, and a pop-up dialog is displayed informing the player of her missed guess. Focus is then placed on the textbox control used to collect player guesses.

Finally, a bitmap is loaded into the window's graphicbox control. The game determines what bitmap image to load based on the value assigned to totalMissed. For example, if this is the first time that the player has guessed an incorrect letter, a bitmap showing a head with no body parts is loaded. If, on the other hand, this is the player's sixth miss, a bitmap showing a complete body is displayed, notifying the player that she has lost the game. In addition, the Submit button is disabled, and the New Game button is enabled.

If the player's guess did match up against at least one of the letters in the mystery word, the else portion of the if…then…else code block is executed. If this is the case, a for…next loop is set up that repeats once for each letter in the mystery word. Upon each iteration of the loop, the mid$() function is used to retrieve a letter from the mystery word. Once a letter has been retrieved, an if statement code block is set up that checks to see if the player's guess is equal to that letter in the word. If a match is found, a print statement is executed that displays that letter. Because the for…next loop iterates through every letter in the mystery word, every matching instance of the player's guess is displayed. Note also that the totalCorrect variable is incremented for each matching letter that is found in the mystery word.

Once the entire word has been processed, the value of totalCorrect is checked to see if it is equal to the length of the secretWord$. If this is the case, the player has guessed every letter that makes up the game's mystery word, and the game is over. After notifying the player of this fact, the Submit button is disabled, and the New Game button is enabled.

Validating Player Guesses

The ValidateInput$() function, shown next, is responsible for validating player guesses and notifying the player when an invalid guess has been submitted:

```
'This subroutine is responsible for validating player guesses
function ValidateInput$(x$)

  'Check to see if the player entered something
  if x$ = "" then  'An empty string is not allowed
    notice "Invalid input: You must enter a letter!"
    ValidateInput$ = "Invalid"  'Return a string indicating invalid input
    print #play.guess, "!setfocus"  'Set focus to the button control
    exit function  'There is no need to go further, so exit the subroutine
  end if

  'Check to see if the player entered more than one character
  if len(x$) > 1 then  'Only one character may be input at a time
    notice "Invalid input: Enter only one letter at a time!"
    ValidateInput$ = "Invalid"  'Return a string indicating invalid input
```

```
      print #play.guess, "!setfocus"   'Set focus to the button control
      exit function  'There is no need to go further, so exit the subroutine
   end if


   'Check to see if the player entered a letter
   if instr("abcdefghijklmnopqrstuvwxyz", lower$(x$)) = 0 then
      notice "Invalid input: Numeric and special character guesses are " _
         + "not valid!"
      ValidateInput$ = "Invalid"   'Return a string indicating invalid input
      print #play.guess, "!setfocus"   'Set focus to the button control
      exit function  'There is no need to go further, so exit the subroutine
   end if


   print #play.guesses, "!contents? guesses$" 'Get the player's guess


   'Check to see if the player has already entered this guess
   if instr(guesses$, lower$(x$)) > 0 then   'Convert the player guess to all
                                             'lowercase characters
      notice "Invalid input: This letter has already been guessed!"
      ValidateInput$ = "Invalid"   'Return a string indicating invalid input
      print #play.guess, "!setfocus"   'Set focus to the button control
      exit function  'There is no need to go further, so exit the subroutine
   end if


end function
```

This function consists of four separate if…then code blocks. The first code block checks to see if the player clicked on the Submit button without entering a guess. The second code block checks to see if the player's guess is more than one character long. The third code block checks to see if the guess is a letter. Finally, the fourth code block checks to see if the player has made the guess before, which is the case if the letter the player submitted is found in the list of guessed letters stored in #play.guesses.

If any of the validation checks proves true, the function returns a value of "Invalid". Otherwise, the function exits without returning anything, signaling a valid guess.

Preparing for a New Game

The PlayAgain function subroutine is called whenever the player clicks on the New Game button. The code statements that make up this subroutine are shown next and should be added to the end of the program file:

```
'This subroutine prepares the game for another round of play
sub PlayAgain handle$

  print #play.button1, "!enable"    'Enable the Submit button
  print #play.button2, "!disable"   'Disable the New Game button

  print #play.guess, "!setfocus"    'Set focus to the button control

  'Reset these variables back to zero to get ready to play again
  totalMissed = 0
  totalCorrect = 0

  call StartNewGame  'Call this subroutine to start a new round of play

end sub
```

When called, the subroutine enables the Submit button and disables the New Game button. It also assigns focus to the textbox control used to collect player guesses. Next, the values assigned to the totalMissed and totalCorrect variables are reset to their initial default settings, and the StartNewGame subroutine is called, allowing the player to play a new game.

Getting Player Confirmation Before Closing the Game

The last procedure in this application, shown next, is a subroutine named ClosePlay. This subroutine is responsible for getting player confirmation before terminating the execution of the game:

```
'This subroutine is called when the player closes the #play window
'and is responsible for ending the game
sub ClosePlay handle$

  'Get confirmation before terminating program execution
  confirm "Are you sure you want to quit?"; answer$

  if answer$ = "yes" then  'The player clicked on Yes

    close #play  'Close the #play window

    end  'Terminate the game

  end if

end sub
```

The Final Result

Okay, this marks the end of yet another successful development project. Assuming that you followed along carefully and did not make typos, your new game should be ready to go. If, on the other hand, you find that things are not working as expected, it is time to put your newly developed debugging skills to work. In fact, even if the game is running just fine, you might want to go ahead and run it once using Just BASIC's debugger, just so that you can observe and verify its proper execution.

Summary

In this chapter, you learned how to track down and fix syntax, logical, and runtime errors. You discovered how to work with the Just BASIC debugger to keep an eye on program statement execution as well as to monitor the status of variable values. You found out how to exercise step-by-step control over the execution of programming statements within your programs. In addition, you learned how to develop error handlers. Finally, you discovered how to create the Hangman game.

Now, before you put this book down and move on to other things, why don't you take a little extra time to make a few improvements to the Hangman game by addressing the following list of challenges.

Challenges

1. Currently, the Hangman game randomly pulls mystery words from an array that contains 10 entries. As a result, it does not take long before players start running into the same word repeatedly. Consider expanding the number of words stored in the array to 40 or 50.

2. To give the game a little more pizzazz, consider adding a splash screen to it. In addition, add a Help window.

3. You might also want to do away with all the pop-up windows displayed by the game and instead communicate with the player by adding another textbox control to the window in which you can post messages.

4. Add a little sound to the Hangman game by setting it up to play different wave files when the player guesses a correct letter or when the player wins or loses a game.

5. It might also be a good idea to let the player know what the mystery word is at the end of each losing game.

PART

IV Appendixes

What's on the Companion Website?

To become an effective programmer with any programming language, you must dedicate yourself to learning the language through the development of new applications. This means that you have to spend time learning about and experimenting with different language features. As you learn more and tackle more challenging programming tasks, it helps to have a collection of source code from which you can draw upon and rely.

If you created each of the applications presented in this book as you went along, you already have access to a good set of examples with which you can experiment and learn. However, if you have not had time to create one or more of the book's applications, you can download them from this book's companion website located at www.cengage.com/downloads.

Assuming that you have read each chapter of the book and you did not skip around too much, you should already have a good understanding of how each game works and what its purpose is. However, in case you jumped around a bit, Table A.1 provides a brief overview of each application

TABLE A.1 JUST BASIC SOURCE CODE LOCATED ON THE COMPANION WEBSITE

Chapter	Game	Description
Chapter 1	Knock Knock Joke	This game provides an introduction to BASIC programming and demonstrates the steps involved in creating a small Just BASIC application that tells the player knock-knock jokes.
Chapter 2	The Legend of Mighty Molly	This game demonstrates how to collect and process user input through the creation of a mad-lib-style computer game.
Chapter 3	BASIC Crazy 8 Ball	This game simulates a magic 8-ball that provides randomly selected answers to player questions.
Chapter 4	Ask Genie	This game pits you against a willful genie named Tabethia, who is determined not to grant any of your wishes.
Chapter 5	Rock, Paper, Scissors	This game demonstrates how to use conditional logic to create a player versus computer game based on the popular Rock, Paper, Scissors game.
Chapter 6	Guess My Number	This game demonstrates how to use a loop to control the overall operation of a number-guessing game.
Chapter 7	BASIC BlackJack	This card game demonstrates how to improve the organization of BASIC applications through the use of functions and subroutines.
Chapter 8	Tic-Tac-Toe	This is a two-player implementation of the classic Tic-Tac-Toe game.
Chapter 9	BASIC Slot Machine	This game pits the player against a computer-simulated Las Vegas-style slot machine, complete with animation and sound effects.
Chapter 10	Just Bricks	This is a breakout-style arcade game that demonstrates Just BASIC's ability to generate advanced computer games.
Chapter 11	Hangman	This game ties together all the programming concepts demonstrated in this book through the development of a game that challenges the player to guess mystery words in five or fewer wrong guesses.

B

What's Next?

Now that you have completed this book and know the fundamentals of programming, you may be wondering what to do next. Although you have learned much already, there is still plenty left to be learned. You should not view this book as the end of your programming education. Instead, think of it as the beginning. To become an effective programmer, you must continue to expand your knowledge and skills.

Fortunately, there is no end to the number of different opportunities open to you. For starters, you may want to continue to work and experiment with Just BASIC to see how far it will take you. Or you may want to move on to any number of alternative and more advanced BASIC programming languages, such as Liberty BASIC or Visual Basic. Alternatively, you might want to apply your BASIC programming skills to other avenues such as VBScript (a Visual Basic–like scripting language).

This appendix has been designed to help you keep your momentum going by pointing you to different resources that you can tap into to learn more about BASIC programming in its many forms. You will learn where to go to learn more about Just BASIC, as well as where to find information about other programming languages.

Locating Just BASIC Resources Online

The Internet provides access to an abundance of information on Just BASIC. The first place to start is the Just BASIC website, which you will find at www.justbasic.com. This website has plenty of useful information, including the latest news about Just BASIC, access to download the current release of Just BASIC, and upgrade information to Liberty BASIC, the big brother commercial version to Just BASIC.

The Just BASIC Forum

Another excellent source for learning more about Just BASIC is the Just BASIC forum located at http://justbasic.conforums.com. At the Just BASIC Forum, you can access different discussion forums and view thousands of topics and postings made by other Just BASIC programmers. You can also post your own questions and answers if you want. There are forums specifically dedicated to novice programmers, games and graphics development, tip sharing, and much more.

The Just BASIC Files Archive

Another excellent source of Just BASIC information can be found on the Just BASIC Files Archive located at http://jbfilesarchive.com/phpBB3/viewforum.php?f=35. Here you can get access to forum discussions regarding a host of topics, including game development, utilities, database access, and Internet application development.

If you run into a problem with a Just BASIC application that you cannot figure out on your own, you might want to join this site and post your question to see if other programmers have already run into the same problem and figured out a way to fix it.

Liberty BASIC

As you have already been informed, Liberty BASIC is Just BASIC's big brother. Liberty BASIC is marketed as a commercial implementation of the BASIC programming language. Although it's not as robust and powerful as other BASIC programming languages like Visual Basic, Liberty BASIC is a low-cost option that is well suited as a programming language for computer hobbyists and individuals just getting started in BASIC programming.

To download a trial copy of Liberty BASIC, visit the Liberty BASIC website at www.libertybasic.com. Here you can access online documentation, tutorials, and training videos. Registered users can even take an online Liberty BASIC programming class.

Because of its close relationship to Just BASIC, you will find that the transition from Just BASIC to Liberty BASIC is straightforward. You will also find that Liberty BASIC provides all the capabilities provided by Just BASIC—and much more.

Liberty BASIC benefits from the support of a large and active online community, which includes third-party developers who provide add-ons designed to extend or enhance Liberty BASIC's capabilities. One area of third-party development that may interest you is applications that are designed to simplify the development of *graphical user interfaces (GUIs)* for Liberty BASIC applications. Two such third-party applications are Liberty BASIC Workshop and Liberty BASIC Quick Visual Designer.

Liberty BASIC Workshop

Liberty BASIC Workshop is an integrated development environment that is distributed as freeware. You can download a copy of it from http://alycesrestaurant.com/workshop.htm. Its features include a GUI builder that is designed to assist you in the development of Liberty BASIC window interfaces.

Run BASIC

Run BASIC is a web development tool that allows you to create web applications using a version of BASIC that is based on Just BASIC and Liberty BASIC. Run BASIC installs as an online web interface and a web service, consisting of the BASIC programming language, an SQLite database, and a small web server, which provides multisession support. Run BASIC applications are created without *Hypertext Markup Language (HTML)*. Instead, Run BASIC automatically generates the HTML for you. Applications created using Run BASIC are written as BASIC programs, as is done with Just BASIC.

Run BASIC offers an alternative to more complex web development languages and environment list PHP, Perl, and Apache. You can install it on your own computer, setting up a Run BASIC web server. If your Internet service provider permits it, you can install Run BASIC on one of its web servers.

Run BASIC install using a simple installer program. Installation packages are available for Windows, Mac OS X, and Linux. Once it's installed, you can interact with and program Run BASIC using your web browser, which automatically connects to the Run BASIC server that is installed on your computer. You can learn more about and download a copy of Run BASIC at www.runbasic.com.

Visual Basic

For programmers whose customers are Microsoft Windows users, Microsoft Visual Basic is the dominant BASIC programming language. Visual Basic is a Rapid Application Development (RAD) application development tool that is closely integrated with the Microsoft .NET framework, upon which it depends to run and access system and network resources. As far as BASIC programming languages go, Visual Basic is as complicated as it gets. As a result, it takes longer to learn and master than other BASIC programming languages. To help address this issue, Microsoft has developed a scaled-down version of Visual Basic called Microsoft Visual Basic Express 2013, which is a little easier to learn.

You can download a copy of Microsoft Visual Basic Express 2013 at http://msdn.microsoft.com/vstudio/express/vb/, where it is made freely available as a component of Visual Studio Express 2013.

Other BASIC Programming Languages

In addition to Just BASIC, Liberty BASIC, Visual Basic, and NS Basic, there are dozens of other programming languages that are based on BASIC. Although it is well beyond the scope of this book to attempt to cover each of these BASIC dialects, some deserve a mention. Table B.1 shows a list of seven additional BASIC programming languages and provides the address of the language's website. Also included in Table B.1 is a listing of the operating system that each of these BASIC programming languages supports.

TABLE B.1 ALTERNATIVE BASIC PROGRAMMING LANGUAGES

Name	URL	Supported Platforms
DarkBASIC	www.thegamecreators.com	Windows (game development)
PowerBASIC	www.powerbasic.com/	Windows
Kbasic	www.kbasic.com/	Windows, Linux, Mac OS X
Yabasic	www.yabasic.de/	Windows, Linux, UNIX
SmallBASIC	http://smallbasic.sourceforge.net/	Linux, Windows
True BASIC	www.truebasic.com/	Windows
XBasic	www.xbasic.org/	Windows, Linux

Non-BASIC Programming Languages

Of course, there is nothing that says you have to apply your newly developed programming skills to BASIC programming. You can apply the programming techniques and principles that you learned in this book to any programming language, including such languages as these:

- Microsoft C#
- Microsoft C++
- Perl
- Python
- JavaScript
- Java
- Ruby

Each of these programming is separate and distinct and has its own set of strengths and weaknesses. You can obtain more information about these and other programming languages by spending a little time searching the Internet.

www.tech-publishing.com

Last but not least, you may want to check out the author's website, which is located at www.tech-publishing.com, as shown in Figure B.1. Here you will find other books offering additional information regarding many of the programming languages introduced in this book.

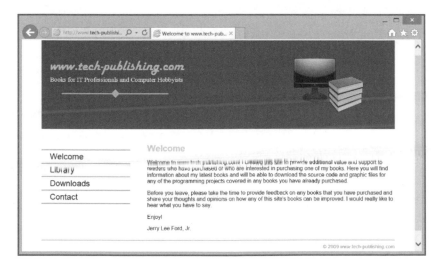

Figure B.1 The author's website at www.tech-publishing.com.

Glossary

absolute path. A path specification in which the complete path to a file or folder, including the drive letter and any folders, is included in the path between the drive specification and the target file or folder.

accelerator key. A key that can be used to activate a menu or menu item when pressed in conjunction with another key, such as Alt.

AppleScript. A scripting programming language run on Mac OS X.

applets. Java programs embedded inside web pages that are loaded and executed by a web browser.

application window. A window that can contain interface controls and that supports optional features such as resizing and menus.

argument. A value, literal, or variable that is passed to a subroutine or function for processing.

array. An index list of values stored and managed as a unit.

assembler. A program used to compile assembly language programs, line for line, into machine code.

assembly language. A low-level programming language that uses mneumonic codes to represent specific machine code commands.

BASIC (Beginner's All-Purpose Symbolic Instruction Code). A programming language initially created to teach people how to program.

binary file. A file that is capable of storing text, graphics files, sound files, and so on.

binary operator. An operator that performs a calculation on two values, such as addition, subtraction, multiplication, and division.

bmpbutton control. A user interface control similar to the button control but which supports the display of a graphics image in place of a text string.

break point. A designated location within a program that pauses the execution of an application to facilitate debugging and the observation of variable values.

button control. A user interface control that displays a graphical representation of a button users can click on to send a command to a program.

by reference. A state in which the value of an argument passed to a procedure for processing is changed if the corresponding procedure parameter is changed during the execution of the procedure.

bytecode. An intermediate level of compilation (sometimes referred to as *p-code*) used by programming languages such as Java to run an application in a virtual machine, allowing for greater portability with minimal loss of time and minimal use of resources during runtime compilation.

by value. A state in which the value of an argument passed to a procedure for processing remains unchanged if the corresponding procedure parameter is changed during the execution of the procedure.

C. A general-purpose programming language developed in the early 1970s at Bell Telephone Laboratories for use on UNIX operating systems.

C++. An object-oriented programming language that views system and key language resources as objects that provide everything needed to access and manipulate them.

checkbox control. A user interface control that gives the user a choice between two options, which when set displays a check box inside a square field.

COBOL (Common Business-Oriented Language). A programming language developed in the 1950s to support the development of business applications.

code editor. A text editor used to enter and save program source code.

collision detection. An event that occurs when two objects (sprites) make contact with one another during the execution of a computer game.

combobox control. A user interface control that includes features provided by the listbox and textbox controls that can be used to present users with a list of options from which to select.

compiler. A program that translates program language statements into machine code.

concatenation. The process of joining two or more strings to create a new string.

constant. A descriptive name assigned to a known value that does not change during program execution.

counter. A variable used to keep count of iterations in a loop.

cross-platform. The ability to run an application on more than one operating system.

data. The information that your applications collect, store, process, and modify during execution.

database. An application that is designed to facilitate the storage and retrieval of large amounts of data.

debugger. A software program used to locate and analyze errors that occur during the application development process, thus enabling programmers to trace and pause program execution to check the status of program variables.

dialog. A special pop-up window designed to collect user information or to notify the user of an event or result.

do...until. A programming statement that creates a loop that repeats until a specified condition is true.

do...while. A programming statement that creates a loop that repeats as long as a specified condition is true.

endless loop. A loop that never ends.

event. An occurrence of a predefined activity such as a mouse click or the closing of a window.

event handler. A mechanism for triggering subroutine or function execution based on the occurrence of a specified event, such as a mouse click or the closing of a window.

expression. A statement that is evaluated and produces a result.

flowchart. A tool used by programmers to graphically depict the logical flow of all or part of a program.

focus. A state in which a user interface control has been set up to accept any incoming keyboard input.

for...next. A programming statement that creates a loop that repeats a set number of times.

Fortran (FORmula TRANslator). A programming language created in the 1950s for the purpose of performing complex mathematic calculations.

FreeForm-J. A Just BASIC application that assists Just BASIC programmers in visually designing graphical user interfaces (GUIs).

function. A collection of statements that is called and executed as a unit and which has the ability to return a value to the statement that called upon it.

game state. A term that describes the different stages a computer game goes through during its execution.

global variable. A variable that is accessible throughout the program.

graphicbox control. A user interface control that can display bitmap images and draw shapes such as squares, circles, and text characters.

graphics window. A window designed to display graphics and sprite animation.

groupbox control. A programming statement that consists of a box with a label that is used to group and organize other controls.

HTML (Hypertext Markup Language). A web development language used to provide and display content on the World Wide Web.

IDE (integrated development environment). An application or group of applications designed to facilitate application development, which usually includes a code editor, compiler, and debugger.

if…then. A programming statement that tests a condition and then alters the execution flow of an application based on the result of its analysis.

interpreter. A program that converts script statements into machine code at runtime.

Java. A cross-platform programming language, developed by Sun Microsystems in the early 1990s, that is based heavily on C and C++.

JavaScript. A scripting language used to develop scripts embedded within web pages to add dynamic content to websites.

Just BASIC. A free BASIC programming language used to create standalone Windows applications.

Liberty BASIC. A commercial programming language based on BASIC that provides all the same functionality as Just BASIC plus a number of additional features.

listbox control. A user interface control used to display a list of items from which the user can make a selection.

local variable. A variable that is accessible only within the scope in which it is created.

logical error. An error created when a programmer makes a mistake laying out the logic used to perform a given task.

loop. A set of programming statements that is repeatedly executed as a unit.

machine code. The basic language of a computer, which is made up of binary patterns that the CPU can understand and process.

mainwin. A text window automatically created as part of every Just BASIC program.

menus. Drop-down lists of commands located at the top of the window, just underneath the window's title bar.

Microsoft .NET Framework. A collection of resources designed to support the development and execution of Windows applications that run on desktop computers, local area networks, and the Internet.

MIDI (Musical Instrument Digital Interface). A communications protocol that enables electronic musical instruments and computers to communicate.

Objective-C. An object-oriented programming language based on C that runs on Mac OS X.

object-oriented. A type of programming language that views resources as objects containing methods and properties that can be used to manipulate and configure their behavior.

order of precedence. A set of rules that determines the order in which a programming language evaluates a numeric expression.

parameter. A variable defined within a subroutine or function that maps to an argument that the subroutine or function is called on to execute.

p-code. An intermediate level of compilation (sometimes referred to as *bytecode*) used by programming languages such as Java to run an application inside a virtual machine, thus allowing for greater application portability.

pen. A virtualized writing instrument that can be used to draw on a graphics window or a graphicbox control.

Perl. A scripting language originally developed to run on UNIX but later ported over to every major operating system platform.

pixel (Picture Element). The smallest addressable area that can be written to on the screen or window.

point. 1/72 of an inch.

procedure. A collection of programming statements that can be called upon to execute from different locations within an application.

program. A file containing code statements that, when executed, tell the computer to do something.

pseudo code. A term that refers to an English-like outline of all or part of the programming logic that makes up a computer program.

Python. A scripting language similar to Perl that is known for its emphasis on easing programmer development, sometimes at the cost of speed and efficiency.

RAD (Rapid Application Development). A programming technique in which the programmer begins application development using a drag-and-drop tool that facilitates the creation of graphical user interfaces. Once the interface has been designed, the program code required to finish building the application is added.

radiobutton control. A user interface control that gives users a choice between two or more mutually exclusive choices.

random access file. A file that can be read from or written to at any location within the file.

RBScript. A scripting language derived from REALbasic.

relative path. A path specification that identifies the location of a file or folder relative to the location of the current working directory (folder).

reserved word. A programming language keyword that has been defined as having a special purpose.

Rexx (Restructured eXtended eXecution). A scripting language developed by IBM and later ported over to every major computing platform.

Ruby. An object-oriented scripting language similar to Perl.

Run BASIC. A web development service that supports the development of web applications using a version of BASIC that is based on Just BASIC and Liberty BASIC.

runtime error. An error that occurs when an application performs an illegal action.

scripting language. A computer language that is interpreted into machine code at execution time.

select…case. A programming statement used to set up a series of conditional tests, each of which is compared to a single value.

sequential file. A file that contains plain text and that is processed sequentially, from beginning to end.

source code. The statements that make up a program.

special variables. A collection of variables created and managed by a programming language that provides access to commonly used information.

sprite. An image that is integrated into a larger background scene and forms the basis of computer animation.

SQL (Structured Query Language). A specialized programming language designed to support the creation, modification, and retrieval of data stored in a database.

statements. The instructions that make up a computer program.

statictext control. A user interface control used to display a text string on a window.

subroutine. A collection of one or more code statements that can be called upon to execute.

syntax error. An error that occurs when you do not write a code statement according to the rules of the programming language.

textbox control. A user interface control that provides a single-line input field that can be used to display or to collect small amounts of text input the user provides.

texteditor control. A user interface control that provides a multiline text field that can be used to display text or to collect text input by the user.

text window. A window designed specifically for the purpose of displaying text, which always includes a menu bar containing File and Edit menus.

token file. A file used as the basis for creating Just BASIC applications that can run as standalone applications.

trapclose. An event that automatically occurs when the user clicks on the system menu close button or otherwise closes the application window.

variable. A pointer to a location in memory (address) where a value is stored.

VBA (Visual Basic for Applications). A Microsoft programming language based on BASIC that can be used to automate the execution of an application.

VBScript. A scripting language based on BASIC.

wave. A digital audio file with a .wav file extension that stores uncompressed raw audio data.

while...wend. A programming statement that creates a loop that repeats for as long as a specified condition is true.

Index

Symbols

- operator, 173
! character, 82
$ character, 145
* operator, 173
/ operator, 173
// comment character, 25
^ operator, 173
{} (curly braces), 167
" (double quotes), 25, 281
+ operator, 173
< operator, 172
<= operator, 172
<> operator, 172
= operator, 172
> operator, 172
>= operator, 172

A

AboutGame subroutine, 331
ABS() numeric function, explained, 142
absolute path, explained, 251
accelerator keys, using with menus, 106
adaptive applications. *See* conditional logic
AddBallToGame subroutine, 337
AddBricksToGame subroutine, 336–337
addition operator, description and example, 173
Agentix Installer program, 63
AnalyzeAndUpdateBallLocation subroutine, 339–341
and operator, type and example, 176

application menus
    adding to windows, 106
    building, 106–107
    defined, 106
    naming, 106
    naming items, 106
    separator line, 106
    standards, 107
    users' expectations, 107
    See also window menus
application windows
    ! character, 82
    accelerator keys, 106
    adding programming logic to, 81
    closing, 80–82
    designing with FreeForm-J, 108–111
    device parameter, 80
    dialog type, 76, 78
    displaying, 80
    event programming, 82
    graphics type, 76–78
    #handle parameter, 80–81
    #main handle, 81
    opening, 80–82
    specifying size and location, 83–84
    style suffixes, 78–79
    text type, 76–77
    UpperLeftX variable, 83
    UpperLeftY variable, 83
    window type, 76–77
    WindowHeight variable, 83
    WindowWidth variable, 83–84
    See also windows
applications. *See* programs